The Braddock Expedition
and
Fox's Gap
in
Maryland

Curtis L. Older

HERITAGE BOOKS
2008

HERITAGE BOOKS

AN IMPRINT OF HERITAGE BOOKS, INC.

Books, CDs, and more—Worldwide

For our listing of thousands of titles see our website
at
www.HeritageBooks.com

Published 2008 by
HERITAGE BOOKS, INC.
Publishing Division
100 Railroad Ave. #104
Westminster, Maryland 21157

Other books by the author:

The Land Tracts of the Battlefield of South Mountain:
Including Many Other Tracts near the Area from Land Records of
Frederick County, Washington County, and the Maryland Archives

Cover: "On the Great Trail" by Robert Griffing

International Standard Book Numbers
Paperbound: 978-1-58549-301-2
Clothbound: 978-0-7884-7486-6

To Rachael

Table of Contents

Maps

Preface

The old Sharpsburg Road, from Middletown, Maryland, through Sharpsburg to Shepherdstown, Virginia [now West Virginia], crossed South Mountain at Fox's Gap. It also bore the name of Fox's Road for many years. From early 1755 until at least mid 1763, it was the main road from Frederick Town to Swearingen's Ferry. After the creation of Sharpsburg in 1763, the road became the Sharpsburg Road.

The route of this road exists today, as it has for over 250 years, but is known by a number of names along its path. Heading east from Sharpsburg to just north of Middletown are Geeting Road, Dog Street Road, Reno Monument Road, and Marker Road. This road played a role in historic events with worldwide significance. There is no work published that documents the history of this road and the Fox family that lived along it.

An objective of mine is to describe and document the most historic events connected with the old Sharpsburg Road, Fox's Gap, and the life of Frederick Fox. These events include the Braddock Expedition of 1755, which perhaps included more men who would go on to achieve high acclaim than in any other venture in American history. The Braddock Expedition was a truly remarkable undertaking. The part Maryland played in it deserves review. It seems fitting to document the route of the Braddock Road in time for its 250th anniversary.

I will present information about the Fox family as well as other families who had some connection with Fox's Gap and the old Sharpsburg Road. An analysis of the land tracts in the Fox's Gap area will help document the families along the road as well. Much of the material will be presented in the words of the participants in the events. It is their story. The reader can make his or her own interpretation of the words of those participants.

Forever embedded in the history of our Civil War is the name of Fox's Gap. On the other hand, the history of the Braddock Expedition has become lost to both visitor and area resident. Indeed, many a hiker on the Appalachian Trail has come to Fox's Gap unaware of its long history. It is the history of the American journey, from early settlers and founding fathers to the agony of civil strife and reconstruction. It is this history, this Fox's Gap, this old Sharpsburg Road, the author seeks to preserve.

This book would not have been possible without the assistance of Susanne Flowers of Frederick, Maryland. Susanne worked in the office of the Clerk of the Circuit Court for 16 years before retiring in 1990. Her efforts went beyond the call of duty. She deserves credit for documenting many of the land tracts mentioned in this book. She provided materials that led me to sources of information that otherwise were unknown to me. Any misuse or misinterpretation of her information is entirely mine.

The quality of this book would have been diminished without the contributions of Robert H. Fox of Cincinnati, Ohio. An ardent student of the history of the Fox family, Robert provided information that was invaluable. He provided pictures of Daniel Booker Fox, the pitcher used by George Washington at the Fox Inn, a rifle owned by Frederick Fox, and the Fox Inn from about 1940. He provided genealogical information as well.

My mother's membership in the Daughters of the American Revolution led me to join the Sons of the American Revolution and the Society of the Descendants of Washington's Army at Valley Forge. It was the patriotic flavor of these organizations and their concern for our national heritage, when coupled with things of a military nature, that led me to this point.

Perhaps an old adage, "I would rather be lucky than good any day," might be most appropriate at this point. Divine intervention must have taken place when I stumbled upon some of the material used in this book.

Reviewers of this book include Doug Bast, Director of the Boonsborough Museum of History, Boonsboro, Md.; John Frye of the Washington County Free Library, Hagerstown, Md.; Jay Graybeal of the Historical Society of Carroll County, Westminster, Md.; and Allan Powell of Hagerstown. Of course, any errors, oversights, or omissions are entirely mine.

Curtis L. Older
Gastonia, North Carolina
May 2, 1995

Introduction

Prelude to the Braddock Expedition

Strong forces were at work upon Fox's Gap during the mid 1700s. The adventure of the frontier led settlers into western Maryland and Virginia. Investment motives of men of wealth led them to speculate in the land sought by the pioneers. Wealthy investors usually had close ties to officials in government. In the mid 1700s a very small group of men, along with the governor, wielded most of the power in the colony. The British government, the ruling power in the colonies, sought to preserve and strengthen its claim to the land being sought by the pioneers and investors.

Roads built across the sparsely populated land were another force. Roads allowed settlers to penetrate farther into the frontier. They provided for communication and transportation between people on the frontier and those living farther east. The building of roads served the interests of the settlers, investors, and the government. One of the most significant roads in western Maryland in the early 1700s passed through Fox's Gap on its way from Philadelphia to Winchester, Virginia.

Which of the forces was the most significant in the development of the frontier? Perhaps each depended to a degree upon the others. However, another force already was at work. It seems almost unimaginable to think this force existed in the 1740s and 1750s. This force was the impetus towards national unity. It was common to all the colonies, not just Maryland or Pennsylvania or any one colony. Events in 1755 showed a movement towards assistance and cooperation underway among the colonies in America. The Albany Convention of 1754 is noteworthy in this regard.[1]

The forces acting on a regional and national scale also acted on an international scale. English and French interests in the Ohio Valley lead us to yet another force. What is clear is that there was a sixth force acting over all the other forces. The sixth force was the struggle for power by the leading nations of the world. Of course, all of the forces previously mentioned were in direct conflict with the Indians. Only armed conflict could resolve the opposing interests.

The Ohio Company and Its Maryland Members

The Ohio Company best represents the culmination of all the forces enumerated. The Ohio Company brought together, and was driven by, the forces of the frontier, land speculation, government, roads, the unity of the colonies, and international competition.

The formation of the Ohio Company in 1747 was for the general purpose of promoting the interests of the English and the Colonials in the region west of the Allegheny mountains, in the immediate vicinity of the forks of the Ohio River. The Ohio Company "secured a royal grant of 500,000 acres on the Ohio between the Monongahela and Kanawha Rivers."[2] It sought to secure a large share of the Indian and skin trade in the Ohio country and to establish a permanent settlement west of the mountains.[3] The Ohio Company represented the concerns of investors and government leaders alike.

The Ohio Valley, in the 1740s and 50s, was virtually uninhabited. Few questions in Colonial America were more confusing than the one, in the late 1740s, as to what power controlled the Ohio country. Not only was the Ohio Valley the focus of English concern, the French had their eye on it as well. The prevention of a French occupation of the Ohio Valley was the objective of the British government and of the Ohio Company.

A group of Virginians, Marylanders, and a few influential London traders organized the Ohio Company. Many historians overlook the role of Maryland in the Ohio Company and westward expansion. Fox's Gap played a significant role during this era. Fox's Gap was on two major routes through western Maryland before 1756.

Non-Maryland members of the Ohio Company at one time or another included Col. Thomas Lee, Col. Thomas Nelson, Lawrence Washington, Augustine Washington, George Washington, John Mercer, George Mercer, James Mercer, John Francis Mercer, Francis Thornton, Presley Thornton, John Carlyle, George Fairfax, George Mason, William Nimmo, Robert Carter, Lunsford Lomax, John Edward Lomax, John Tayloe, James Scott, Gawin Corbin, Samuel Smith, Richard Lee, Philip Ludwell Lee, and Thomas Ludwell Lee, all of Virginia; and Robert Dinwiddie, Arthur Dobbs, John Hanbury, Capel Hanbury, Osgood Hanbury, and Samuel Smith of Great Britain (see Appendix F - Biographical Listing, for biographies of many individuals mentioned in this book).[4]

Maryland members of the Ohio Company were Thomas Cresap, Daniel Cresap, Nathaniel Chapman, Jacob Giles, and James Wardrop. "Thomas Cresap arrived in America as a boy about 1715. He apparently always had his home in Maryland. In 1739 he acquired 500 acres called 'Long Meadows,' located on the Antietam, approximately two miles from present-day Hagerstown.[5] In 1744 he secured 'Skipton in Craven,' a section of one hundred acres, lying on the Antietam creek near the Potomac."[6]

Thomas Cresap lived near Old Town in 1755.[7] "Cresap had left his home at Long Meadows near the present site of Hagerstown and established a hunting lodge for himself on the Potomac River, several miles west of the mouth of the South Branch."[8] Land records indicate Thomas Cresap surveyed a number of tracts in the Fox's Gap area. Daniel Cresap was a son of Thomas:

> Nathaniel Chapman is listed in the Ohio Company petition as being from Virginia but, as a matter of fact, he lived in Charles County, Maryland, and was an extensive landowner in that colony. He did, however, own large tracts of land in Virginia, particularly in Prince William and in Fairfax Counties. He was born about 1710 and died in 1760.[9] His importance to the company rested largely on the fact that he held land of

such extensive proportions that he was able to be of influence both in Maryland and Virginia. His stock in the company was later inherited by his son, Pearson Chapman.[10]

Jacob Giles and James Wardrop, like Nathaniel Chapman, were listed as Marylanders. While both actually did live in Maryland, they were members of Virginia families. James Wardrop owned considerable property in both colonies. He was listed in the original Ohio Company petition as being from Virginia,[11] yet in the instructions of the Ohio Company to Christopher Gist[12] on April 28, 1752, he, along with Jacob Giles and Thomas Cresap, was listed as being from the province of Maryland.[13]

Excerpts from the *Maryland Gazette* indicate a Jacob Giles was engaged in an iron works near the Susquehannah and lived at the mouth of the Susquehannah. He may have bought other iron works near Baltimore. A Jacob Giles also owned a number of ships and was engaged in shipping.[14] Perhaps he was the father of James Giles and Nathaniel Giles, both of whom served in the Maryland Assembly.[15]

"James Wardrop was a signer of a petition[16] sent in 1754 to the king's council requesting a definition of the company's boundaries."[17] Wardrop acquired a number of land tracts in the vicinity of Fox's Gap. These tracts included Wooden Platter, Oxford, The Cool Spring, Bloomsbury, Curry's Old Place, and John's Delight.[18]

Other men of influence in Maryland owned land near the routes through Fox's Gap as well. These men included Gov. Samuel Ogle, Benjamin Tasker Sr., Joseph Chapline Sr., Daniel Dulaney Sr., Dr. Charles Carroll, and Charles Carroll.[19] John Francis Mercer, a Virginia member of the Ohio Company, was governor of Maryland from 1801 to 1803.[20]

Daniel Dulaney Sr. founded Frederick Town, Maryland, in 1745.[21] Joseph Chapline Sr. (Sept. 7, 1707 - 1768) founded Sharpsburg, Maryland, on July 9, 1763, naming the town in honor of Governor Horatio Sharpe.[22] Chapline was a lawyer and a member of the Lower House of the Maryland Assembly, representing Frederick County from 1749 to 1763, 65-6, and 68. He was a member of the Arms and Ammunition Committee during the French and Indian War years of 1758 to 1762.[23]

The Road to Ft. Cumberland and Ft. Duquesne

Relations between England and France were under considerable stress in 1754. Not only in Europe, but on the North American continent as well, the two powers struggled for supremacy. Tension between them was no higher than in the Ohio Valley. It was in this remote area where armed conflict between them erupted. Perhaps it was an indication of a larger struggle to come in 1776.

The Ohio Company erected a fort in 1754 at the Forks of the Ohio, today the site of Pittsburgh, Pennsylvania. Ft. Cumberland at Wills' Creek was the connecting link between the fort on the Ohio and the settled areas to the east. Ft. Cumberland, today the site of Cumberland, Maryland, was built in late 1754. "The orders of the King were obeyed with alacrity by Colonel Innes, and under his supervision Fort Cumberland was erected and garrisoned, during the winter of 1754-1755."[24]

The term *road* is inappropriate to describe the route between Ft. Cumberland and Ft. Duquesne in early 1755. At best it was a path. There was only one road by which one could reach Ft. Cumberland, the road from Winchester, Virginia. This was desolate territory and the road between Winchester and Ft. Cumberland also was terrible. The roads to Winchester were the only links to Ft. Cumberland and the Ohio Valley at that time from the east.

The Conococheague Creek enters the Potomac River at Williamsport, Maryland. During the French and Indian War, the Williamsport area was known as Conococheague. A multitude of spellings of the word Conococheague exist in writings during the 1700s. These include Conogogee, Conocogogee, Conogochieg, etc. There was no adequate wagon road in early 1755 by which one could go directly west from Conococheague to Wills' Creek, site of Ft. Cumberland.

A land tract record supported a Maryland wagon road leading west from Conococheague towards Wills' Creek by 1743. The patent for Colemore's Ramble, February 28, 1743, included the following: "Near a small branch of the Little Tonoloway and on the left side of the main road that goes from said creek to the old town and near where said wagon road crosses Tonoloway Hill." This road was inadequate for military purposes, such as transporting supply wagons. George Washington traveled the route in 1747. "Travell'd up Maryland side all the Day in a continued Rain to Collo. Cresaps right against the Mouth of the South Branch about 40 miles from Polks. I believe the worst Road that ever was trod by Man or Beast."[25]

The strategic importance of the three roads to Winchester, by way of Conococheague, Alexandria, and Shepherdstown, became apparent during the Braddock Expedition and the French and Indian War that followed. Men and supplies passed over these routes on their way to the areas of conflict. The Indians used these routes as well. Western Maryland was a strategic area in the contest between the English and French.

The erection of the fort at the Forks of the Ohio was sufficient provocation, as viewed by the French, to require a response. The fall of the Ohio Company fort, April 17, 1754, resulted in a group led by Joshua Fry, with George Washington second in command, being ordered to recapture it. Fry died May 31, while leading his Virginia forces to the Ohio. He was buried near Wills' Creek. George Washington assumed command and first met and defeated Jumonville and his men on May 28. However, on July 3-4, Washington and his men found themselves besieged at Ft. Necessity. Washington's capitulation led to yet another British response.[26]

One result of the French and Indian War was supremacy over the North American continent for the English and the largest land transfer in the history of the world. The French and Indian War provided military training to the men who would lead both the American and British forces in the American Revolution. It was a struggle with worldwide implications. One of the most important chapters in this struggle was . . . the Braddock Expedition.

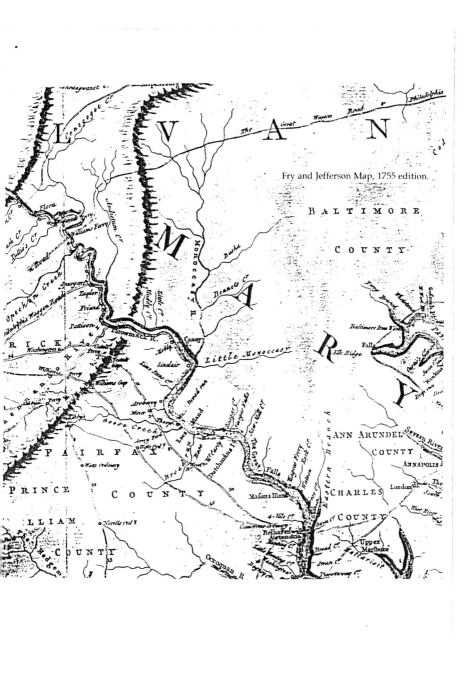

Fry and Jefferson Map, 1755 edition.

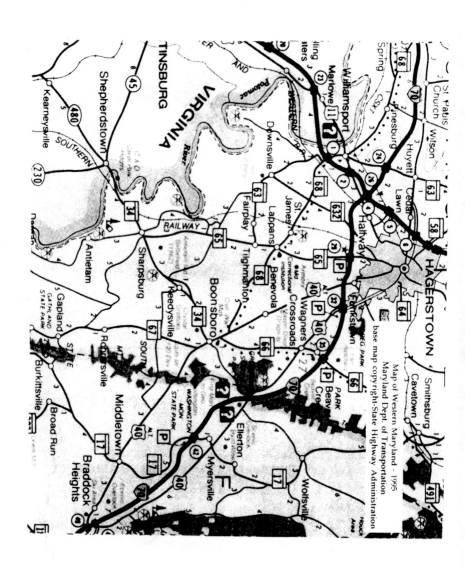

Map of Western Maryland - 1995
Maryland Dept. of Transportation
base map copyright-State Highway Administration

Chapter One

Preparations are Made

British and American concern over their loss in the Ohio Valley mounted during the remainder of 1754. In the later part of that year, the British embarked on an effort to divest the French of their tenuous hold in the Ohio Valley. The effort came in the form of the Braddock Expedition, consisting of both British and American troops under the command of British General Edward Braddock.[1] The participants read like a Who's Who of men who found a place in history during the American Revolution. It included those who earned everlasting fame in America's westward expansion. Daniel Boone, Daniel Morgan, Thomas Cresap, Thomas Gage, Christopher Gist, Horatio Gates, Henry Gladwin, Charles Lee, Adam Stephen, Hugh Mercer, Andrew Lewis, Dr. Thomas Walker, and George Washington were the most prominent. General Braddock declined the services of Richard Henry Lee.[2]

Colonial governors in 1755 included Robert Dinwiddie[3] of Virginia, Horatio Sharpe of Maryland, Arthur Dobbs of North Carolina, William Shirley of Massachusetts, James De Lancey of New York, and Robert Hunter Morris of Pennsylvania.[4] Until the arrival of General Braddock, Governor Sharpe of Maryland was the Commander-in-Chief of British forces in North America.[5]

The territory of Virginia in the late 1750s included what is now western Pennsylvania and the present states of West Virginia, Kentucky, Ohio, Indiana, Illinois, Michigan, and Wisconsin.[6] Williamsburg was the seat of government for the Virginia colony that stretched to the Ohio and beyond. Winchester, Virginia, 194 miles northwest from Williamsburg, was a post on the way to Ft. Cumberland at Wills' Creek.[7]

Ft. Cumberland, "named in honor of the Duke of Cumberland, Captain-General of the British Army, (sometimes called Fort Mt. Pleasant), stood on the Bank of Wills' Creek, near its junction with the Potomac, on the site of the present city of Cumberland, in Alleghany county, Md. In ancient days the site of the fortification had been a Shawanese village, with the Indian name of Cucucvetuc."[8] The road between Winchester and Ft. Cumberland was almost nonexistent. "From Winchester to this place which is seventy miles is almost uninhabited, but by a parcel of Banditti who call themselves Indian Traders, and no Road passable but what we were obliged to make ourselves with infinite Labour."[9] A trail led from Wills' Creek to Ft. Duquesne.

The British evaluation of the state of affairs left them three courses of action.[10] First, British, American, and Indian forces could drive the French from the forts they had built or captured in the Ohio Valley. Second, forces could attack other places simultaneously with the attacks on the French forts considered in alternative one. Third, they could create a diversion, weakening, or abandonment of the French locations mentioned in alternative one by a principal attack in another place. The British were concerned about French forts at Niagara and Crown Point on the New York frontier as well. There also was the possibility of French encroachment in the Carolinas.

Benjamin Franklin, who played an important role in the Braddock Expedition, provided insight as to British reasoning. "The British Government not chusing to permit the Union of the Colonies, as propos'd at Albany,[11] and to trust that Union with their Defence, lest they should thereby grow too military, and feel their own Strength, Suspicions & Jealousies at this time being entertain'd of them; sent over General Braddock with two Regiments of Regular English Troops for that purpose."[12]

The specific plans of the British appeared in a *Sketch of Regulations & Orders Proposed Relating to Affairs of North America, November, 1754 and Quaeries Relating to the Same.*[13] Major General Edward Braddock was to command His Majesty's Forces. The forces included two regiments. Sir Peter Halkett commanded the 44th Regiment of Foot, and Colonel Dunbar commanded the 48th Regiment of Foot. "For the expedition he was given two of the army's poorest infantry regiments."[14] Each consisted of 30 sergeants, 30 corporals, 20 drummers, and 500 privates, to be augmented to 700 rank and file from Virginia, North and South Carolina, Maryland, and Pennsylvania. The Deputy Quarter Master General was Sir John St. Clair.[15] Mr. Pitcher was Commissary of the Musters.[16]

Commodore Keppel commanded the British naval component of the Expedition. The British Navy supplied two ships of the line and two frigates for this venture, as well as transports. The HMS Centurion and HMS Norwich transported Commodore Keppel and Major General Braddock, respectively, to Hampton, Virginia:

Instructions from the Lords of the Admiralty to Admiral Keppel

Two of His Ships of the Line, and two Frigats, should be got ready to be employed in North America for the Protection of His Colonies, and that a sufficient Number of Transport Ships should be provided and Victualled, for carrying from Cork in Ireland to Virginia in North America Sir Peter Halket's & Colonel Dunbar's Regiments of Foot, each consisting of 644 Persons, together with 74 Commission Officers their Servants and Baggage: and 354 Tuns of Arms, Accoutrements &ca for Colo Shirley's and Sir William Pepperel's Regiments to be raised in New England; to proceed under Convoy of the Two aforementioned Frigats; And Thirteen Transport Ships being provided for this purpose. The said Thirteen Ships, with Three others laden with Ordnance Stores in the Service of that Office, are ordered to proceed directly from Cork to Virginia, under Convoy of His Majesty's Ships the Seahorse and Nightingale, commanded by Captains Pallisser and Diggs.

The troops are to be immediately brigaded in the following manner - orders given at Fort Cumberland:
The First Brigade, Commanded by Sir Peter Halket.
44th Regiment of Foot - 700 men
Captain Rutherford's - Independent Company of New York - 100 men
Captain Gates - Independent Company of New York.

Captain Polson's - Carpenters - 50
Captain Peronnee's - Virginia Rangers - 50
Captain Wagner's - Virginia Rangers - 50
Captain Dagworthy's - Maryland Rangers - 50
Second Brigade, Commanded by Colonel Dunbar
48th Regiment of Foot - 700
Captain Demerie's - South Carolina Detachment - 100
Captain Dobb's - North Carolina Rangers - 100
Captain Mercer's - Company of Carpenters - 50
Captain Stevens's - Virginia Rangers - 50
Captain Hogg's - Virginia Rangers - 50
Captain Cox's - Virginia Rangers - 50

The Detachment of Seamen to encamp with the Second Brigade and the Troop of light horse separately.

When you arrive at Virginia, in the Centurion, you will probably find there the Three other aforementioned Men of War, with the Transports; and also the Ships named in the Margin, which are Stationed in North America, and ordered to rendezvous at Virginia.[17]

The British identified three routes in America by which to transport men and supplies to the Ohio Valley.[18] The first route was through Virginia. The second was by way of the Potomac River. The third was through New York, Philadelphia, Lancaster, and on to Winchester, Virginia.

The third route implies there was no road through western Maryland or Pennsylvania to Ft. Cumberland in late 1754. The third route is interesting because there were two routes from Lancaster to Winchester. One route was the Great Wagon Road to Philadelphia.[19] This route led from Philadelphia through Lancaster, York, Conococheague, and on to Winchester, Virginia.[20] The 1751 Fry and Jefferson Map indicates the Great Wagon Road from Philadelphia went south from Winchester, Virginia, to Charlotte, North Carolina.

The second route between Winchester and Philadelphia went from Philadelphia through Lancaster and Wright's Ferry in Pennsylvania, Frederick Town and Fox's Gap in Maryland,

Shepherdstown in Virginia, and on to Winchester. This route was the Great Philadelphia Wagon Road, also known as the road from Conestoga to Opequon. The route passed through the areas that became Taney Town and Woodsborough in Maryland. This route appeared on the 1794 Map of Maryland by Dennis Griffith.

Nead, in *The Pennsylvania-German in the Settlement of Maryland,* included the courses of the Pennsylvania portion of the Great Philadelphia Wagon Road as recorded in the February 6, 1740, Minutes of the Court of General Quarter Sessions. Nead indicated the Maryland assembly continued the road to the Potomac River. However, he stated, "thence to the Potomac river, crossing the South Mountain through a gap known as Crampton's Gap."[21] Although a route through Crampton's Gap did lead from the Frederick and Middletown area to Harper's Ferry, it was not the main route. The road through Crampton's Gap was only a horse trail until at least the late 1760s. The main route continued through Fox's Gap to Winchester and was a wagon road by the early 1730s.

Conestoga was in Pennsylvania near Lancaster.[22] Opequon was about 5 miles southwest of Winchester, Virginia. Tracey and Dern, in *Pioneers of Old Monocacy,* indicated the road from Conestoga to Opequon went through Turner's Gap, about one mile north of Fox's Gap.[23] These authors were mistaken, as will be shown later. The road went through Fox's Gap:

Different Routes in North America [1754] (copy)

Route from Williamsburg to the French Fort upon Lake Erie near the Ohio by Land
From Williamsburg to Fredericksburg across two Ferries, one over Pamunkey River, the other over Mattapony River at the Places marked in the Map. 100 Miles. From Fredericksburg to Winchester 90 Miles, i.e., 70 to the Mountains and 20 beyond them. From Winchester to Wills' Creek. 50 Miles. Thus far the Road is very good, and passable with all sorts of Carriages. From Wills' Creek to Gist's Plantation on the Monongehela 70 Miles.

From Gists's Plantation to the Forks 50 Miles. Here the Fort built by Us and taken by the French is situated.

Route to the Ohio by Water
From the Mouth of Potomack river to the Great Falls is 170 Miles, navigable for Vessels of 200 or 300 Tons. From Alexandria at the lower part of the Falls to where the River is again navigable, a Land Carriage of 30 Miles good Road. From hence to next Falls thro' the blue Ridge 60 Miles, navigable for Canoes carrying 1000 Wt. Land Carriage of 3 or 4 Miles to where the River is again navigable. From hence to Wills' Creek 200 Miles, navigable for small boats, which will carry about 1000 Weight.

Route from Winchester to New York.
From Winchester to Lancaster 100 Miles. From Lancaster to Philadelphia 68 Miles. From Philadelphia to Trenton 30 Miles. From Trenton to New York 66 Miles. N. B. A Good Wagon Road passable for all sorts of Carriages.[24]

The 1755 version of the Fry and Jefferson Map included the following table, added to the map in that year:

These Distances with the course of the Roads on the map I carefully collected on the spot and entered them in my journal from whence they are now inserted.
J. Dalrymple
London Jan. 1st 1755

	Williamsburg	Fredericksburg	Alexandria
Fredericksburg	107 1/2 N miles		
Alexandria	168 N	60 1/2	
Lord Fairfax	186 NW	76 NW	78 E
Winchester	194 NW	84 NW	86 E
Wills' Creek	281 NW	171 NW	173 E to N
Ft. Necesity or			
The Great Meadow		238 NW	238 E to N
Ft. Duquesne	591 NW	281 NW	283 E to N

A unit of measure used by the English during this period, relating time and distance, seems useful to point out. According to Michel, "three English miles make an hour."[25]

Included in a *Sketch for the Operations in North America* on November 16, 1754, we find additional British strategic plans:

> The French will, in all Probability, endeavour to reinforce the several Posts they now have on the River Ohio; & on the Lakes to the Westward of it, by sending Troops up the River Mississipi: as the season will allow the King's Troops to take the Field much sooner in those southern Parts than in any other Part of the Colonies; the operations should begin there as soon as the Weather will permit. The Troops should therefore be carried up to Potomach River, as high as Wills' Creek, where Covering is ordered to be erected for them by Deputy Quarter Master General Sir John St. Clair; as also Magazines & a Park for the amunition & artillery, which may be necessary upon this first Part of the Expedition: the Quarter Master general having likewise orders to prepare conveniencies for the genl Hospital at Hampton, & for a flying one at the Creek before mentioned.[26]

Concern with the French on the Ohio was not far from the minds of colonial governors as well. In this context, Governor Dinwiddie of Virginia addressed the House of Burgesses at Williamsburg on September 4, 1754. He admonished them for their failure to support a campaign against the French on the Ohio and dismissed them until October 17. Despite their unwillingness to address the situation presented by the French and the growing number of their Indian allies, the House of Burgesses soon concluded they must support a campaign to reclaim the Ohio Valley.

Governor Sharpe of Maryland was a strong proponent of English interests. He was a critical player at this time on the stage of world events. "In the correspondence of Governor Sharpe, the earlier portion of which is now for the first time published, we have one of the most precious sources of information concerning a momentous period in our colonial history, the final struggle between England and France for the possession of North America."[27] The 1755 Census gave Baltimore County a population of 17,238 and Frederick County 13,970.[28]

Efforts by Governor Sharpe to join with other Colonies in a common defense against the French met with resistance from the Assembly. "The Revival of the Law for Arms & Ammunition I did my utmost to promote but neither my Exhortations nor the Secretary of State's Letter requiring them to join in the Defence of the neighbouring Colonies against any hostile Attempts of the French or Indians could induce them to think such a timely provision reasonable & necessary."[29]

Sharpe's efforts to persuade the Maryland Assembly to join the effort against the French and Indians continued to be difficult during much of 1754. "A Bill also was sent from the Lower House with the specious Preamble of being for His Majesty's Service, whereby the Sum of £3000 was to be granted for the support of the neighbouring Colonies against any Attempts of the French or other hostile Troops: but the old Clause concerning Hawkers & Pedlars (whereby your Lordships Right to forfeitures is disputed) being inserted therein & the Lower House in many Conferences obstinately persisting that not the least Concession should on their part be made with respect to that Article the Bill was returned them with a negative & so the Affair Dropt."[30] Finally, in mid July 1754, Sharpe prevailed upon his Assembly for the sum of £6,000.[31] The Assembly passed the measure without inserting the clause concerning hawkers and pedlars.[32]

In New York, Governor DeLancey obtained a pledge of cooperation. "The Assembly have also resolved (upon my laying before them the letter from the Earl of Holdeness one of his Majesty's principal Secretaries of state) that they will make a suitable Provision for Assisting any of the Neighbouring Colonies to repell force by force in case they be invaded in an Hostile manner by any armed force whatsoever."[33]

Governor Sharpe's itinerary showed his involvement with the state of affairs. Announcements in the *Maryland Gazette* indicated his travels, many of which involved military considerations in the Ohio Valley. On September 12, Sharpe left for Calvert, St. Mary's, Charles, Prince George's, and Frederick Counties. He was to tour Wills' Creek before returning home the middle of October.[34] However, Governor Sharpe postponed his trip to Wills' Creek and returned home September 27.[35]

On October 17, Governor Sharpe went to Williamsburg.[36] "As soon as Governor Dinwiddie signified to me that Mr Dobbs was arrived & that His Majesty's Pleasure would be obeyed by my coming to Williamsburg before Governor Dobbs should depart for North Carolina I immediately took the Liberty to leave Annapolis & came hither the 19th Instant where I have been entirely taken up ever since in consulting with those Gentlemen on the most expedient Measures for promoting His Majesty's Service & in making preparations for putting those measures in Execution."[37] Sharpe returned to Annapolis November 3.[38]

Sharpe departed for Wills' Creek on November 12:[39]

The making some necessary preparations for my Journey will detain me this week at Annapolis but the beginning of next I propose to set out for Wills' Creek & if there appears a probability of effecting any thing with such a Body of Troops as can be drawn together before the severe Season come on, I hope by the next opportunity of Conveyance that will probably offer to give you a Satisfactory account of my Winters Campaign. But if a Council of War which I intend to hold as soon as I reach Wills' Creek shall find it most expedient to postpone any Attack till the Neighbouring Governments can be persuaded to send us proper Reinforcements I shall return again as soon as I have regulated & disposed of the Companies for the security of our Frontiers this winter against the Incursions of the French Indians who were seen Governor Morris advises me on their March towards the French Fort on Ohio to be employed this winter as was apprehended against our Back Inhabitants.[40]

Sharpe returned to Annapolis on December 5.[41]

Logistics was the one great problem confronting the Braddock Expedition. The transportation of men and material from Alexandria to Ft. Cumberland and beyond was a monumental endeavor. British plans did not envision the task required. In retrospect, the success of transporting the materials, including cannons weighing thousands of pounds, to Ft. Cumberland and beyond was perhaps the most significant achievement of the Braddock Expedition.

Food for the troops was a problem from Alexandria to the Ohio Valley. Governor Dinwiddie appointed Charles Dick and Thomas Walker commissaries. "Dr. Thomas Walker (1715-1794) was one of the leading land speculators of colonial times."[42] These men played a significant role in feeding the troops and moving the supplies:

Governor Dinwiddie's Commission to Charles Dick and Thomas Walker

R. D., Esq'r., Gov'r, &c., To Chas. Dick and Thomas Walker, Esq'rs: By Virtue of the Power and Authority given me by His M'y's imediate Com'ds to conduct the present Expedit'n to the Ohio ag'st the French and encroachments on the King's Lands, I, reposing especital Trust and confidence in the Fidelity, knowledge and good Conduct of You, C.D. and T. W., Do hereby appoint You to be joint Comissaries for Provis's and Stores, to be purchas'd and provided for the Forces intended for the Ohio. And I hereby give You full Power and Authority to contract, agree for and purchase such Provis's as may be tho't necessary for a due and proper Supply for the afores'd Forces. And you hereby have Power and Authority to press Horses, Wagons, Boats, &c., y't may be necessary for convey'g the Provis's to the Camp or to attend the Forces on their March, Conduct'g Yourselves agreeable to the Act of Assembly in like Cases provided. And I further hereby order and Command all Officers, Civil and Military, to be aiding and assist'g to You in the discharge of Y'r Appointm't. Given, &c., 28th Dec'r, 1754.[43]

In January 1755, Annapolis welcomed members of the British forces. "Last Monday, Lt. Col. Elliston, of Col. Shirley's Regiment, and Lt. Col. Mercer, of Sir William Pepperell's

Regiment (who came from England in the Gibraltar Man of War
recently), came into Annapolis."[44] Sir John St. Clair, Deputy
Quarter Master General, arrived at Hampton, Virginia, shortly
after the new year as well. 'The Gilbraltar Ship of War arrived
here the 9th curr't, and bro't Passengers S'r Jno. St. Clair and two
L't. Colo's and two Adjut'ts for the two Regim'ts to be rais'd in N.
Engl'd, ect."[45]

Activities of Sir John St. Clair and Governor Sharpe

The role played by Sir John St. Clair in the Braddock
Expedition was substantial. He made the initial preparations
for the Expedition to the Ohio Valley. Sir John reconnoitered
much of the territory before the arrival of General Braddock and
formulated a plan for the disposition of the troops upon their
arrival. On January 10, Sir John traveled to Williamsburg where
he delivered dispatches to Governor Dinwiddie and spent
January 11 consulting with the Governor regarding the
Expedition.[46] The next day, St. Clair and Governor Dinwiddie
went to Hampton to implement St. Clair's order to establish a
hospital sufficient to accommodate 150 sick. Upon their return to
Williamsburg the 14th, St. Clair wrote letters to the Governors
of all the provinces. St. Clair and Governor Dinwiddie agreed
the Expedition could save three weeks by landing all the troops
at Alexandria instead of Hampton.

Governor Sharpe left Annapolis January 13 bound for the
camp at Mount Pleasant on Wills' Creek.[47] His intent was to
remain at the camp for a month, unless something required his
return to Annapolis.[48] St. Clair arrived at Ft. Cumberland on
January 26, two days after Sharpe.[49]

St. Clair described his plan to visit Wills' Creek in a
letter to General Braddock. "I propose going tomorrow morning
from hence to Wills' Creek, I shall go the one Road and return
the other; my Journey will take me at least twelve Days going
and coming back, being 600 Miles with the same Horses; I shall
stay there about Six Days which I hope will be Sufficient to see
our Barracks in a fair way of being built. Shall return hither the
2d Day of Febry or sooner if I can do my business."[50] St. Clair
intended to average 50 miles per day by horse between
Williamsburg and Wills' Creek.

The following account of St. Clair's trip gives a vivid picture of the condition of the roads. "The 16th of January set out for Fredericksbourg, and got to that place the 18th being 104 Miles of very good Road. From the 19th to the 22d getting to Winchester which is 93 Miles of very bad Road. From the 23d to the 26th I was on the Road to Wills' Creek, this is 85 miles of the worst Road I ever travelled; and greatly lengthen'd by the Roads being in the Channells of the Rivers, when they might be shorten'd by cutting them along the Ridges of the Mountains. Cut road to avoid Patersons Creek."[51]

Sir John gave no indication of what he meant by going to Wills' Creek by one road and returning by the other. Conococheague, however, was on his return route. Sharpe and St. Clair came down the Potomac by canoe. St. Clair and Governor Sharpe were with Governor Dinwiddie on February 8, presumably in Williamsburg.[52]

Sharpe entertained hopes for a winter campaign, led by him, against the French. He gave up the hope for such after his arrival at Wills' Creek:

> ... but whatever were my wishes at that time I was soon convinced of their Vanity when I arrived at Wills' Creek. there I learnt that the Number of the French at their Fort exceeded 600 beside several Parties of Indians who were at their Devotion & submitted to their Command. The Fort tho small was rendered pretty defensible by a Ditch & two Out works before the curtains that faced the Land on the side of the rivers it was surrounded with Stoccadoes or Palisades & the Garrison had laid in a sufficient Stock of Provision for at least the whole winter.
>
> The Troops that I must have commanded were three Independant Companies that did not in the least answer the Expectations I had entertained of them, the Remains of the Virginia Forces amounted to about 120 discontented unruly & mutinous; the Maryland Company was at that time incompleat & undiciplined but I may without vanity declaire they were equal to any there. The Officers who bore his Majesty's Commission would

not deign to rank with those who served under his Governor's Commissions; in vain were my Attempts to persuade them to agree tho I proposed the same Scheme which I find is now come with a Sanction from home.[53]

The journey to Wills' Creek gave Sir John an indication of the navigation problems on the Potomac:

> That part of my Instructions which regards the building of Batteaus or Floats on the Pattommack at the Falls of Alexandria, I am obliged to delay executing, as I am informed the doing of it wou'd be in vain, for that in Winter the Stream is so rapid that there is no rowing heavy Boats against the Current, and that in Summer there are many flatts and Shoals which will render the Navigation almost impracticable.[54]
>
> I acquainted you that Governor Dinwiddie told me that the Navigation of the Pattommack is impracticable, this I can now affirm from Experience, for Governour Sharp and I found it so for all other Vessells but Canoes cut out of a Single Tree; We attempted to go down the River in this sort of boat, but we were obliged to get on Shore and walk on foot expecially at the Shannondeau Falls: So that the getting Batteaus or floats made for the transport of the Artillery and the Baggage of the Regiments, cou'd serve for no other thing, but to throw away the Government's Money to no purpose, and loose a great deal of time.[55]

The Different Routes in North America, previously listed, included a *Route to the Ohio by Water.* There should be no doubt the British planned to use the Potomac River to the extent possible. St. Clair's remarks indicated any usage of the Potomac was limited.

Sharpe confirmed his and St. Clair's trip down the Potomac. ". . . we set off to explore Potowmack River which proved from the number of shoals & falls be of no Service in transporting either Artillery or other Baggage in our passage down Sr. John contracted for all the Forrage Flour & Calavances[56] on the Banks of that River the next thing we went

upon was a proper Disposition for Quartering the Troops of all
which Sir John St. Clair having given you a distinct Account I
shall not trouble you with a Repetition."[57]

Sharpe explained his activities on his trip to Ft.
Cumberland in a letter to Lord Baltimore:

> After I had been there a week I had the pleasure
> to see Sir John St. Clair arrive, also after which we
> tarried there only one Day & in Order to examine the
> Channel of that River we came down Potowmack by
> water for the Distance of about 250 Miles,[58] the many
> Falls & Shoals in that River will we find render the
> conveyance of Artillery & other Stores to the Camp by
> water impracticable, the 5th Day from our leaving the
> Camp we reached Alexandria or Belhaven a Town on the
> South Bank of Potowmack just below the great Falls of
> that River having purchased & secured all the
> Provisions & Forrage that was to be gotten on each side
> the Water as we came down, staying a Day at Belhaven
> we proceeded to Dumfries & Fredericksburg in Virginia
> providing & engaging Quarters for the Troops in each of
> those places & from thence we journyed to Williamsburg
> where we hope to find General Braddock by that time
> arrived. We have agreed to quarter 5 of the Companies
> from Europe for a month or so to refresh themselves after
> their Voyage if the General approves thereof, in your
> Ldp's province, one Company at Marlboro, one at
> Bladensburg, a third at Rock Creek, three Towns in
> Prince George Cty & two at Frederick Town which stands
> on Monoceasy River in Frederick Cty.[59]

The February 9 letter from St. Clair to Braddock also is
significant because it outlined St. Clair's, and Sharpe's, plan of
dispersing the forces upon their arrival:

> As I have seen most of this country, I shall more
> freely give my opinion with regard to the Dispostion of
> the Troops on their Arrival, both for the Security of our
> Magazines, Subsistance of the Troops, ease of the

Inhabitants and that as few Countermarches may be made as possible.

The first thing to be done at all Events is to have our Artillery, Baggage and Provisions carried up to Winchester from Alexandria. During the Transport of the Artillery to Winchester, there will be sufficient time to cut the Road to Savage River.

That the Transports which have on board one Regiment may stop in the River Pattommack as near Fredericksbourg as they can, that Regiment may be quartered in the following manner.

3 1/2 Companys at Winchester 6 Days march from Fredericksbourg

1/2 of a Company at Conogogee 8 Days by Winchester

6 Companys at Fredericksbourg & Falmouth,[60] one march from their landing

The other Regiment

5 Companys at Alexandria with the Company of Artillery & Stores of all kind.

1 Company at Dumfries 2 Days march from Alexandria.

1 Compy at Upper Marlbro' 1 Days march (in Maryland)

1 Company at Bladensbourg 1 Days March (in Maryland)

2 Companys at Frederick 6 Days march (in Maryland)

By this disposition the Companys which are quartered at Winchester Conogogee and Frederick form the Chains, to cover our Magazines, and will be near at Hand to advance either to Wills' Creek or Savage River as you shall Judge most proper.[61]

Ft. Cumberland was poorly situated in St. Clair's opinion. "The Fort and Magazine at W. Creek is tho't by S'r Jno. St. Clair not to be in a proper Situat'n, yet of much Use as a Magazine."[62] Sir John's plan included using Conococheague as part of the supply route. He planned on half of a company at Conococheague, "8 Days by Winchester," and two companies at Frederick Town in Maryland. "I expect 100 Wagons with Flower from Pensilvania at Winchester by the 15th of March, which Wagons will serve for carrying the Amunition and Stores from Alexandria, least the Horses of this Country employ'd before that time shou'd fall off."[63]

St. Clair and Sharpe expected General Braddock to be at Williamsburg upon their return from Wills' Creek. "As Governour Sharpe expected to have found you arrived, he came to this place (Williamsburg) by Alexandria and Fredericksbourg, at the latter I saw him review 80 men of the Virginia Troops."[64] Governor Sharpe returned home, by way of "Fredericksbourg and Alexandria" on Tuesday afternoon, February 18, to meet with his Assembly on the 20th.[65]

St. Clair was in the Williamsburg area February 8 through 16. He again set out for Winchester on February 18. "This may take me up some Days. Then will go to Alexandria either to wait General Braddock or to where the service requires."[66] According to Governor Dinwiddie, "S'r Jono is gone to W. Creek to review the Independents and the Recruits raised for this Province, and to form them into Companies."[67] Sir John St. Clair returned to Alexandria by early March. Governor Sharpe received a letter from St. Clair and went to Alexandria to meet him.[68] Sharpe returned to Annapolis on Saturday morning, March 8.[69]

The Arrival of General Braddock

Two journals, written by participants to the Braddock Expedition, appeared in *The History of An Expedition against Fort DuQuesne, in 1755,* edited by Winthrop Sargent. The journalists provided a contemporary account of the Expedition. Robert Orme (? - Feb. 1781), an aide-de-camp of General Braddock, was the author of the Orme Journal. He "entered the army as an ensign in the 35th Foot. On 16th Sept. 1745, he exchanged into the Coldstreams, of which he became a lieutenant, April 24, 1751. He was never raised to a captaincy, though always spoken of as such."[70] The dates provided by Orme in his journal are not precise. Orme wrote his journal as a recapitulation of events, days or perhaps months, after they happened.[71]

The Morris, or Seaman's, Journal begins at Alexandria on April 10 and runs to August 18, 1755. "The author of this Journal is unknown. It was not General Braddock Aide-de-Camp Captain Roger Morris. The author was one of the naval officers detached for this service by Commodore Keppel."[72] He was member of the detachment of seamen ordered to accompany the army to Ft. Duquesne. The journalist marched with Dunbar's Regiment through Frederick Town and Conococheague in Maryland, providing a narrative of the route.

General Braddock arrived at Hampton, Virginia, on February 20, 1755. He proceeded to Williamsburg where he met with Governor Dinwiddie:

> Gen'l Braddock came to my Ho. last Sunday Night, and he expects the forces from Irel'd in a Fortnight. He has formed the Virg'a Forces as follows: Two Compa's of Carpenters, chose from the whole; four Compa's of Rangers, and one Compa. of light Horse, and w't may rem'n and are suitable, are to Augm't the two Regim'ts from Irel'd.[73]

General Braddock and Commodore Keppel agreed to disembark the troops at Alexandria. All the troops arrived before General Braddock reached Alexandria in early April (OR, 297). A considerable quantity of beef was brought on the transports as 1000 barrels were unloaded at Alexandria (OR, 288). General Braddock requested Governors Shirley, Delancey, Morris, and Sharpe to meet him at Annapolis in early April (OR, 288).

Supplies and the ability to transport them remained a critical issue. Pennsylvania agreed to supply flour for the Expedition, to be delivered at Conococheague:

> I congratulate You on Y'r Assembly's voting £10,000, w'ch will be of great Service. Three more of the Transports are arrived at Hampton, and I expect they will all be there this Week. Pensylvania has ordered the purchase of 14,000 Bush's of Wheat, to be bolted into Flour and delivered at Conegocheek, w'ch, with the Qu'ty already engag'd, [I] am in hopes will be sufficient for Bread. I have sent of Alex'a and Fredericksb'g, 800 bls. Pork and 1,000 bls. Beef on board the Transports. I conceive, with Bacon and Butter in the back Counties, will answer for Provis's; the greatest strait we shall be

under will be the want of Horses and Carriages, this is
an Affair of the greatest Consequence.[74]

Governor Dinwiddie, on March 9, received Governor
Morris's letter of February 26, indicating the proposed delivery
of 14,000 bushels of wheat at Conococheague.[75] This was a major
triumph for Governor Dinwiddie. He promptly wrote Governors
Morris and Sharpe. "Y'r favo. of the 26th Ult'o I rec'd
Yesterday. I am very glad You prevail'd with Y'r Committee for
the Flour of 14,000 bush's of Wheat, to be delivered at
Conegocheek."[76] Conococheague became a major supply point to
the Braddock Expedition.

Governor Dinwiddie expressed his concern for the
Braddock Expedition in early March:

> As the Transports are most of them arrived, I
> believe the Gen'l will take the Field soon, but the want
> of Carriages for Ordnance Stores is w't I have much in
> Tho'ts. I have ordered 16 Wagons to be built, but we
> shall want 100 . . . What may be expected from the Six
> Nat's? I fear the N. York Colony has not managed well
> with these People. You know Washington's Conduct was
> in many Steps wrong, and did not conform to his Orders
> from me, or he had not engaged till the other Forces had
> joined him . . . I shall wait on the Gen'l to Annapolis,
> where he expects to meet Gov'r Shirley, to consult the
> General Plan of Operations, and I doubt not Niagara will
> be greatly the Object of their Consultat's, as I think y't
> Fort to be of the greatest Consequ'ce . . . Pray favo. me
> with a Letter to Annapolis, describ'g the Wensh Ferry
> Carriage for convey'g Provis's, &c. over the Mount's. The
> heavy Guns of 4,000 lbs. will require great Care and
> Labour to get them over, tho' the Number of Ingineers
> now here may be supposed well qualified for such
> Work.[77]

General Braddock wrote Robert Napier from
Williamsburg on March 17. "Have pack'd them all up to
Alexandria with very little grumbling, whither I propose to

follow them the day after to morrow, and in all probability be there a day or two before them."[78] Braddock indicated to Napier his decision concerning the disposition of his forces:

> I at first intended to have canton'd the Troops according to the Account sent you by Sir John St. Clair, but as the Winter seems to be now so far broke up as to admit of their encamping without any ill consequence, I have order'd those that first arriv'd, as I have the others since, to proceed up the River Potomack to Alexandria, there to disembark and encamp immediatly.
>
> The Levies [troops] of Virginia and Maryland are likewise to join me at Alexandria: After I have augmented the two English Regiments to 700 Men each with the best of 'em, I purpose to form the others to the following Establishmt which has been agreed to by Govr Dinwiddie; vizt Two Companies of Carpenters, consisting each of a Captain, two Subalterns, three Serjeants, three Corporals, and fifty Men; Four Companies of Foot Rangers or six, if I can get them, upon the same Establishment; One troop of Horse Rangers, consisting of one Captain, two Subalterns, two Serjeants and thirty Men: These companies are to receive from the Province the same nominal pay in the Currency of the Country . . . I have also settled a Company of Guides, one Captain two Aids and ten Men. I have fix'd posts from the Head Quarters to Philadelphia, Annapolis and Williamsburg, to facilitate the Correspondence necessary for me with those several Governments.[79]

In late March General Braddock indicated, "I have appointed Captain Morris of Dunbar's my other Aide-de-Camp, and have given the Major of Brigade's Commission to Captain Halket at Sir John St. Clair's Recommendation."[80]

It was early March when the General sought the services of a young man with experience in dealing with the French on the Ohio. Until March 14, George Washington had been out of the service, but on that date he received the following letter:

Williamsburg, March 2, 1755

Sir: The General having been informed that you
expressed some desire to make the campaign, but that
you declined it upon the disagreeableness that you
thought might arise from the regulation of command,
has ordered me to acquaint you that he will be very glad
of your company in his family by which all
inconveniences of that kind will be obviated. I shall
think myself very happy to form an acquaintance with a
person so universally esteemed and shall use every
opportunity of assuring you how much I am . . Sir . . Your
most obedient servant, Robert Orme, aide-de-camp[81]

St. Clair attended to his own schedule during this time.
A letter from St. Clair to Napier indicated, "In my last letter to
you I acquainted you that I was to review the Independent
Companys and to form the Provincial Troops of Virginia and
Maryland in which Service I was employd till the 24th of
March, they being scattered all about the County. On my coming
that Day to Alexandria I found the British Troops disembarked
and beginning to land their Stores."[82]

St. Clair departed Alexandria for Ft. Cumberland on
April 2. His purpose was to assist the transport of the artillery
and stores to Wills' Creek. He did not arrive at the fort until the
16th because he helped repair old roads and cut a new one.[83] The
roads to the fort were not passable until May 1.[84]

The Governor's Conference at Alexandria

The General, accompanied by Governor Dinwiddie and
Commodore Keppel, set out from Williamsburg for Alexandria on
March 22. They arrived in Alexandria on the 26th.[85] The group
arrived at Annapolis the afternoon of April 3, in preparation for
the Governor's Conference.[86] The Governors did not arrive by
Monday the 7th, so the General returned to Alexandria. While
at Annapolis, the General learned no wagons were available on
the Maryland side of the Potomac. He appealed to Governor
Sharpe, who promised more than one hundred at Rock Creek
(OR, 282).

Sharpe indicated to Calvert, on April 10, that the Governor's Conference had been moved to Alexandria. "Governor Shirley has not yet reached Annapolis but I expect him & Governor Morris to Morrow & shall the next morning accompany them to Alexandria where the General proposes to tarry till the Middle or End of next week whence he will proceed to Frederick Town in his way with the Regiments to Wills' Creek."[87]

Governor Sharpe, in company with some of the other governors, departed Annapolis for Alexandria on April 12. The Governors, as well as Colonel Johnston, arrived at Alexandria on the 13th. General Braddock, Commodore Keppel, and Governors Shirley, Delancy, Dinwiddie, Sharpe, and Morris held their conference on the 14th[88] in the Carlisle House, often called the Braddock House.[89]

The Governors reported to the General that they had tried to establish a common fund for the support of the Expedition, but were unsuccessful with their Assemblies (OR, 300-1). Governor Morris of Pennsylvania presented the report of his road commissioners.[90] The members of the conference decided to attack Crown Point and Niagara at the same time as Ft. Duquesne (OR, 300).

The governors were of the opinion that Pennsylvania, Virginia, and Maryland should maintain a garrison at Ft. Duquesne as well as on Lake Erie, if General Braddock achieved success. Sharpe solicited his brother John, "I hope your good Offices will procure me the Command thereof as I have good reason to think neither of the other Governors will be found my Opponents."[91]

> Mr. Dinwiddie laid before the General contracts made for eleven hundred head of cattle, eight hundred of which were to be delivered in June and July, and three hundred in August; he said that he had also written Governor Shirley, for a large quantity of salt fish, that a great deal of flour was already at Fort Cumberland, and that the assembly of Pennsylvania had promised to deliver flour, to the amount of five thousand pounds of their currency, at the mouth of Conegogee, in April, which was to be carried up the Potomack to Fort Cumberland (OR, 287).

General Braddock ordered Halket's and Dunbar's
Regiments to march to Ft. Cumberland by different routes.
Braddock ordered Halket to march to Winchester with six
companies. Lt. Col. Thomas Gage was to remain with four
companies to escort the artillery (OR, 298). Halkett's regiment
and the artillery were to go through Virginia by way of
Alexandria and Winchester. Dunbar's Regiment, with the stores
and the ammunition, were to go through Maryland by way of
Frederick Town and Conococheague.

St. Clair "proposed that one regiment with all the
powder and ordnance [artillery] should go by Winchester, and
the other regiment with the ammunition, military and hospital
stores by Frederick in Maryland. That these should be carried
ten miles up the Potomack to Rock Creek, and then up the
Potomack to Ft. Cumberland" (OR, 296).

Sharpe returned to Annapolis on the 17th after the
Conference.[92] A letter to Lord Baltimore, April 19, described
Sharpe's agenda and that of General Braddock:

> . . . at present two Virginia and the Maryland
> Company are engaged in opening a Road to Wills' Creek
> & thence towards Juniata River in Pensilva which flows
> into Susquehanna . . . The three Governors above
> mentioned from the Northward came hither the 11th &
> 12th Inst, & this Day Sennight I proceeded with them to
> Alexandria, which place we left again Thursday
> morning & they are now on their way returning to their
> respective Governts General Braddock departs from
> Alexandria to Day & I have promised to be with him
> next Tuesday Evening at Frederickton where I shall
> tarry till the 1st of May when all the Troops will be in
> Motion & he will proceed to Wills' Creek & thence
> without any Stop or Delay for the Ohio.[93]

Initially, Sharpe planned to accompany General
Braddock to Wills' Creek. "Governor Shirley departed hence for
N England this Morning after having had an Interview with
General Braddock at Alexandria which place the General

proposed also to leave this Day & proceed to Frederick Town on this Side Potowmack where I shall do myself the honour to wait on him next Tuesday & with his permission attend him to Wills' Creek for which place the two Regiments will receive his Orders to march the end of this Month."[94]

Dunbar's Regiment from Alexandria to Frederick Town

General Braddock intended to use the sailors to assist Halkett's Regiment in transporting the artillery. Braddock mistook his orders regarding the assignment of the sailors and later corrected his oversight. The orders from England indicated the sailors were to assist Dunbar's Regiment.

The seamen received orders on April 10 to march the following day with six companies of Sir Peter Halkett's Regiment to Wills' Creek. On the 11th, Braddock countermanded the orders. The seamen proceeded to Rock Creek, eight miles from Alexandria, in the Sea Horse and Nightingale's boats on the 12th. There they put themselves under Colonel Dunbar. The seamen assisted in loading wagons the next day (MR, 367). Rock Creek probably was the site of current day Georgetown.[95] Halkett left Alexandria April 9 (OR, 298-9).

Shortly before the Governor's Conference got underway, some of Dunbar's troops marched for Frederick Town in Maryland. Members of Dunbar's Regiment continued their march to Frederick Town on April 14 at six in the morning. The seamen received orders to march at the front and arrived at Lawrence Owen's about two o'clock.[96] Owen's Ordinary was about fifteen miles from Rock Creek and eight miles from the upper falls of the Potomac (MR, 367). The march began the following day at 5:00 a.m. The troops marched to Dowden's, a public-house fifteen miles from Owen's.[97] An abrupt change of weather greeted them on their arrival and caused them to halt the next day.

The march to Frederick Town resumed the morning of April 17 (MR, 368). Orme gives the date as the 18th (OR, 299). It was fifteen miles to Frederick Town from Dowden's. The roads were mountainous (MR, 368). The troops crossed the Monocacy River about four miles before arriving in Frederick Town. Daniel Kennedy helped ferry 55 wagons with stores, as well as Col. Dunbar's Regiment, over the river.[98] The army arrived in

Frederick Town at 3:00 p.m. "This town has not been settled above 7 years, and there are about 200 houses and 2 churches, one English, one Dutch [German] the inhabitants, chiefly Dutch, are industrious but imposing people: here we got plenty of provisions and forage (MR, 368)."

The seamen camped on the north side of Frederick Town on the 18th, after staying in quarters "which were very indifferent" the night before.[99] "We found here an Independent Vessel belonging to New York under the command of Captain Goss (MR, 368)."

Colonel Dunbar received orders to send one company to Conococheague to assist in forwarding the stores from there to Ft. Cumberland. He was to remain with the corps at Frederick Town until further orders. Thirty men received orders to remain with the officer at Rock Creek (OR, 299).

General Braddock at Frederick Town in Maryland

The General departed Alexandria on April 20th. He left Lt. Col. Gage with four companies of Halkett's 44th regiment to dispatch the powder and artillery as fast as any horses or wagons arrived. Braddock arrived in Frederick Town at noon on April 21, accompanied by aides-de-camp Orme and Morris and Secretary Shirley (MR, 369). Shirley was the son of Governor, and later General, Shirley. The General stayed at a house provided for him. Sir John St. Clair also arrived in Frederick Town the 21st (MR, 369).

General Braddock found few supplies available for his troops upon his arrival in Frederick Town (OR, 307). As a result, the troops tried to find cattle, most likely seeking them a number of miles outside the town (OR, 307). The troops not only collected cattle, as we learn from Daniel Dulaney Jr. "Soon after the General's arrival at Frederick Town, orders were issued to the recruiting officers to enlist all able-bodied men, servants not excepted. These orders were punctually executed by the officers of Dunbar's Regiment, to the great injury and oppression of many poor people, whose livelihood depended in great measure upon their property in their servants."[100]

The following is the first entry in General Braddock's Orderly Book at Frederick Town in Maryland:

> Frederick Town, Tuesday, April 22, 1755. Parole-Westminster.
>
> One Sergeant, one Corporal and 12 men to parade immediately at the Town Guard to march with the Wagons laden with artillery stores to Conocogee and to return back with the Wagons to Frederick as soon as they are unloaded.[101]

Some wagons passed through Frederick Town on their way from Rock Creek to Conococheague, where they were unloaded. The unloading of these wagons at Conococheague supported the opinion of St. Clair and Braddock. They believed Maryland wagon owners would provide their services only on the Maryland side of the Potomac River.

A bridge was built across the Antietam to accomodate the wagons. It took more than a month to move the ammunition and supplies from Rock Creek to Conococheague (OR, 307). Because the Potomac was "not then navigable, even by the smallest canoes, new difficulties arose in providing wagons to send them to Ft. Cumberland." There are, however, indications some supplies traveled from Conococheague to Wills' Creek by water.[102]

Governor Sharpe departed Annapolis Tuesday morning, April 22,[103] for Frederick Town, where he arrived the 23rd.[104] Sharpe gave the distance from Annapolis to Frederick Town as 80 miles.[105] General Braddock's orders for the 23rd directed some of his troops to meet Governor Sharpe at the Antietam on the road to Conococheague. Governor Sharpe probably went to the bridge on the Antietam between April 23 and 27. What orders he gave the troops at the Antietam are unknown.

Another famous American entered the affairs of the Braddock Expedition at this time. On the morning of March 18, Governor Morris of Pennsylvania sent his Assembly a message announcing the arrival of General Braddock in Virginia. He urged the Assembly to display "Vigour, Unanimity and Dispatch" in supplying men, provisions, and money for the army's use. Morris mentioned to the Assembly the roads to be opened between the settled parts of the province and the Ohio country, as well as a postal service between Philadelphia and Winchester. Benjamin Franklin was appointed, March 22, to consider and report on establishing the postal service.[106] Another fascinating episode was about to begin in Franklin's life:

> Our Assembly apprehending, from some Information, that he had conceived violent Prejudices against them, as averse to the Service, wish'd me to wait upon him, not as from them, but as Postmaster General, under the guise of proposing to settle with him the Mode of conducting with most Celerity and Certainty the Dispatches between him and the Governors of the several Provinces, with whom he must necessarily have continual Correspondence, and of which they propos'd to pay the Expence. My Son accompanied me on this Journaey. We found the General at Frederick Town, waiting impatiently for the Return of those he had sent thro' the back Parts of Maryland & Virginia to collect Wagons. I staid with him several Days, Din'd with him daily, and had full Opportunity of removing all his Prejudices, by the Information of what the Assembly had before his Arrival actually done and were still willing to do to facilitate his Operations.[107]

Franklin described his trip and future plans to his wife, Deborah, in a letter from Annapolis, April 13, 1755. "We got well over here last Night about 8 aClock I believe I shall not return the same Road with the Company, but go round by Winchester, and so to Carlisle, in order to settle the Posts, which the Assembly agreed to Support for a Year between the Camp and Philadelphia." Governor Sharpe, on April 17, 1756, submitted expenses for horses and couriers from Wills' Creek to Annapolis "agreeable to the desire of General Braddock in the spring of 1755."[108]

Franklin went only as far as Annapolis with the governor. He did not attend the Governor's Conference in Alexandria. "I did not reach home till the 12th Instant, from the

Journey, in which I had the Honor to accompany your Excy. as far as Annapolis. In my way I have had the good Fortune to do an acceptable Piece of Service to the Forces under General Braddock."[109]

It was at Frederick Town where Benjamin Franklin met with General Braddock. Heusser, in 1921, indicated, "The inn where their deliberations were held is one block west of the Baltimore & Ohio station."[110] When Franklin "was about to depart, the returns of wagons to be obain'd were brought in, by which it appear'g that they amounted only to twenty-five, and not all of those were in serviceable condition." In an accounting a t Frederick, April 23, 1755, Franklin received about £800 from General Braddock.

Another record of Franklin, *Proceedings at Lancaster in the Wagon Affair*, April 26, 1755, indicated he did not go to Winchester as planned. If Franklin had gone to Winchester from Frederick Town, he undoubtedly would have gone through Fox's Gap. A letter to Susanna Wright, April 28, 1755, placed Franklin at Lancaster, Pennsylvania. He stated, "On the Road from your House hither . . ." "The Wright homestead, at Wright's Ferry [now Columbia] was near the Susquehanna crossing on the road from Frederick and York to Lancaster." Wrightsville, Pennsylvania, is near this site today.[111]

A newspaper notice by Franklin on May 6 directed some wagons to proceed to Wills' Creek. "The Wagons that are valued at York and Forney's, are to set out immediately after the Valuation from thence for Wills' Creek, under the Conduct and Direction of Persons I shall appoint for that Purpose."[112] General Braddock wanted 150 wagons and 1500 horses at Ft. Cumberland by May 10 (OR, 307). Franklin succeeded in raising about 150 wagons and 500 horses.

The horses and wagons were to travel by way of Conococheague (OR, 308). Nead indicated, "the 150 wagons were sent over the Monocacy Road from Wrightsville to Braddock's Camp at Frederick."[113] Franklin apparently took this route to the Wright home and on to Lancaster after he left the General a t Frederick Town. This route was part of the "road from Conestoga to Opequon." It was over this trail that the first Germans went from Pennsylvania to Maryland, in 1710, and later when the movement became more extensive the same route was used."[114]

"In addition to supplying wagons Franklin contributed to Braddock's campaign by helping to organize the construction of a road between army headquarters at Fort Cumberland on Wills' Creek and the Pennsylvania back settlements."[115] Shippen indicated, on March 13, 1755, the government of Pennsylvania had directions to cut a road 100 feet wide from Conococheague to Wills' Creek. In March 1755, at Sir John St. Clair's request, Governor Morris appointed James Burd and four other commissioners to survey a route westward from Shippensburg to the head of the Youghiogheny.[116] Roads were undertaken from Shippensburg to both Ft. Cumberland and Ft. Duquesne.[117] A road from Shippensburg to the Turkey Foot of the Youghiogheny was discussed in April 1755.[118] General Braddock ordered a magazine of stores to be laid in at Shippensburg.[119]

Lady Edgar confused Frederick Town and Ft. Frederick when she stated, "On the 22nd of that month Sharpe joined him (Braddock) at Fort Frederick, Maryland, where a part of the army was quartered. It is to be noted that at this place and time two of the foremost figures of the century first met—George Washington and Benjamin Franklin."[120] Ft. Frederick was not built until 1756. It is on the Potomac River between Williamsport and Cumberland, Maryland. Washington and Franklin did not meet at this time.

While General Braddock and Governor Sharpe were at Frederick Town, another man prepared to join the Braddock Expedition. This man felt the military might give him the opportunity to be of service to his fellow citizens. On April 23, George Washington left Mt. Vernon for Bullskin, a Virginia plantation of his, intent on meeting General Braddock at Wills' Creek. Bullskin Creek is between Shepherdstown, West Virginia, and Winchester, Virginia. (see "Washington" on Fry and Jefferson Map). As events turned out, Washington officially became a member of the General's family at Frederick Town in Maryland.

Chapter Two

Journey to the Monongahela

Preparations neared completion by late April for Dunbar's Regiment to begin the march from Frederick Town in Maryland to Ft. Cumberland. The transportation of supplies remained a significant problem. The following order indicated Braddock's troops unloaded some supplies in Frederick Town that came from Rock Creek:

> Frederick, Friday, April 25, 1755. Parole-Appleby.
> Col. Dunbar's Regiment to hold themselves in readines to March by 29th.
> After Orders.
> One Corporal and four men to march tomorrow morning to Rock Creek, with four wagons that came up this evening; when the party comes to Rock Creek they are to put themselves under command of Ensign Hench.[1]

Ordnance stores arrived on Friday as well as eighty recruits (MR, 370).[2]

Another journal to survive the Braddock Expedition was "The Journal of Captain Robert Cholmley's Batman," also known as "The Batman's Journal." The author of this journal was with Dunbar's Regiment on the march through Maryland. A *batman* was a military servant assigned to a particular officer.[3] The Batman's Journal indicated on the 25th all the troops received enough Indian corn to last for six days, while several men received a whipping for drinking.[4]

On Sunday, Dunbar's troops prepared for their departure. Maryland supplied at least 45 troops for the Expedition that day, one officer, two drummers, and 42 recruits.

The Maryland men were recruited during a period of 20 days. Sir Peter Halkett's Regiment received the same number of troops.[5] Dunbar's Regiment received the following order to march April 29:

> Frederick, Sunday, April 27, 1755. Parole-Chester.
> Col. Dunbar's Regiment is to march ye 29th and to proceed to Wills' Creek agreeable to the following route:
>
> | | Miles. |
> |---|---|
> | 29th From Fredk. on the Road to Conogogee . . . . . | 17 |
> | 30th From that halting place to Conogogee . . . . . | 18 |
> | 1st from Conocogogee to John Even's . . . . | 16 |
> | 2nd Rest | |
> | 3rd To the Widow Baringer . . [before Winchester] | 18 |
> | 4th To George Poll's . . . . [after Winchester] | 9 |
> | 5th To Henry Enock's . . . . | 15 |
> | 6th Rest . . . . | |
> | 7th To Cox's at ye Mouth of Little Cacaph . . . . . . | 12 |
> | 8th To Col. Cresap's . . . . | 8 |
> | 9th To Wills' Creek . . . . | 16 |
> | Total . . . . | 129 |

The men are to take from this place three Days provisions; at Conogogee they will have more, at the Widow Baringers 5 Days. at Colo. Cresap's one or more Days and at all these places Oats or Indian Corn must be had for the Horses but no Hay. At Conogogee the Troops cross the Potomack in a float. When the troops have marched 14 miles from John Evans they are to make the new road to their right which leads from Opeckon Bridge. When the troops have marched 14 miles from George Polle's they come to the Great Cacapepon they are to pass that river in a float, after passing they take the road to the Right. If the water in the little Cacappon is high the Troops must encamp opposite to Cox's.

At the mouth of the little Cacapepon the Potomack is to be crossed in a Float. Four miles beyond this they cross

Town Creek if the the Float should not be finished canoes will be provided. If the bridges are not finished over Wills' Creek and Evans Creek, wagons will be ordered to carry the men over. It will be proper to get 2 Days Provisions at Colo. Cresap's ye whole shd. not arrive till ye 10th.

A subaltern and 30 men are to be left behind with a proper number of tents which will be carried for them; these men are to have six days Provisions.

The General's Guard is not to be relieved to morrow but proper centrys are to be found from the 30 men ordered to remain.[6]

These orders did not require Dunbar's troops to halt for any period of time or to perform any tasks at Conococheague.

The route assigned Dunbar's Regiment from Frederick Town to Wills' Creek was interesting for several reasons. The only stopping point on the route with no proper name assigned to it was during the first night out of Frederick Town. The orders simply stated "on the road to Conogogee," a distance of 17 miles from Frederick Town. The second point, perhaps easily missed, was that Dunbar received no order to stop at Winchester. Braddock's men cut a new road, about six miles north, to bypass Winchester. Therefore, Dunbar's Regiment did not take supplies to Winchester or pick up supplies at Winchester. Lastly, as early as the date of these orders, April 27, Dunbar's Regiment was to march to near Winchester from Conococheague. There was no order to march to Ft. Cumberland by a direct road that led west from Conococheague through Maryland.

The General ordered a bridge built over the Antietam and provisions laid in on the road (Orme 308). Several records of the Braddock Expedition made reference to "provisions laid in on the road." A letter by Governor Dinwiddie indicated some provisions might have been placed along the route of march for the troops.[7] There is no order of General Braddock, however, that indicated the unloading of wagons at the Antietam or along the road. The order of April 27 at Frederick Town refered to the bridge over the Opeckon. Hough indicated Dunbar did not cross the Opeckon in Virginia.

The entry in General Braddock's Orderly Book on the 28th indicated Dunbar's Regiment was to march the next day. Both the Morris and Batman Journals indicated the men received orders on Monday, April 28, to march from Frederick Town. General Braddock's orders indicated the troops should carry three days of provisions. The Batman's Journal indicated they were to carry five days provisions:[8]

> Frederick, Monday, April 28th, 1755. Parole-Deventry.
> The Detachment of sailors and the Provost Marshalls Guard consisting of one Sergeant, one Corporal and 10 men to march with Colo. Dunbar's Regiment tomorrow morning and to make the rear guard.[9]

The orders to Captain Gates indicated the significance of Conococheague. Conococheague served as a magazine for the Expedition. Braddock's men unloaded wagons arriving at Conococheague from Frederick Town and sent them back to Rock Creek for more supplies:

> To Captn Gates, 28th, April, 1755.
> You are directed by his Excellency, Genl. Braddock, to proceed with your Company to Conogogee where you are to act as a covering party for the Magazines and you are to remain there till further orders, unless all the Stores, Ammunition, &c., should be come up from Rock Creek and forwarded to Wills' Creek, in that case you are to join the General at Wills' Creek as soon as possible. You are to give all possible assistance and use your utmost endeavors in transporting the several Stores, Ammunition, Provision, &c. to Wills' Creek with the utmost expedition. Whilst you remain at Conogogee you are to send a Sergeant or Corporal with such of your men as are to be trusted with all the wagons which arrive at that place from Rock Creek, allowing one man to each wagon, and you are send them immediately back to Rock Creek for more stores till you shall be informed from the officers there that everything is sent up.[10]

"A proper Commissary was appointed at Conococheague, with orders to send up all the flour to Fort Cumberland, and directions were given for gathering to that place all the provision which had been left for want of carriages at Alexandria, Rock Creek, Frederick, and Winchester. Thus two Magazines were formed in different parts of the county, from either of which the General might supply himself as he should find most convenient (OR, 325)." It is evident from the above statement that some supplies went from Winchester to Conococheague.

Col. Thomas Cresap and his oldest son, Daniel, helped supply food to the forces. Daniel lived at, or near, Conococheague. His father, the Colonel, lived at that time in Old Town, west of Conococheague. Daniel, whose home at Conococheague was along the line of march, was made an agent to supply meat and flour to Braddock's men.

Records in the Maryland Archives indicated Thomas Cresap transported items by water and by road from Conococheague to Old Town:

March 18, 1755. That a Charge is Likewise made in the same Account of £59: 6: 7 for Carrying 29667 lb of Flour from Conigocheeg to Old Town by Water, at 4/p Hundred and from thence by Land to the New Store at 1/6 p Hundred amounting to £22: 5: 0 and for Carrying 16400 lb of Flour from Conigocheeg to New Store by Land at 7/6 p Hundred the Sum of £16: 10: 0. all which Charges and several other Articles for Carriage in the same Account Your Committee apprehend are Extravagant.[11]

Sharpe indicated, "the provisions were to go to Wills' Creek by water from Conegoge:"[12]

To Ensign French at Rock Creek, 28th April, 1755.
You are ordered by His Excellency Genl. Braddock to forward with all expedition the Ammunition, Stores, &c. at Rock Creek to Mr. Cresap, Conogogee, taking care to send the Ammunition Train, Stores, &c. first, then the Hospital Stores and salt fish. You are not to wait for the

Beeves [cattle] but as soon as the afore-mentioned things are gone up you will move with your party and join the Regiment at Wills' Creek agreeable to the following march route; as you will find Provisions very scarce on the Road you must take with you as many days of salt Provisions as the men can carry: Miles.

From Rock Creek to Owens Ordy	15	
To Dowdens	15	
To Frederick	15	
On the Road to Conogogee.	17	
To Conogogee	18	[Daniel Cresap's][13]
To John Evan's	16	
To Widow Baringer's	18	
To Geo. Polle's	9	
To Henry Enocks'	15	
To Mr. Cox's	12	
To Colo Cresaps	8	[at Old Town]
To Wills' Creek	16	
	————	
Total	174	

You must if you should find it necessary, take with you Guides from place to place and make such halts as you shall find absolutely necessary being careful not to lose any time. If the Wagons should come in very slowly make your application to the Civil Officers and if that should not succeed send Parties to fetch in any Wagons you shall hear of. Inform Lieut. Breerton of the March Route and tell him it is the General's orders that he make all imaginable dispatch. As soon as the Paymaster arrives he must also victual his men when the last stores of all kinds which are to be sent and dismissed at Rock Creek. You are to send a letter to Captain Gates at Conogogee informing him of it. The hand barrows and wheel barrows of the train except 6 of each are to be left behind all but the wheels and the iron work which are to be forwarded.[14]

Dunbar's Regiment from Frederick Town to Conococheague

On Tuesday, April 29, Dunbar's Regiment marched early in the morning from Frederick Town (OR, 308). The Orderly Book of General Braddock refers to the route as "the road to Conocogee." The route led from Frederick Town through present day Middletown. Dunbar's Regiment crossed the Catoctin Creek and marched along the wagon road through Fox's Gap. After passing the crest of South Mountain, the regiment continued for a distance of about two miles until they came to the area of Moses Chapline Sr.'s property. It was in this area they spent their first night out of Frederick Town. Moses Chapline Sr., brother of Joseph Chapline Sr., probably established his home about two miles west of Fox's Gap during the early 1740's.[15]

Not far beyond the Chapline homestead, just south of present-day Keedysville, the road forked. The road to the right led to Conococheague. The road to the left led to Swearingen's Ferry and Shepherdstown on the Potomac River. The morning of the 30th, Dunbar's men took the road to Conococheague. They crossed the Antietam by means of a bridge near the present Hitt (or Upper) Bridge northwest of Keedysville. There was no indication Dunbar's men escorted wagons or supplies to Conococheague from Frederick Town during their march.

Braddock and Washington from Frederick Town to Winchester

George Washington arrived in late April at his Bullskin Plantation in Virginia, between Swearingen's Ferry and Winchester. On May 1, Washington traveled from Bullskin to Frederick Town in Maryland. He crossed the Potomac River by way of Swearingen's Ferry at Shepherdstown (see Appendix F - Biographical Listing, Thomas Van Swearingen the Elder of the Ferry). The route traveled by Washington to Frederick Town was by way of the old Sharpsburg Road through Fox's Gap. He stayed in a home in Frederick Town the night of May 1. In his book, Albert Heusser included a picture of an old building labeled "Washington's Headquarters, Frederick, Md."[16]

The second of May, General Braddock, Governor Sharpe, Washington, aides-de-camp Orme and Morris, and secretary

Shirley, set out for Winchester, Virginia, by way of
Swearingen's Ferry.[17] They took the main road from Frederick
Town to Swearingen's Ferry (i.e., the old Sharpsburg Road). The
road passed through the present sites of Middletown, Fox's Gap,
the Middle Bridge on the Antietam, and the square in
Sharpsburg. Braddock traveled in a coach he purchased from
Governor Sharpe, until he arrived at Ft. Cumberland.[18]

The routes taken by General Braddock and Dunbar's
Regiment were the same from Frederick Town to just south of
present-day Keedysville, where the roads forked. Braddock and
Washington continued west to Swearingen's Ferry while
Dunbar's Regiment went northwest to the mouth of the
Conococheague.

Bartholomew and Margaret Booker lived near Fox's Gap
at the time of the Braddock Expedition.[19] Bartholomew later
became the father-in-law of Frederick Fox. He acquired a tract
named Mendall in 1754 from Joseph Chapline Sr.[20] This tract
was northeast of Fox's Gap. It is possible Bartholomew Booker
provided the Braddock Expedition with supplies. Records
indicated he received £22 in 1757 in payment for supplies
provided during the French and Indian War.[21] Sharpe indicated
£2000 remained outstanding to the citizens of Frederick County,
in 1758, for expenses related to the Braddock Expedition.[22]

Swearingen's Ferry began operation just in time to
accomodate General Braddock and his party.[23] "In May, 1755
Thomas Swearingen was authorized to conduct a ferry over the
Potomac somewhere in Frederick County."[24] However, a 1754
Frederick County Court record indicated Captain Swearingen
operated a ferry on the Potomac at that time:

> Thom Smith petitions the Court "that on the
> west side of Antieatum Ford on the main road that goes
> from Frederick Town to Capt. Swearingham's Ferry on
> Potomack, the road being washed into such deep ruts and
> uneven places by the continual course of water in wet
> seasons descending from the hills on each side that it
> hath made it very difficult for travelers to go with
> wagons".[25]

The ferry operated until 1849 at the site of the present Rumsey Bridge at Shepherdstown.

Governor Sharpe left the General at the ferry on the Potomac. Perhaps Sharpe stayed that night with Joseph Chapline Sr. whose home was near the present site of Sharpsburg. The area that became Sharpsburg probably was the home of several traders or settlers in 1755.[26]

Shepherdstown, on the Virginia side of the Potomac, dates to about 1734. "Old records indicate" that Thomas Shepherd "lived near Antietam Furnace several years prior to 1734. In that year he bought 222 acres from Jost Hite and established the village of Shepherdstown, the oldest village in West Virginia."[27]

The General's party took the road from Shepherdstown to Winchester. They arrived at Winchester on May 3.[28] They remained until the 7th when they departed for Ft. Cumberland at Wills' Creek. "The 31st of April the General set out for Winchester hoping to meet the Indians, but as none were, or had been there, he proceeded to Fort Cumberland, where he arrived the 10th of May, and also the 48th Regiment. Sir Peter Halket with six companies of the 44th, two independant companies and the Virginia troops were already encamped at this place (OR, 309)."

Why Through Maryland?

The reason Dunbar's Regiment marched through Maryland needs clarification. Why did any troops or supplies pass through Maryland when there was no road on the Maryland side of the Potomac to Ft. Cumberland? All of the troops under the commands of Halkett and Dunbar ultimately went through, or near, Winchester, Virginia, on their way to Wills' Creek. Why didn't Dunbar's troops march directly to Winchester from Alexandria? The answer lies with the transportation of supplies to Wills' Creek and beyond.

St. Clair suggested using Conococheague as a magazine and supply base. Conococheague was on the Great Wagon Road from Philadelphia to Winchester, as well as on the road from Frederick Town, Maryland, through Fox's Gap. It also was on the Potomac. It offered significant advantages for these reasons.

Without a road through to the west, however, Conococheague could serve only as a base from which to send supplies to Wills' Creek by way of the Potomac River or by road through Winchester.

During the return from his initial trip to Ft. Cumberland, St. Clair heard of many Dutch [German] settlers at the foot of the Blue Ridge. They were willing to carry provisions and perhaps supply 200 wagons and 1500 horses. However, as early as the middle of February, St. Clair was aware of a severe limitation in using these people. They did not wish to work outside Maryland. They would not cross the Potomac River.[29]

In a rather blunt letter to General Braddock, written in February, St. Clair vented his frustration with the Maryland Germans:[30]

> . . . and I may say where the Inhabitants are totally ignorant of Military Affairs: Their Sloth & Ignorance is not to be discribed; I wish General Braddock may be able to make them shake it off. I shall undertake to talk to the Germans in the language they have been brought up under in Germany. There is no such thing as to perswade any of them to enlist in the Virginia Companys.[31]

Governor Sharpe expressed his reservations about the Germans in a letter to his brothers. "It is expected I apprehend from your Letter that the Germans who have imported themselves into these Provinces will be found as ready as they are capable of bearing Arms on this Occasion, but I can assure you that whatever Character they may deserve for Courage or military Skill I despair of seeing any of them so forward as to offer themselves Volunteers under my Command unless the Enemy was to approach so far as actually to deprive them of their Habitations & Possessions of which alone they are found tenacious."[32]

General Braddock expressed his reason for passing through Maryland in a letter to Robert Napier, April 19, 1755:

I shall set out to morrow for Frederick in my way to Ft. Cumberland at Wills' Creek, where I shall join the two Columns which are now upon their March at about fifty Miles distance: This Disposition I was oblig'd to make for the Conveniency of Horses and Wagons, by which means I employ those of Maryland which would not be prevail'd upon to cross the Potomack.[33]

The movement of men and supplies to the Ohio Valley required more wagons and teams than Virginia could supply. This was the primary reason for the inclusion of a Maryland route in Braddock's plan. Maryland wagon owners and drivers, many of whom were German, did not desire to cross the Potomac into Virginia. They were, however, willing to participate if they could work in Maryland. It was very unlikely Maryland wagons went beyond Conococheague. Their primary use probably was the transportation of supplies from Rock Creek to Conococheague. Wagon teams from Pennsylvania proved necessary as well. General Braddock initially viewed the route through Maryland as essential.

Another point of interest in the April 19 letter by Braddock was the confirmation the General spent little time with his troops between Alexandria and Wills' Creek. Braddock indicated his troops were 50 miles ahead of him at the time he wrote Napier. He planned to join them at Ft. Cumberland.

Governor Dinwiddie, in a letter to Sir Thomas Robinson on March 17, identified the key constraint to the expedition. ". . . the only Difficulty is providing Carriages for the Ordnance Stores, &c., but as I hope by Diligence we shall be able to surmount y't, tho' the passing the Allegany Mount's will be troublesome, but those better acquaint'd with these Things y'n I am, seem to make light of it."[34]

Governor Sharpe proposed the use of a Maryland route to Governor Dinwiddie in December 1754. Governor Sharpe was the first to propose the movement of supplies by wagon to Conococheague and then by water up the Potomac River. "I cannot but think that the several Rivers & waters that occur & intersect the Road from Belhaven (Alexandria) to Wills' Creek on the South Side of Potowmack will render the Conveyance of Stores that way expensive & very uncertain wherefore I apprehend it will be the best & easiest way to land every thing that shall be sent up Potowmack for the Troops at Rock Creek whence our wagons will carry them to Conegocheek where Battoes may be made to convey every thing thence by water."[35]

Perhaps the letter from Sharpe to Dinwiddie was enough to convince Dinwiddie of the desirability of the Maryland route:

> I have only agreed for 6 Wagons with four Horses & Harness to each to be delivered all of them for £280, & each of them will come loaded to the Camp with 20 Ct of flour, at the price of 12/ Currency p Ct these according to the Directions I gave at the Camp were to be emploed two of them there in drawing Timber for the Fort or otherwise as should be found expedient, & the other four to be employed in carrying up to Conegogeek the Stores that now are or may be landed at Rock-Creek, but I will contradict the Orders I left, that they may be employed between Winchester & Wills' Creek since you prefer that Route, tho from the Observations that I had an Opportunity of making by journying to the Camp one way & returning the other I am satisfied that you will find the Carriage thro Winchester much more expensive than on the North shore of Potowmack, especially if you take into the Account the Charge of building such a number of Boats & of opening such a Road as you propose to shorten the Distance by the way of Winchester.[36]

Dinwiddie indicated to Sharpe the preceding September, "I am glad you have directed the opening the new road from Rock Creek, which must be of great Service."[37] Perhaps this was the creation of a road from Rock Creek to Frederick Town or an improvement in an existing route.

How Was Conococheague Used?

Part of the reason for the use of a Maryland route related to how the Braddock Expedition used Conococheague and the

Potomac River. Conococheague was on several important roads. It also was on a river that flowed by way of Ft. Cumberland. If a t all navigable, it was imperative to use the Potomac River.[38] Conococheague played a part in moving some items to Ft. Cumberland by water. The degree of use of the Potomac River, however, is difficult to determine.

Governor Morris of Pennsylvania made note of the lack of a road to the Ohio in late 1754. "Tho the People of this Province have for Thirty years past carried on a Trade to the River Ohio and were seated at the very Place where the French have built their last Fort, yet I cannot learn that we have any thing more than a Horse Way thither through the Woods and over the Mountains, by which I am told it will be very difficult if not impracticable to transport any considerable Quantity of Provisions; but there is a very good Wagon Road from this City to Watkin's Ferry on Patowmack by which any Goods may be carried very commodiously to that Place."[39]

Conococheague served as an important strategic site. A wagon road to Conococheague from Frederick Town in Maryland passed through Fox's Gap. The road through Fox's Gap was critical if supplies were to be taken through Maryland to Conococheague.

The road through Pennsylvania from Philadelphia to Conococheague was important to the movement of supplies to Ft. Cumberland. This road, in 1758, may not have been in as good condition as the road through Fox's Gap to Conococheague:

> As the Roads from Lancaster in Pensilvania to Williams' Ferry upon the Potowmack, may want considerable Repairs, & Widening for the Carriages of Cannon &c...
>
> I will give orders for clearing & repairing the Road between Pensa & Williams' Ferry according to Your Desire.[40]

Governor Dinwiddie, in early January, asked Governor Morris of Pennsylvania to arrange for the delivery of 600,000 pounds of flour at Wills' Creek:[41]

... but the Flour, if possible, must be had, and if
sent from Y'r Place to Winchester, w'ch is a Wagon Road,
will answer.[42]

Winchester is now proposed for the Magazine of
Provis's, &c. There is a Wagon Road from Y'r Place to it.
Can You engage Quantities of Flour to be delivered there,
and the Price?[43]

The Flour from Phila'a will come dear; but as
there is a Wagon Road from thence to Winchester, it's
tho't Proper to make y't Place the Magazine . . .[44]

There also was a record of two chests of medicines delivered to
Conococheague for use in the Expedition.[45]

Dunbar's Regiment from Conococheague to Wills' Creek

Dunbar's Regiment departed Conococheague May 1 and
arrived at Ft. Cumberland on May 10. Their route crossed into
Virginia, passed near Winchester, and proceeded to Ft.
Cumberland. Walter Hough, in his book *Braddock's Road
Through the Virginia Colony,* presented an in-depth
documentation of the route traveled by Dunbar's Regiment from
May 1 to May 10. Hough also documented the route of Sir Peter
Halkett's Regiment through Virginia.

Dunbar's troops took no supplies with them from
Conococheague, other than their food rations. The regiment
departed Conococheague on May 1. "Begain ferrying people
across the Potomac into Virginia and was completed by 10
o'clock. Marched 17 miles to John Evans and were 20 Miles from
Winchester (MR, 370)."[46] Perhaps the troops with the writer of
the Morris Journal were ferried across by Evan Watkins or crossed
using canoes collected on the Antietam or elsewhere.[47]
"Thursday May ye 1st. We marched Cross the River Portwomack
Into Virginia to Widow Evens and Carried three days provisions
along with us it being 18 miles (BJ, 12-3)." Troops with the
batman "marched" across the river, indicating its shallowness.
The roads soon became "indifferent" (MR, 371).

The crossing of Dunbar's Regiment back into Virginia was
news to Governor Dinwiddie.[48] Perhaps Dinwiddie thought a

road went through Maryland from Rock Creek to Wills' Creek. He apparently was informed by Sharpe about a proposed road in 1754. "The road you are pleased to mention from Rock Creek to Wills' Creek will be of very great use & Advantage & therefore desire you will please give your orders to execute it immediately."[49]

Sharpe also had informed Dinwiddie of the possibility of transporting goods by means of the Potomac. However, Dinwiddie was aware of the potential limitations on the use of the Potomac between Conococheague and Wills' Creek. "I shall be glad if the Method you propose for Conveying Provisions &c from Belhaven by Rock Creek, Conegocheek &c may prove Successful, but I fear in Freshes [spring rains, but rocks are a problem] the Battoes [a flat-bottomed boat] cannot go up, & in Summer they will want Water, but a Tryal will not be amiss."[50]

On May 2, the first division of the troops, part of Halkett's Regiment, arrived at Wills' Creek.[51] Dunbar's troops rested along the route of march on May 2 (MR, 370). On May 3 they marched to Widow Barringer's, 18 miles from Evans and 5 from Winchester. The regiment never stopped at Winchester. "Satterday May the 3d. We marched to Widow Billingers about 19 miles and Rec'd two days Provisions and drumed a woman out of the camp. May 4th - March to one Potts, 9 miles from the Widow's. Sunday May the 4th. We marched to Potses [Pott's] Camp, it Beeing 9 miles."[52]

"May 5th - Marched at 5 in our way to Henry Enocks, being 16 miles from Potts. After going 15 miles we came to a river called Kahapetin, where we ferried the Army over and got to our ground where we found a company of Peter Halket's encamped (MR, 371). Munday May the 5th. We marched to Kennets [Henry Enoch's] Camp after a very Rainy Night and Morning. The tents being very wet made the Baggage very heavy, it being 18 miles."[53]

Dunbar's Regiment, on May 8, crossed the Potomac for the third time. "May 8th - Ferried over into Maryland. Marched to Jackson's, 8 miles from Cox's. Colonel Cressop, a Rattle Snake Colonel, lived there. The General arrived at 6 with his Attendants, and a Company of Light Horse for his guard, and lay at Cresop's. The General ordered the Army to halt tomorrow" (MR, 372-3).

"May 10th - Marched at 5 to Wills' Creek, 16 miles from Cressop's. At 12 the General passed by. We marched again, and heard 17 guns fired at the Fort to salute the General. At 2 we arrived at Wills' Creek. Found 6 companies of Sir Peter Halket's Regiment, 9 companies of Virginians, and a Maryland Company" (MR, 373-4).

The first entry in General Braddock's Orderly Book, after the entry of April 28 at Frederick Town in Maryland, was at Ft. Cumberland on Saturday, May 10. The first line of that entry recorded the appointment of a third aide-de-camp to the General. "Mr. Washington is appointed Aid de Camp to His Excellency Genl. Braddock."

The Month of May at Wills' Creek

The remainder of the month of May saw the consolidation of Braddock's forces at Wills' Creek. The writer of the Morris Journal visited an Indian camp the 13th. General Braddock met with some of the Indians but had little success enlisting many of them in his cause.

An entry on the 14th indicated Frederick Town in Maryland served as a hospital as early as the time that Dunbar's Regiment and the General were there. "This day 2 of our men arrived from Frederick hospital, and our men from Connecockieg that were left to assist the Artillery." The reference by this entry to artillery is interesting. The date of this entry seemed to be too early to refer to the ten cannon sent by Dinwiddie to Ft. Cumberland by way of Rock Creek and Conococheague.

Supplies remained a problem. Some of the casks of beef were condemned. Governor Dinwiddie wrote Orme on May 16. "I hear y't Provis's at F't Cumerl'd begin to be scarce; surely if Pensyl'a'a has performed their Promis, Flour cannot be want'g, and if salt Provis's are wnat'g. You know there is a good Qu'ty at Alexa'a, w'ch can be sent if Wagons can be had."54

"Lt. Col. Gage, with 2 companies of Sir Peter Halket's, and the last division of the train, consisting of 3 field pieces, 4 howitzers, a number of cohorns, and 42 wagons with stores arrived." According to a letter by General Braddock to Napier on

June 8, the artillery, after nearly a month on their march, arrived the 17th. Captain Gate's New York Company arrived the 19th. About the 20th eighty wagons from Pennsylvania and eleven wagons from Philadelphia arrived (OR, 312 and MR, 379). "But in Consequence of the difficulty of procuring teams, the artillery, &c., did not arrive until May the 20."[55]

On the 21st, a troop of light-horse and 2 companies of Halkett's Regiment, under the command of Major Chapman, arrived from Winchester. All the troops were now at Wills' Creek, except the North Carolina company commanded by Captain Dobbs. Both Regiments took part in military drills. "Our Force here now consists of 2 Regiments of 700 men each; 9 companies (Virginia) of 50 men each; 3 Independent Companies of 100 men each; one Maryland Company of 50 men; 60 of the train and 30 seamen (MR, 380)." ". . . and the whole of the Forces are now assembled, making about two thousand Effectives, the greatest part Virginians."[56]

The company of 100 men from North Carolina under the command of Capt. Edward Brice Dobbs, son of North Carolina Gov. Arthur Dobbs, arrived on May 30. The orders prepared in England assigned the North Carolina unit to Dunbar's Regiment. The unit was late in arriving at Ft. Cumberland. Perhaps they traveled directly from Alexandria to Wills' Creek, rather than by way of Frederick Town in Maryland.

The North Carolina company employed a young wagon driver named Daniel Boone (see Appendix F - Biographical Listing).[57] The cabin of Daniel Boone's father was at that time in the Yadkin Valley of North Carolina. George and William Boone, cousins of Daniel, founded Boonsboro, Maryland, not far from Fox's Gap, in the early 1790s.[58] One of the leading scouts in the Expedition was Christopher Gist, the veteran woodsman who had been Washington's guide, a neighbor of the Boones in the Yadkin Valley.[59]

Daniel Morgan participated in the Braddock Expedition as well.[60] Morgan probably lived at Winchester at the time. Lt. Henry Gladwyn was part of Dunbar's 48th Regiment.[61] Capt. Horatio Gates led an independent company from New York.[62] Capt. George Mercer served as an artificer from Virginia. Lt. Col. Thomas Gage was with Halkett's 44th Regiment. Andrew Lewis also was a participant in the Braddock Expedition.[63]

The departure of the first troops from Ft. Cumberland towards Ft. Duquesne took place in late May. A detachment of 600 men, commanded by Major Chapman, marched for Ft. Duquesne on May 29. They took 21 field pieces and 50 wagons with provisions. Sir John St. Clair, 2 engineers, Mr. Spendlowe, six seamen, and some Indians received orders to clear the roads for them:

> Sr Peter Halket with the 44th Regiment was to march with the first division, taking with him about a hundred wagons of provisions, stores and powder. Lt. Col. Burton with the independent Companies, Virginia, Maryland and Carolina rangers, was to march with the artillery, ammunition, some stores and provision, and to form the second division. Colonel Dunbar, with the 48th, was to make the third division, and to take with him the provision wagons from Winchester, the returned wagons from the advanced party, and all the carrying horses (OR, 322).

Commodore Keppel apparently became ill and was detained at Ft. Cumberland.

The Month of June

Braddock's troops spent much of the month of June clearing the road towards Ft. Duquesne. The work of clearing an adequate route was laborious and progress was painfully slow. Dunbar's Regiment marched from Ft. Cumberland the morning of June 10. The general anticipated an easy, though an important capture, and already looked forward after all his victories, to spending a merry Christmas with Morris at Philadelphia.[64]

Governor Dinwiddie expressed frustration at the cooperation received from the other colonies. ". . . the Backwardness of M'yl'd and Pensylvania is a great Bar in my way; . . . When did You part with the Gen'l? Do you not think he will be ready to march by y's Time? He sent Co. Washington for Money, who carried up £4,000 St'r. He says he will want £10,000 more in two Mo's . . . The Train of Artillery has greatly contributed to the Delay of the Expedit'n, but hope every Thing now is in proper Order for their March."[65]

Virginia sent ten ship-cannon by way of Rock Creek and Conococheague to Wills' Creek. Their intended destination was Ft. Duquesne:[66]

> I shall send up ten Pss. of Cannon from Hampton, w'th their appurtenances, to be mounted on the Fort, and shall do my utmost in provid'g necessary Provis's for the People y't may be left there . . . I am much surprized You were not better supplied with Wagons from Virg'a . . . The Flour from Pennsylva'a I tho't a Person had been appointed to receive it to prevent its fall'g into improper Hands, y't on y's Occasion are too apt, from lucrative Views, to make the most of every Thing they can; but I hope You will be able to discover some of these wicked People to make some Examples by a proper Punishm't, to deter others from such bad Practices.[67]

> Please pres't my kind Respects to the Gen'l, and acqu't him y't I have ordered 10 Cannon, with their Appurtenances to Rock Creek, with 24 b'ls of Rice, from thence to be carried to Conegacheeg, from thence to F't Cumberland. I shall write to G'r Sharpe to procure Wagons to convey them there.[68]

Governor Dinwiddie requested Governor Sharpe to take responsibility for these guns between Rock Creek and Conococheague:

> I have order'd 10 Cannon and 20 bls. of Rice to Rock Creek. I must desire You will, at a proper Time, order Wagons to carry them to Conneegocheeg, from thence to be carried to Fort Cumb'l'd, Y't if the Gen'l succeeds in tak'g the Fort these Cannon are design'd to be mounted there, and I do not doubt You will give the necessary Dirct's for transport'g of them, and send Y'r Orders to the Store Keeper at Rock Creek to receive and take Care of them.[69]

The Morris Journal describes Braddock's march towards
Ft. Duquesne during late June and early July:

> The General and all the Army arrived at the
> little Meadows, which is 22 miles from the Fort. He
> found here that the number of carriages, &c., that he
> had with him occasioned his marches to be very short,
> and that in all probability if they continued to do so, the
> French fort would be reinforced before he got before it.
> He therefore thought proper to take 1200 of the choicest
> men, besides Artillery and Sailors, with the most
> necessary stores that would be wanted to attack the Fort,
> making up in all 51 carriages, and left all the heavy
> baggage, &c. with Col. Dunbar, and the rest of the forces
> to follow him as fast as possible, and marched
> accordingly, and continued so to do without being
> molested (except now and then losing a scalp, which in
> the whole amounted to 8 or 9, a number far less expected),
> til the 8th of July, when he encamped within 8 miles of
> the French Fort, and there held a Council of War, which
> agreed that as they were to pass over the Mongohela
> River twice (this river is a 1/4 mile broad, and 6 miles
> from the French Fort), that the Advance party should
> parade at 2 o'clock to secure that pass, as on the contrary
> if the Enemy should have possession of it, they would
> not be able to get over without a great loss (MR, 383-4).

Governor Dinwiddie received advice from General
Braddock to prepare for French and Indian attacks:

> Whereas it has been signified to me by his Ex'y'
> Gen'l Braddock, y't is suspected w'n our Army is far
> advanc'd the French and their Ind's will fall upon the
> frontier Settlements of y's Colony, for the better guarding
> ag'st the dangerous Consequences of such an Attempt You
> are hereby required to keep a diligent Lookout and have
> a number of Y'r Militia constantly on the watch by way
> of Patrolers, and to send me spedy Advice if any number

of Men shall appear in Arms on our Frontiers, and give a proper Alarm to the Neighbouring Counties.[70]

The attacks by the enemy Indians on the settlers began by at least the middle of June, as noted in the Morris Journal.

British advances upon Niagara and Crown Point were underway, as well, at this time. "I hope Maj'r Gen'l Shirley's Regim't, S'r W'm Pepperell's, and the Jersey Forces, are on their March to Niagara. I shall be glad to hear the Forces destined for Crown Point were in readiness to begin their March."[71]

Intelligence reports available to Governor Dinwiddie in late June indicated the number of French and Indians at Ft. Duquesne was growing. "I think his Army consists of 3,000 Men, and from the best Intelligence I can have, the Fr. have reinforced their Men on the Ohio w'th 700, so y't their Forces there are ab't 1,200 Men, besides Ind's; y't I am in great hopes Gen'l Braddock will soon retke the Fort they took from us last Sumer, and y't his next Let'r will be dated from y't Fort."[72]

The Battle of the Monongahela

The main portion of the army crossed the Monongahela River the morning of July 9. The entire army was across by noon. Just beyond the river the advance party, under the command of Lt. Col. Thomas Gage, came under attack. The main body of the army advanced towards the point of action, while the advance party chose to retreat.

Shortly after the attack began on the front of the column, Braddock's forces found themselves under attack on their flanks. Some of the French and Indians were on a hill from which they attacked the right flank of Braddock's troops. Braddock's men were unable to take this hill during the battle that lasted several hours. The number of French probably was 300 or 400. Perhaps as many (or more) Indians fought along side the French:

The General had five horses shot under him and at last receiv'd a wound through his right arm into his Lungs . . . Poor Shirley was shot thro' the head, Capt Morris wounded, Mr Washington had two horses shot under him and his cloaths shot thro in several places behaving the whole time with the greatest courage and resolution. Sr Peter Halket was killed upon the spot Coll Burton and Sr John St Clair wounded, & Inclosed I have sent you a list of the Killed and wounded according to as exact an account as we are yet able to get.[73]

The Seaman's Journal gave the losses in the battle as follows:

> The number killed, wounded, and left on the Field, as appeared by the returns from the different companies, was 896, besides Officers, but cannot say any particular Company suffered more than another, except the Grenadier Companies and Carpenters; for out of Colonel Dunbar's Grenadiers, who were 79 complete that day, only 9 returned untouched, and out of 70 of Halket's only 13. Amongst the rest, I believe I may say the Seamen did their duty, for out of 33, only 15 escaped untouched: and every Grenadier Officer either killed or wounded. Our loss that day consisted of 4 field pieces, 3 Howitzers, and 2 wagons, with Cohorns, together with the 51 carriages of provisions and Ammuniton, &c., and Hospital stores, and the General's private chest with £1000 in it, and about 200 horses with officers' baggage.[74]

The French and Indians pursued Braddock's retreating force as far as the river. The retreat continued throughout the night. The survivors reached Dunbar's camp, about 50 miles from the scene of the battle. The wounded general's condition continued to deteriorate. On July 13, George Washington buried General Braddock's body in the road. Orme gives the date as the 18th.

Details of the engagement at the Monongahela appeared in various sources. George Washington gave his account late in his life.[75] St. Clair, wounded early in the engagement, admitted to knowing little after the first minutes of the battle. Governor Dinwiddie's account of the battle appeared in a letter to the Earl of Halifax.[76] A letter by Orme to Robert Napier gave his account of the action of July 9.[77] A brief account of the battle also appeared in a letter from Orme to Governor Sharpe.[78] Dunbar's account of the battle appeared in a letter to Robert Napier.[79] Also of note was a letter by William Shirley to Robert Hunter Morris of Pennsylvania, dated at Ft. Cumberland, May 23, 1755. Shirley, of course, was killed in the battle. Pargellis included numerous papers related to logistics after the battle.[80]

Other participants in the Braddock Expedition included William Baird (? - May, 1792), who escaped and was afterwards coroner of Washington County, Maryland, from its formation to his death.[81] Also surviving the Expedition was Thomas Older (1728 - 1805), not an ancestor of the author. Older was captured by the Indians, escaped, and ultimately settled at Fort Ticonderoga, New York.[82]

Dunbar's Retreat

Colonel Dunbar took command of the remaing force. He was responsible for the destruction or abandonment of all the cannon and many supplies. This was done to expedite the retreat. Dunbar, with the remains of the army, returned to Ft. Cumberland July 20.

Dinwiddie wrote Orme, "can History produce where so many British Forces were defeated by so few of the Enemy?"[83] Dinwiddie wrote Governor Dobbs of North Carolina to inform him of his son's whereabouts:

> Y'r Son was not in the Engagem't, but was with Colo. Dunbar by some stink'g Weeds in the Woods. Y'r Son's Sight is hurt, but he will soon recover it. If Mr. Glen, agreeable to promise, had prevail'd over a Number of the Cherokee and Catawba Warriors to join our Forces we sh'd not in all probability been defeat'd, as they w'd have attack'd the Ind's in their Bush way of fight'g, w'ch the Regulars are Strangers to; . . . Comod. Kepple sail'd Yesterday for Engl'd . . . P.S.-It's natural to believe these Banditti will endeav'r to Rob and murder our frontier Settlem'ts. I therefore have three Compa's of Rangers to oppose their Wicked Designs.[84]

Governor Sharpe was quick to lend his assistance to Dunbar and the remains of Braddock's army. "Tuesday morning last His Excellency our Governor set out from hence for Frederick County and lodged that night at Colonel Tasker's seat at Bellair. We hear His Excellency intends for Fort Cumberland."[85] Sharpe arrived at Ft. Cumberland only to find Dunbar had made plans to march for Philadelphia. Sharpe was adamant Dunbar's plan did not meet with his approval:

> The 23d of July I took the Liberty to acquaint you with General Braddock's Misfortune & that I was proceeding to Fort Cumberland to tender my Services to Colo Dunbar & his Majesty's Troops that were returned thither I was glad to find at my Arrival that there was no want of fresh provisions among them but the Colo had given Orders to the two Regiments & the Independant Companies to hold themselves in readiness to march for Phila last Saturday sennight . . . The several Companies that have been raised & supported by the Govts of Virga N Carolina & Maryland are left to garrison Fort Cumberland & to protect the Frontiers of these Provinces till something farther can be done for their security & for this Majestys Service.[86]

Sharpe returned to Annapolis on August 7.[87]

A second attempt against Ft. Duquesne by Dunbar's troops appeared to Sharpe to be out of the question:

> . . . but Friday morning he sent to me desiring I would give my Attendance at a Council that he had called upon the Receipt of your Letter. The proposition or question submitted to us was whether he should march again immediately to attack Fort DuQuesne against which we were unanimous & I think you would not have been of a contrary Opinion had you seen the Troops & been acquainted with their Disposition & wants.[88]

> The inclosed Copy of my Letter to Governor Dinwiddie on my Return from Fort Cumberland will

support what I writ to you about the same time & will shew I presume that Colonel Dunbar never consulted any of us on the propriety of marching the Regiments to Phila immediately after the Action & leaving the Frontiers of these provinces exposed, had he asked my Opinion thereon He would not I assure you have obtained my Consent for I thought then as I do now that there was a wide Difference between marching such an Army as his was then to attack Fort Du Quesne without Artillery or other Stores & remaining on the Defensive at Fort Cumberland or any other advanced post between that & the Ohio.[89]

The Morris, or Seaman's, Journal ended on August 1. The seamen left the army on the 3rd and arrived in Hampton the 18th, by way of Winchester, Virginia.[90]

Several sources discussed the march of Dunbar's troops to Philadelphia by way of Shippensburg.[91] It was likely Shippensburg served as a supply base as early as May.[92] 1) "Dunbar marched to Philadelphia by way of Winchester, a most roundabout route, for he had been unwilling to wait two weeks for the Raystown-Ft. Cumberland road to be opened."[93] 2) "Dunbar, with his wagon train and artillery, went by way of Winchester, but his infantry marched along the river to Conegogee, where Dunbar crossed the Potomac & marched for Shippensburg."[94] 3) "From Winchester Dunbar marched to Philadelphia by way of Conegogee, Shippensburg, Carlisle and Lancaster, and on Aug. 28 he arrived and encamped his troops on Society Hill."[95]

George Washington Assumes Command

Governor Dinwiddie could not believe the turn of events. "Our People were as much alarm'd at the march of the Regulars to Phila'a as at the Defeat on Monongahela, and general Consternation among them."[96] Little more than a month after the battle at the Monongahela, Governor Dinwiddie made the following appointment:

Commission from Governor Dinwidde to Colonel George Washington, Given under my Hand, &c, Aug'st 14th, 1755

. . . do by these Presents appoit You COLONEL of the Virg'a Regim't and Com'd'r-in-Chief of all the Forces now rais'd and to be rais'd for the Defence of y's H. M'y's Colony, and for repell'g the unjust and hostile Invasions of the Fr. and their Ind'n Allies . . .[97]

Instructions for Colonel Washington

. . . As Winchester is the highest Place of rendezvous w'ch is expos'd to the Enemy, You are hereby requir'd to make y't Y'r head quarters[98]

Mrs. Browne

Another journal that survived the Braddock Expedition was "Mrs. Browne's Diary."[99] This journal recorded the account of an English lady who accompanied her brother, a commissary officer attached to Braddock's forces. Her journal ran from November 17, 1754, to January 19, 1757. She made the following entry at Alexandria on April 22. "All the Troops march'd to Wills' Creek. Left behind 1 Officer and 40 Men, my Brother and self in care of the Sick, having 50 ill." It was the first of June before Mrs. Browne and her brother departed for Wills' Creek.

Mrs. Browne and her brother traveled only as far as Ft. Cumberland. It was there, on July 17, her brother died of the "bloody flux" [dysentery]. Mrs. Browne almost met the same fate herself, becoming quite ill.

August 30 she arrived in Frederick Town in Maryland:

I was very ill and not able to march with the rest. Mr. Anderson was so kind as to leave his Servant to attend me. We march'd at 10 and at 6 we arriv'd at Frederick's Town in Maryland. Mr. Bass came to meet me, he had taken a Lodging for me at the Widow DeButts.[100] I was very much fatigued having marched since I left the Fort 150 Miles, very ill with a Fever and Flux.

Mrs. Browne was among the few who would travel to Ft. Cumberland through Virginia from Alexandria and return by way of Frederick Town in Maryland. It is interesting to speculate by which route she returned to Frederick Town in Maryland. Did she go through Winchester to Conococheague and then down to Frederick or did she cross at Swearingen's Ferry. The latter certainly was the shortest route.

Mrs. Browne's entries for the month of October follow. They show the sick came from Ft. Cumberland to Frederick Town in Maryland. ". . . the Hospital is removed down to Frederick-town in this province . . .":101

October the 1. The Director is arrived from Philadelphia, but no Letters from England. We are to march as soon as the sick come from Fort Cumberland.

Octr. the 5. All the Sick are come from Fort Cumberland, but they were obliged to leave some of the Baggage behind, being alarm'd by the Indians.

Octr. the 7. An Express is arriv'd from near Fort Cumberland with an Account that the Indians have scalp'd 5 Families, and that they are in the greatest Distress having Bread but for 3 Days and cannot go out for more.

Octr. the 8. An Express is arriv'd from Fort Cumberland with an Account that the Indians are near them, and beg some Assistance.

Octr. the 9. Very busy packing up to go to Philadelphia having but 2 days notice . . .

In Conclusion

"Washington saw from the first, with Dinwiddie, that the Ohio Valley was the key to the possession of the North American continent, and that Fort Duquesne was the key to the Ohio Valley,--hence to lose that fort or to hold that fort meant to lose or to hold the continent of America."102 It seems appropriate to add the name of Horatio Sharpe to those of Washington and Dinwiddie.

Osgood, in his major work entitled *American Colonies in the Eighteenth Century* stated, "An initial error of serious importance had been made in planning Braddock's part of the campaign before he left England. It consisted in the decision that he should land in Virginia and proceed thence toward Fort Duquesne. The distance by that route was much greater, more rugged and less settled than the one which would have been followed if the expedition had started from Philadelphia."[103]

Braddock apparently supported Osgood's opinion. "I have order'd a Road of Communication to be cut from Philadelphia to the Crossing of the Yantghyanghain, which is the Road we ought to have taken, being nearer, and thro' an inhabited and well cultivated Country, and a Road as good as from Harwich to London . . ."[104] St. Clair was of the same opinion. "Thus far I do affirm that no time has been lost in pursuing the Scheme laid down in England for our Expedition' had it been undertaken at the beginning from Pensylvania it might have been carried on with greater Dispatch and less expence . . ."[105]

Osgood did not recognize there was no way to reach Ft. Cumberland or Ft. Duquesne other than by way of Winchester. Braddock and St. Clair could only speculate on the Pennsylvania route since they had not traveled the route. The creation of the desired road through Pennsylvania could not have been completed in time for their use.

The conclusion of Nichols seems best. "The expedition sailed to Virginia because the Potomac Route to the Forks of the Ohio was immeasurably superior to any conceivable Pennsylvania route."[106] The wagon road through Fox's Gap was critical to the Braddock Expedition. It provided an adequate route for wagons and led to a strategic point on the Potomac at Conococheague.

In the wake of the Braddock Expedition, the determined efforts of the brave men who met the challenge of the French and their Indian allies won most of the North American continent for the British. George Washington never forgot the road he traveled with General Braddock from Frederick Town to

Swearingen's Ferry. He probably traveled the road again in later years. The cape of General Braddock remains at Mt. Vernon. One can only wonder how many times George Washington relived in his mind the events of . . . the Braddock Expedition.

Society of Colonial Wars and Maryland Historical Society
Marker. Photo by Allan Powell.

Braddock Boulder. Photo by Susanne Flowers.

Chapter Three

Documentation of the Braddock Road through Fox's Gap

A number of authors contend Dunbar's Regiment went through Turner's Gap near Boonsboro, Maryland, during the Braddock Expedition. Most of these authors place General Braddock and George Washington on the same route as Dunbar's Regiment, although perhaps a day behind. A point many of these authors miss is that General Braddock did not travel with his troops from Williamsburg to Wills's Creek. A careful reading of the various journals that have survived supports this statement.

At Frederick Town in Maryland, General Braddock ordered Dunbar's Regiment to leave the morning of April 29, 1755, on the road to Conococheague.[1] His orders indicate Dunbar was to take the road to Winchester after arriving in Conococheague. The General had to have known at the time he gave the orders there was no road through Maryland to Ft. Cumberland.

It is not obvious why Dunbar's Regiment did not march directly to Winchester, Virginia, from Frederick Town. Perhaps Dunbar's Regiment accompanied supplies or ammunition to Conococheague. Some material did go from Conococheague up the Potomac to Ft. Cumberland. Conococheague also served as a magazine.

Nothing written by any of the participants to the Braddock Expedition indicates General Braddock accompanied Dunbar's Regiment when it left Frederick Town. According to the Orme Journal, "The 31 of April the General set out for Winchester."[2] General Braddock apparently had no reason to go to Conococheague. He knew the only route to Ft. Cumberland a t

Wills's Creek was through Winchester. It is reasonable to think
he took the most direct route from Frederick Town to Winchester.
Thus, we have two routes from Frederick Town to identify. Let us
first look at the route taken by General Braddock.

The Braddock and Washington Route

General Braddock and George Washington traveled from
Frederick Town to Swearingen's Ferry on May 2, 1755, on their
way to Winchester, Virginia.[3] Governor Sharpe of Maryland
accompanied them. The route they took went through Fox's Gap.
The data to document the route of Braddock and Washington is
significant and conclusive. The writings of Governor Sharpe and
George Washington provide information about the route. We
begin with George Washington, who left his Virginia home of
Mt. Vernon, in Fairfax County, on April 23. The train to which
he refers is the train of artillery:

> *To William Fairfax
>
>   Mount Vernon, April 23, 1755.
>   Dear Sir:
>   I cannot think of quitting Fairfax without
> embracing this last opportunity of bidding you farewell.
> I this day set out for Wills Creek, where I expect to meet
> the Gen'l. and to stay, I fear too long, as our March must
> be regulated by the slow movements of the Train . . .[4]

The following letter indicates Washington was at
Bullskin, another Virginia plantation of his, on April 30.
Bullskin was between Swearingen's Ferry and Winchester. The
1775 *Fry and Jefferson Map* shows "Washington" west of Vestal's
Ferry on the Shenandoah River and east of Frederick Town
[Winchester], Virginia. Swearingen's Ferry, on the Potomac, was
near the site of the present Rumsey Bridge at Shepherdstown,
West Virginia:

*To Mrs. George William Fairfax
Bullskin, April 30, 1755.
... out of 4 Horses which we brought from home,
one was kill'd outright, and the other 3 render'd unfit for
use; so that I have been detain'd here three days
already.⁵

This letter indicates Washington arrived at Bullskin by
April 27. Perhaps at this time his plans changed from meeting
the General at Wills's Creek to meeting him at Frederick Town
in Maryland. Whatever the cause of the alteration of his plans,
the next writing of Washington occurs on May 5 at Winchester:

*To William Fairfax
Winchester, May 5, 1755.
Dear Sir: I overtook the General at Frederick
Town in Maryland and from thence we proceeded to this
place, where we shall remain till the arrival of the 2nd
Division of the Train, (which we hear left Alexandria
on Tuesday last); after that we shall continue our march
to Wills Creek; from whence it is imagined we shall not
stir till the latter end of this Month, for want of Wagons,
and other conveniences to Transport our Baggage &c. over
the Mount'n.
You will naturally conclude that to pass through
Maryl'd. (when no business requir'd it,) was an
uncommon, and extraordinary route for the Gen'l. and
Colo. Dunbar's Regiment to this place; but at the same
time the reason, however, was obvious to say that those
who promoted it had rather have the communication
should be that way, than through Virginia; but I now
believe the Imposition has to evidently appeared for
the Imposer's to subject us to the same Inconveniences
again. please to make my Compt's to Colo. G. [George
William Fairfax] to whom I shall write by the next
oppertunity, and excuse haste. I am &c.⁶

It would be easy to assume from this letter that
Braddock and Dunbar were traveling together. However, we
know that was not the case. From the letters of Washington we

know he traveled from Bullskin to Frederick Town, Maryland, sometime after April 30. We know he arrived in Winchester, Virginia, on or before May 5.

Another Washington letter, similar in content to the above, but this time to his brother, who apparently traveled to Bullskin with him, appears below:

> *To John Augustine Washington
>   Winchester, May 6, 1755
>
> Dear Brother
>   A very fatiguing Ride and long round about brought me to the General (the day I parted with you) at Frederick Town; a small Village 15 Miles below the blue Ridge in Maryland from thence we proceeded to this place, where we have halted since Saturday last, and shall depart for Wills Creek to morrow.[7]

In a footnote, Fitzpatrick interprets this letter for us. "George apparently took leave of John Augustine Washington 1 May 1755 at or near Bullskin plantation. John Augustine must have set out on his return journey to Mount Vernon that same day or soon afterwards. Washington's route to Frederick, Md., was probably by way of Swearingen's ferry on the Potomac and through the South and Catoctin mountains in Maryland."

The 1775 *Fry and Jefferson Map* indicates Washington may have had to travel a few miles west from his Bullskin property before reaching the wagon road which led from Winchester to Swearingen's Ferry and on to Frederick Town in Maryland.

The date of the letter, May 6, was a Tuesday. Saturday last would have been May 3. Thus, the date of arrival at Winchester by the General and his party was Saturday, May 3. It is interesting Washington identifies Frederick Town as 15 miles below the Blue Ridge. Undoubtedly he was giving the distance from Fox's Gap to Frederick Town as 15 miles. We shall have occasion to refer to this distance later.

Another letter of Washington also may confuse people who have not done a thorough job of researching the Braddock and Washington route:

*To Major John Carlyle

                                   Ft. Cumberland, May 14, 1755
Sir:

         I Overtook the General at Frederick Town in
Maryl'd. and proceeded with him by way of Winchester
to this place; which gave him a good oppertunity to see
the absurdity of the Route, and of Damning it very
heartily. Col. Dunbar's Regiment was also oblig'd to
cross over at Connogogee and come down within 6 Miles of
Winchester to take the new road up, which gave me
infinite satisfaction . . . [8]

Washington wrote this letter from Ft. Cumberland at Wills's
Creek. Washington did not mean General Braddock and Dunbar's
Regiment both crossed the Potomac at Conococheague.
Washington's main point in this letter was the unreasonableness
of going through Maryland in the first place. By going into
Maryland, Dunbar's Regiment and the supply wagons had to
cross the Potomac at Rock Creek, near present day Georgetown.
They would then cross back into Virginia at Conococheague.
Still, they would have to cross the Potomac at Wills's Creek. If
they had avoided Maryland, they would have crossed the
Potomac only at Wills's Creek. Crossing the Potomac with many
horses and wagons in 1755 was no easy task.
         Washington left Bullskin to meet the General in
Frederick Town, Maryland. The most direct route to Frederick
Town from Bullskin was by way of Swearingen's Ferry. Indeed,
that route was a long roundabout, as Washington states. It is only
speculation why Washington went to Frederick Town to meet the
General. How did he find out he was to meet the General there?
         Only one document written by a participant to the events
identifies the Braddock and Washington route from Frederick
Town in Maryland to Winchester, Virginia. The route was by
way of Swearingen's Ferry at Shepherd's Town. It is probably for
this reason many authors fail to identify the Braddock and
Washington route. The letter from Governor Sharpe to Governor
Dinwiddie of Virginia follows in its entirety:

May 9th 1755.

Dr Sr

I take this Opportunity of acquainting you that I left the General Capt. Orme & Morris Col. Washington & Mr Shirley this Day Sen'net at Swerengen's Ferry on their way to Winchester. I suppose they will reach Wills-Creek to morrow. Col. Dunbar's Regiment marched from Frederick Town the 29th of April, Col. Halketts & the Virga Companies had I hear left Winchester some Days before there was a good Deal of Difficulty in procuring a Sufficient number of Wagons to carry the Stores that were sent up on this Side Potowmack but they are all at last at Conegogee whence they will be conveyed by Water to Wills-Creek. Inclosed is my Accot against you; I have not heard any thing from the northward; that you have succeeded to your wishes with your Assembly, I am desirous & impatient to hear, send me early Advice thereof & oblige.   Your &c[9]

The word *sen'net* is critical in understanding the dates of the various documents related to the Braddock and Washington route. The *Oxford English Dictionary* gives the following. "Sen'net: Sennight, now archaic, originally two words, seven and night; a period of seven (days and) nights, a week." It is similar to the word fortnight that means a period of two weeks.

One may restate the first sentence in Governor Sharpe's letter as follows without changing the meaning:

I left the General, Captain Orme, Morris, Colonel Washington, and Mr. Shirley one week ago today, Friday, May 2, at Swearingen's Ferry, on their way to Winchester. Their plan was to reach Wills's Creek on Monday, May 10.

Note that Sharpe distinguishes among three groups in his letter: Sharpe's group, which included General Braddock and Washington, the group of Dunbar, and the group with Halkett. From the dates assigned to Dunbar's orders and from the Morris Journal, we know Dunbar's Regiment was one day beyond

Conococheague and taking a day of rest on May 2. We know from the letter of Sharpe that Braddock and Washington were at Swearingen's Ferry on May 2.

Because Washington was at Bullskin on April 30 and traveled from Frederick Town to Swearingen's Ferry on May 2, it is evident he traveled from Bullskin to Frederick Town on May 1. Indeed, Washington took the same route from Bullskin to Frederick Town as he and the General took from Frederick Town through Swearingen's Ferry and on to Winchester. Washington, therefore, went through Fox's Gap on May 1 and May 2, 1755.

Governor Dinwiddie acknowledged receipt of Sharpe's letter on June 13:

June 13th, 1755

Sir:

Y'r Let'r of 9th May came to my Hands last Week. I hope by y's the whole Forces are march'd over the Allegany Mount's, and I expect they will soon be in Possess'n of the Fort. I hear Colo. Dunbar's Regim't was obliged to go by Winchester. Etc. . . . It's generally tho't here y't War is inevitable. I wish You Health and Happiness, and am,

Y'r Ex's most ob'd't h'ble serv't.[10]

Additional information about the sequence of events appeared in the *Maryland Gazette,* Thursday, May 8, 1755. The paper indicated Governor Sharpe returned home Tuesday, May 6, from the western parts of Maryland.[11] Undoubtedly, he returned from his trip, during which he accompanied Braddock and Washington to Swearingen's Ferry.

Confirmation that Governor Sharpe accompanied Braddock and Washington to Swearingen's Ferry appears in three other letters. Sharpe wrote Lord Baltimore on May 22, 1755, from Annapolis.[12] "The Regiment could not march from Frederickton before the 29th of April & the General did not leave that place till the first of May [Sharpe used "first of May" loosely, meaning "early May."] when I waited on him over Potowmack in the way to Winchester & then took my Leave." Also on May 22, Sharpe wrote Lord Calvert.[13] "I waited on the

General from Frederickton to Potowmack where he crossed that
River in the Road to Winchester the 2d of May, Colo. Dunbar's
as well as Colo Halketts Regiment had marched a few Days
before for Wills-Creek." Sharpe makes a similar statement in a
letter to his brother John, dated May 24.

There are no orders in General Braddock's Orderly Book
from April 30 through May 9 because during that time the
General was not near any troops to whom he could give any
orders. The General was at Winchester from May 3 until May 7.
Dunbar's Regiment came no closer than five or six miles north of
Winchester on May 4 as they marched from Widow Barringer's
to Potts. They did not stop at Winchester. The General passed
Dunbar's Regiment only a few hours before they reached Wills's
Creek. Halkett's Regiment arrived at Wills's Creek before the
General.

The letters of Governor Sharpe and George Washington
are sufficient to document Sharpe and Washington accompanied
Braddock to Swearingen's Ferry from Frederick Town on May 2,
1755. The next question to be answered is, "By what road or roads
did they travel?" One item that gives specific reference to a
route from Frederick Town to Swearingen's Ferry is the 1762 will
of Moses Chapline Sr.:

> . . . I give and bequeath to my son Josiah
> Chapline, all that part of a Tract called The Resurvey
> on Mount Pleasant, which lyeth to the Southward of the
> Wagon Road, that leads from Swearingens Ferry to
> Frederick Town, as also one other tract of land called
> Josiah Bitt to him and his heirs forever. Imprimis. I give
> and bequeath to my son Moses Chapline all the rest of
> this said tract of land called the Resurvey on Mount
> Pleasant with the Original, that lyeth on the North
> Side of the aforesaid Wagon Road to him & his Heirs
> forever . . .[14]

Moses Chapline Sr. (June 11, 1717 - 1761/2) was born in
Prince Georges County. He was the brother of Joseph Chapline
Sr. He married Janet Caton in 1740, at Annapolis.[15] The Moses
Chapline Sr. homestead was near the base of South Mountain,

about two miles west of Fox's Gap. It was on the road that went through Fox's Gap. Moses and his wife probably moved to this home in the early 1740s.[16] Near the Moses Chapline Sr. home was a family cemetery. Both Moses and his wife are buried in the family cemetery along the old Sharpsburg Road. Moses served at Ft. Frederick during the French and Indian War.[17]

One can identify the Moses Chapline Sr. property on the maps of the Battlefields of South Mountain and Antietam in the *Atlas to Accompany the Official Records of the Union and Confederate Armies.*[18] The United States Army Corps of Engineers prepared these maps. "G. Shiffler" appears on the left side of the Battlefield of South Mountain map. George and Elizabeth Shiffler built a stone wall around the Moses Chapline Sr. cemetery. The cemetery remains today, although the old house burned to the ground January 9, 1901.[19] The map of the Battlefield of Antietam, Plate XXIX, shows the G. Shiffler property on the far right, just east of Springvale. The two maps, placed together so the points marked by "G. Shiffler" touch, create a map of the old Sharpsburg Road. These two maps show the road, from the forks of the roads at the Catoctin Creek just north of Middletown, all the way to Sharpsburg.

The most important strategic point in our study is the area of Fox's Gap itself. The following record, in the Historical Society of Carroll County, Westminster, Maryland, indicates Fox's Gap and the home of John Fox were on the road from Frederick Town to Swearingen's Ferry:

OFW: u-40   Wash. Co.

GRIMS FANCY

2-27-1764   50 A.
6-12-1769 Alexander Grim
   BC & GS 40-114
N.S. Main Road that leads from Frederick Town to Swainingens (Swearingens) Ferry & near to John Fox's house.
On the west side of South Mtn.
On this land is 2 log cabbins 27 x 12 & 14 x 12 & 15 A. cultivated land.
Next to Mt. Atlas.
Wash. Co. near Fox's Gap.
F. C. 1743 Sheet 392

The Grims Fancy survey date was February 27, 1764.
Alexander Grim patented the tract June 12, 1769. This tract began
on the north side of the main road that led from Frederick Town
to Swearingen's Ferry. It was one-half mile west of Fox's Gap.
    The Grim's Fancy land record reads as follows, in part:

> . . . I have carefully surveyed and laid out for
> and in the name of him the said Alexander Grim all that
> tract of land called Grims Fancy lying in the County
> aforesaid beginning at a bounded Black Oak tree
> standing on the north side of the main road that leads
> from Frederick Town to Swearingen's Ferry and near to
> John Fox's House on the West side of the South Mountain
> and running thence . . . fifty acres of Land to be held of
> Conegocheigue Manor Surveyed the 27th of February
> 1764 . . .[20]

The survey record bears an examination date of June 5, 1765. It is
possible to give two interpretations to this record. We can
interpret the record to mean, (1) John Fox's house was near the
road, or (2) the tract called Grim's Fancy was near John Fox's
house. The Grims Fancy land record places John Fox's house at
Fox's Gap between 1764 and 1769.
    John Frederick Fox (Johan Friederich Fuchs) arrived at
the port of Philadelphia on the ship Anderson, Captain Hugh
Campbell, September 27, 1752.[21] John Fox appeared in the state
house in Philadelphia the day of his arrival and "took and
subscribed the usual Qualifications."[22] On the voyage to
America with him was his wife Christina [Christiana in *The
Fox Genealogy*] and at least two children, Daniel and Frederick.
Daniel was the older.[23] Frederick was born May 10, 1751, in
Hesse-Cassel, Germany.[24]
    John Fox was a skin-dresser by trade.[25] He and his wife
were the parents of five children. Magdelin, Michael, and
Rachel probably were born after the arrival of the family in
America. The name of John Fox appears in the Moses Chapline
Sr. Administration Account papers submitted by the executors of
the estate, bearing a date of June 19, 1766.[26] It is possible John

Fox provided some type of services to the estate shortly after the death of Moses Chapline Sr. in 1762. These estate papers place John Fox in the area of South Mountain between 1762 and 1766.

The patent or deed for the land tract John Fox acquired at Fox's Gap is not on record. The name of his tract may have been Friendship. Frederick Fox patented a tract at Fox's Gap called Addition to Friendship in 1805. It is possible John Fox and his family settled in the Pennsylvania German community before coming to Maryland. This author believes they may have settled at Fox's Gap shortly after arriving in Philadelphia.

Alexander Grim, the first owner of Grim's Fancy, also is in the Moses Chapline Sr. will:

> . . . Whereas I have by a Verbal Agreement sold a tract of land called part of the Resurvey on Well Done unto one Alexander Grim for the Sum of thirty pounds current money of Pensilvani, now my will is that if the aforesaid Grim or his heirs do pay or cause to be paid to my Executor the said sum of thirty pounds & interest within three years after my Decease, then I impower my executrix upon Receipt thereof to convey the said land to said Alexander him his heirs or assigns by a Special Deed of Conveyance & the money to become part of my personal Estate, and upon Default of the payment of the money aforesaid by said Alexander Grim then I impower my executrix to sell & convey the land to any other Person & to apply the Money as before mentioned . . .[27]

The homes of Moses Chapline Sr. and John Fox were on the road from Swearingen's Ferry to Frederick Town. Both these homes were on the road that went through Fox's Gap. It is obvious Frederick Town and Swearingen's Ferry were the end points of the road. What other points can we identify along the road?

A map dated August 23, 1792, of the *Road from Swearingen's Ferry on the Potomac River through Sharpsburg to the top of the South Mountain at Fox's Gap* is in the Maryland Archives (see Appendix C - Land Tract Analysis).[28] William Good, Jacob, and Christopher signed the map. "Jacob" probably was Jacob Russell and "Christopher" undoubtedly was

Christopher Orndorff.[29] They most likely prepared the map because they owned property along the road. They may have been road commissioners. The map was recorded at one time in Washington County land records, Liber G, page 867.

William Good[30] and Christopher Orndorff[31] were two very respected citizens of their day. Christopher Orndorff (Nov. 23, 1752 - Sept. 14, 1823) operated a mill at the Orndorff, or Middle, Bridge on the Antietam Creek. Moses Chapline Sr., at his death in 1762, left approximately 1800 acres of land, including the family homestead, to his son Moses Chapline Jr. Moses Jr. sold all of this land and the homestead to William Good. The wife of William Good was Mary Chapline, sister of Moses Jr. The southern portion of this land tract was on the road from Frederick Town to Swearingen's Ferry. William Good and his wife Mary Chapline are buried in the Moses Chapline Sr. cemetery along Dog Street Road (i.e., the old Sharpsburg Road), about two miles west of Fox's Gap.[32]

Christopher Orndorff owned a Mill where the road from Frederick Town to Swearingen's Ferry crossed the Antietam. The Orndorff (or Middle) Bridge crossed the Antietam near the Orndorff Mill. During the Civil War and later it was known as the Middle (or Antietam) Bridge. Alexander Gardner took a picture of the Orndorff Mill at the Middle Bridge shortly after the Battle of Antietam. This picture is in *Antietam: The Photographic Legacy of America's Bloodiest Day* by William Frassinito. The book is about Alexander Gardner and his photography of the Antietam Battlefield. Frassinito, in 1972, took a picture from the same location where Gardner made his 1862 photograph of the Orndorff Mill and the Middle Bridge.

Another critical piece of information about the Braddock route is in the Minutes of the Frederick County Court from the year 1781:

> . . . from the forks of the roads where the Sharpsburgh Road leads out of Braddock's Road to the top of South Mountain, being the direct road from Frederick passing Robert Turner's old place to Fort Frederick . . .[33]

Many readers, aware Dunbar's Regiment marched to Conococheague, place General Braddock on the same route. At the same time, this passage leads many to conclude General Braddock went through Turner's Gap.

The 1781 court minutes indicate the Braddock Road and the Sharpsburg Road met. The fork in the road in 1755 was where the roads through Orr's Gap and Fox's Gap met (i.e. the old Hagerstown Road and the old Sharpsburg Road).

Until at least 1840, the road through Turner's Gap met the road through Fox's Gap about midway between the Fox Inn and the Catoctin Creek. Today, the old National Pike through Turner's Gap crosses the Catoctin Creek just north of Middletown and near the fork of the old Hagerstown and old Sharpsburg Roads. The old National Pike also bears the name of Alternate Route 40 or simply 40A.

At the time of the Braddock Expedition, there was no viable route from Conococheague to Ft. Cumberland. This was the very reason Dunbar's Regiment came down near Winchester after crossing the Potomac at Conococheague. It might be useful to clarify that General Braddock did not go to Ft. Frederick in 1755, since the fort didn't exist at that time. We again turn to George Washington. The date of this letter is June 1756:

> Governor Sharpe is building a fort on Potomac River, about fifteen miles above Conogochieg, which may be of great service towards the protection of our people on that side. It is thought the fort will cost the province of Maryland near thirty thousand pounds, before it is finished.[34]

Fitzpatrick explains in a footnote to the above letter:

> The Governor and Assembly of Maryland had come at last to a temporary reconciliation of their differences, so far as to agree in a bill for raising £40,000 for his Majesty's service. Of this sum £11,000 were to be appropriated to building a fort on the frontiers, near but not beyond the North Mountain; and £25,000 for carrying on any expedition for the public service, in which the

The Road from Swearingen's Ferry on the Potomac River through Sharpsburg to the Top of the South Mountain at Fox's Gap

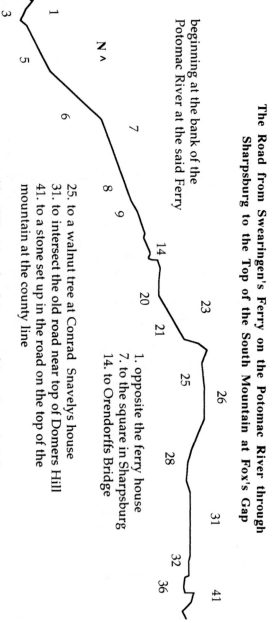

beginning at the bank of the
Potomac River at the said Ferry

N ^

1. opposite the ferry house
7. to the square in Sharpsburg
14. to Orendorffs Bridge

25. to a walnut tree at Conrad Snavelys house
31. to intersect the old road near top of Domers Hill
41. to a stone set up in the road on the top of the
mountain at the county line

August 23, 1792, Maryland State Archives, Special Collections.
MSA G1427-507, B5-1-3.

The Battlefield of South Mountain - 1862

other colonies might join. By the same act the governor was authorized to raise 200 men, to be employed in constructing the fort. (see Acts of Maryland Assembly, May, 1756, and *McMahon's History of Maryland*, vol. 1, p. 305) The fort was called Ft. Frederick. It was a work of considerable magnitude, of a quadrangular form, and constructed of durable materials, situated on an eminence about 500 yards from the Potomac River. Parts of it still remain.

Ft. Frederick is along the Potomac River between Williamsport and Cumberland, Maryland. Today, Ft. Frederick is Maryland's oldest state park.

Swearingen's Ferry began operation in 1755.[35] It operated until 1849. No doubt the Ferry connected roads on both sides of the Potomac. The 1751 and 1775 *Fry and Jefferson Maps* show a road from the area of Shepherdstown to Winchester. The word "Washington" appears on the maps not far from this route. This probably was the site of Washington's Bullskin Plantation.[36]

The previous discussion documented various points along the road from Frederick Town to Swearingen's Ferry. These points include: Swearingen's Ferry, the town square in Sharpsburg, the Orndorff (or Middle) Bridge on the Antietam, the home of Moses Chapline Sr., the home of John Fox at Fox's Gap, and the fork in the road near the Catoctin Creek. The Fox Inn, probably built before 1780, is on this road as well. This was the route of the old Sharpsburg Road that connected Middletown and Sharpsburg.

The Land Tract Records of the Old Sharpsburg Road through Fox's Gap

Land tracts in western Maryland, during the 1700s and early 1800s, were given names. Many early land tracts ran afoul of contiguous tracts. Plotting some of these early tracts is sometimes as much an art as a science. It is often the land tracts of the early 1800s that clarify the location of earlier surveys. Deeds for later transfers of some tracts indicate the level of precision of the earlier survey measurements required an "allowance for variation of the magnetic needle," sometimes up to two degrees. The unit of measure for these early tracts was the "perch." One perch is 16.5 feet. A perch is equal to one pole.

A number of land tracts on the west side of Fox's Gap support the road through Fox's Gap to Shepherdstown before 1755. Smith's Hills had its "beginning at a bounded white oak standing on the side of a hill, within a quarter mile of a wagon road that crosses the Antietam Creek."[37] This tract is near the Lower (or Burnside) Bridge. Fellfoot was "about ten perches from a road commonly called the wagon road."[38] The bounded white oak that was the beginning tree of Mountain was "near the road that leads from Monocice to Teagues Ferry."[39] Mt. Pleasant was "within 30 poles of the wagon road that goes from Shepherd's ford to the Monocacy."[40] The beginning tree of Pile's Grove was "about half a mile above a road commonly called the wagon road."[41]

The land tracts mentioned in the 1762 will of Moses Chapline Sr. are near several of the above mentioned tracts. The Resurvey on Mt. Pleasant began "at the end of the 4th line of the Original."[42] Josiah's Bit had its "beginning at the end of the twelfth line of the second Resurvey on Mt. Pleasant laid out for said Chapline and the end of the second line of a tract of land called Mountain."[43]

Three later tracts in the same area, Old Purchase,[44] Pastures Green,[45] and Miller's Hills,[46] identify the road during the late 1700s and early 1800s. Lines 6, 7, 8, and 9 of Old Purchase identify 142 perches (2343 feet) along "the Wagon Road that leads to Frederick Town." Old Purchase began "at the end of the second line of a tract called Mountain."

The Pastures Green survey mentions a number of the above tracts. Pastures Green encompassed the Old Purchase tract. Line 31 of Pastures Green went "to the Wagon Road twenty feet north of a stone standing in said line." Miller's Hills had its "beginning for the outlines of the whole at the end of the 2nd line of a tract of land called Piles Grove." Line 19 of Miller's Hills went to "the main road leading from Fox's Gap to Sharpsburg." The distance from the beginning tree to the road in 1813 was about 1/2 mile. Security began at a tree "standing on the north side of the South Mountain and about two hundred yards from the main road leading from Frederick Town to Sharpsburg on the south side thereof."[47] The Resurvey of Security is adjacent to Addition to Friendship on the west side of Fox's Gap.[48] Ferry Landing was "on the bank of the Potomac near Swearingen's Ferry."[49] This tract is near the present Rumsey Bridge at Shepherdstown.

Conrad Snavely owned most of the southern portion of Fellfoot Enlarged.[50] Line 25 from the 1792 map of the road ended at Conrad Snavely's house. This reference point agrees with the route of the road identified in the Fellfoot patent.

Also on the west side of Fox's Gap is Mt. Atlas.[51] This patent, consisting of one large tract and two smaller tracts, is contiguous to the Resurvey on Security, Booker's Resurvey on Well Done,[52] and Grim's Fancy, among others.

Three tracts, prior to 1755, on the east side of Fox's Gap support the road through Fox's Gap from the area that became Middletown. The Forrest began "at a bounded hickory standing about half a mile above the wagon road that goes from Conestoga to Opeckin Crosses a creek called Katankin Creek which falls into Potomack River about six miles above Monocacy."[53] This tract begins about 1/2 mile above the bridge over the Catoctin creek. The Forrest was adjacent the south side of Wooden Platter.

The 1794 *Dennis Griffith Map of Maryland* shows the route of the road from Conestoga to Opequon. The road began at Conestoga, Pennsylvania, near Lancaster. It passed through York, Pennsylvania, and Taneytown, Woodsborough, Frederick Town, Middletown, Fox's Gap, and Sharpsburg in Maryland. It crossed the Potomac at Shepherdstown and went on to Opequon, located about five miles southwest of Winchester, Virginia. This route also was known as the German Monocacy Road. Tracey and Dern, page 51 of *Pioneers of Old Monocacy*, indicate the "Road to Opequon" went through Turner's Gap. The road went through Fox's Gap. The old Sharpsburg Road was part of the road from Conestoga to Opequon.

The road from Conestoga to Opequon was the same road as the Great Philadelphia Wagon Road. It was not the same road as the Great Wagon Road to Philadelphia through Conococheague. The *Frye and Jefferson Map* identifies the Great Philadelphia Wagon Road in Virginia. The road crossed the

Potomac at Shepherdstown. The Post Map identifies the Great Philadelphia Wagon Road from Philadelphia to the Maryland line north of Taneytown, Maryland. It is probably the Monocacy Road that is shown on the map as the "Great Philadelphia Wagon Road."[54]

Oxford, surveyed for James Wardrop in 1750, had its "beginning at a bounded black oak standing at the head of a valley that falls into a branch called John Crisles spring branch and about ten or fifteen yards of the main road the leads through Frederick Town by Robert Evans and on the north side of the said road."[55] This tract began about 1000 feet east of the Fox Inn. Wardrop's Cool Spring was near the east side of Oxford.[56] It was surveyed for James Wardrop in 1750 and began "at a bounded white oak standing on the top of a hill about two hundred yards from the Wagon Road that leads through Frederick Town and about a Mile from John Burger's house"

Key to the foldout page of the land tracts on the west side of Fox's Gap

A　　Beginning tree of Fellfoot
B　　Beginning tree of Racon
C　　Beginning tree of Fox's Last Shift
D　　Beginning tree of Flonham
E　　Beginning tree of Piles's Grove
F　　Beginning tree of the Resurvey on Mt. Pleasant
M　　Beginning tree of Mountain
R　　The Reno Monument at Fox's Gap
25　　Line 25 of the 1792 map of the *Road from Swearingen's Ferry to Fox's Gap*
41　　Line 41, last line, of the 1792 map of the *Road to Swearingen's Ferry to Fox's Gap*

Line 39 is not given in the written description on the map. The author estimated line 39 as South, 81 degrees East, 40 perches.

Heavy Black Line - road from Swearingen's Ferry to Fox's Gap

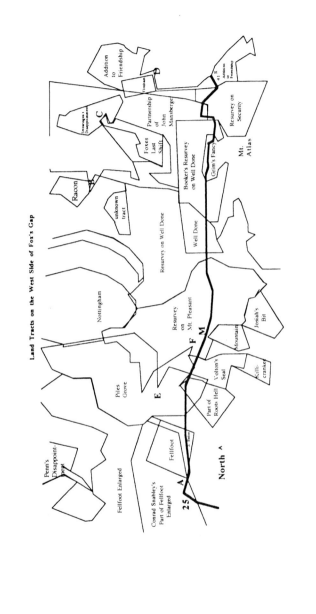

Land Tracts on the West Side of Fox's Gap

Fox's Gap to the Fox Inn Area

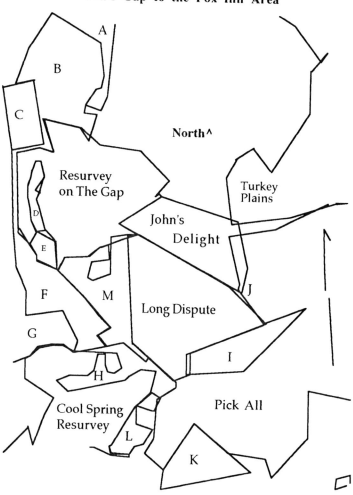

A - Knaves Good Will
B - Addition to Friendship
C - Flonham
D - Apple Brandy
E - Bowser's Addition
F - Addition to Friendship
G - David's Will

H - Daniel's Race Ground
I - Shettle
J - Beginning tree of Pick All
K - Betty's Good Will
L - Mt. Pleasant
M - Fredericksburg

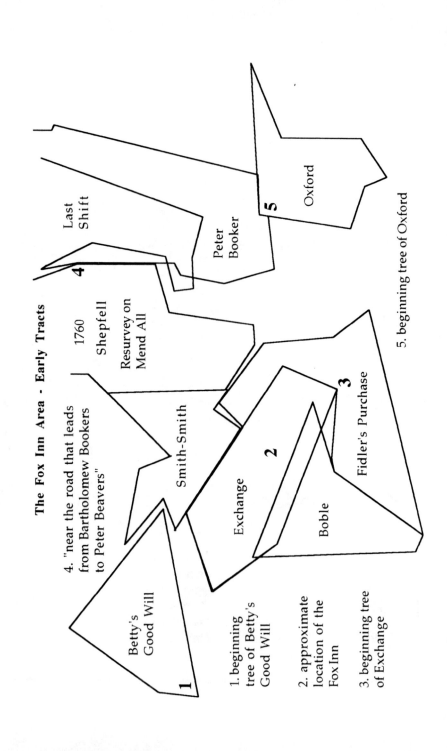

The Fox Inn Area - Early Tracts

Betty's Good Will

Smith-Smith

Exchange

Boble

Fidler's Purchase

1760
Shepfell
Resurvey on
Mend All

Last
Shift

Peter
Booker

Oxford

4. "near the road that leads from Bartholomew Bookers to Peter Beavers"

1. beginning tree of Betty's Good Will

2. approximate location of the Fox Inn

3. beginning tree of Exchange

5. beginning tree of Oxford

The Fox Inn Area - Another View

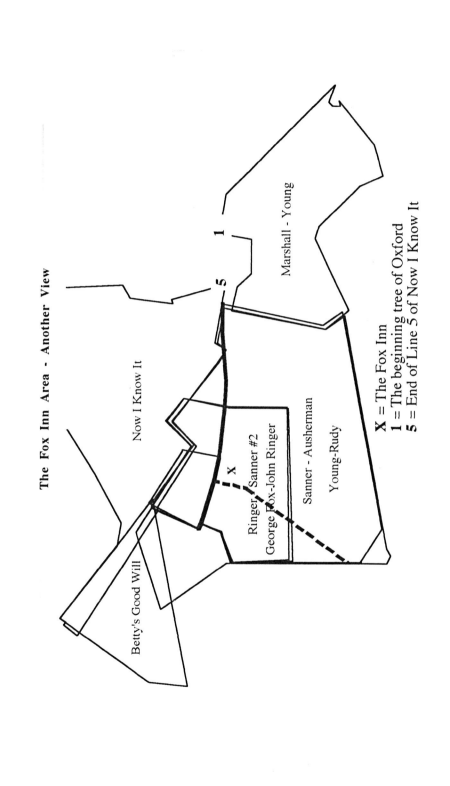

Now I Know It

Betty's Good Will

Ringer, Sanner #2
George Fox-John Ringer

X

Sanner - Ausherman

Young-Rudy

Marshall - Young

5 1

X = The Fox Inn
1 = The beginning tree of Oxford
5 = End of Line 5 of Now I Know It

X   The fork of the old Sharpsburg Road and the old Hagerstown Road, just south of the Catoctin Creek about one mile north of Middletown and near the mouth of Mill Creek on the Catoctin Creek.

Heavy, Broken Black Line - the old Sharpsburg Road

1. The Fox Inn - located on The Exchange, surveyed for Daniel Dulany Sr. in 1749
2. Resurvey on Exchange - patented 1754 to Casper Shaff
3. Jacob Smith Sr. to Jacob Smith Jr., 1795 - I Hope It Is Well Done, 111 acres
4. Bartholomew Booker to George Yeaste, 1760 - Resurvey on Mend All, 52 acres
5. Bartholomew Booker to Christopher Everhart, 1760 - Resurvey on Mend All, 100 acres
6. Bartholomew Booker et al to Christian Koogle, 1791 - Resurvey on Wooden Platter, 327 acres - surveyed for James Wardrop in 1748
7. Wooden Platter - surveyed for Daniel Dulany Sr. in 1742
8. Pick All of Bartholomew Booker - patented in 1764
9. Oxford - surveyed for James Wardrop in 1750
10. Resurvey on Learning, Addition to Learning, and Part of the Resurvey on Learning, 467 1/4 acres - resurveyed 1765
11. Resurvey on Tom's Gift - patented 1764 by Joseph Chapline
12. Cool Spring - surveyed for James Wardrop in 1750
13. Christios Folly - Richard Smith, Innholder, to Peter Beaver, 1755, 100 acres
14. Beginning tree of The Forrest
15. The Forrest - surveyed October 2, 1733
16. Resurvey on Whiskey Alley - 567 acres, May 12, 1762
17. 66 acre tract of Goose Cap - Nicholas Fink to Thomas Welch, 1771
18. Resurvey on Watson's Welfare - Joseph Chapline, 1752
19. Resurvey on Whiskey Alley
20. Beginning tree of Watson's Welfare - "near a mile below the great Road that leads from John Stull's Mill to the mouth of Monocacy"
21. Beginning tree of Cool Spring of James Wardrop

The Fox Inn Area to The Fork of the Roads

Betty's Good Will, surveyed for Robert Evans in 1727, had its "beginning at a bounded white oak standing at the foot of Shannondore Mountain near the wagon road that goes from Teagues Ferry to Minonocee Town."[57] The 1727 date is the earliest date the author found in his research of the land records of western Maryland:

> . . . whereas Robert Evans of Frederick County had on the twentieth day of October seventeen hundred & twenty seven surveyed & laid out for him a tract or parcel of land called Betty's Good Will lying and being formerly in Prince Georges but now in Frederick County containing fifty acres by virtue of so much part of an assignment of a warrant for three hundred acres from John Mills who was assignee of Daniel Oneal by renewment the twenty second day of April seventeen hundrd & forty seven but before the said Evans laid out our grant thereon he did on the fourth day of May seventeen hundred and forty nine assign over all his right title and interest thereto unto Edward Grimes . . .[58]

Various deeds identify the route of the old Sharpsburg Road between Fox's Gap and the Catoctin Creek after 1755. A 1787 deed for part of I Hope It Is Well Done had its "beginning for said part at a stone near the main road that leads from Middle Town to Sharpsburg."[59] This point is about 500 feet north of Betty's Good Will. The deed from Vincent Sanner to Samuel Asherman in 1869, consisting of Part of the Resurvey on Exchange, Bubble, and Deefer Snay,[60] included "Line 17, North 22 degrees east 20 perches into the old Sharpsburg Road." This point is just west of the Fox Inn.

A Resurvey called Now I Know It consisted of portions of Betty's Good Will, the Resurvey on Mend All, the Resurvey on Learning, and I Hope It Is Well Done. The Now I Know It survey mentions Exchange, the Resurvey on Exchange, Pick All, and Pegging Awl.[61] It included "Line 5, South 16 degrees East 46 perches to a stone marked 38 in the main road." This point is just east of the Fox Inn.

Jacob Fluck (Flook) acquired a 50 acre tract called Learning in 1754. An article about Jacob Flook of Middletown shows various tracts on the south side of Marker Road between the Fox Inn and the Catoctin Creek.[62]

According to *The Fox Genealogy* by Daniel G. Fox, the Fox Inn stands on a tract of land transferred from Bartholomew Booker to Frederick Fox on April 4, 1787. This is inaccurate. Frederick Fox never owned the Fox Inn. Daniel G. Fox places the present Fox Inn, visited by him in the early 1900s, on a tract named Turkey Foot (see Appendix C - Land Tract Analysis, The Fox Inn and Appendix D - The Fox Inn). The Turkey Foot[63] tract is surrounded on three sides by a tract named Mt. Pleasant,[64] patented by Frederick Fox on May 27, 1793. These tracts are a short distance north of Betty's Good Will. The Fox Inn is approximately 50 perches south of the end of line three of Betty's Good Will.

The present building known as the Fox Inn stands on a tract named The Exchange, acquired by assignment from Robert Evans by Joseph Chapline Sr. in 1749.[65] Robert Evans acquired the tract by assignment from Daniel Dulany Sr. The original tract was to consist of 100 acres but was 25 acres deficient. Chapline sold the tract to Casper Shaff, a merchant, in 1753.[66] Shaff obtained a patent in 1754 for 275 acres under the name of the Resurvey on Exchange.[67] It is possible to contend, although this author does not do so, the present building known as the Fox Inn dates to the year 1753 or 1754. The patent for the Resurvey on Exchange includes the following statement: ". . . But before the said Joseph Chapline laid out our grant thereon he did on the ninth day of May seventeen hundred and fifty four assign over all his Right Title Interest Claim and Demand whatsoever of in and unto the certificate of Resurvey aforesaid and the land and Premises therein mentioned unto a certain Casper Shaff . . ." Likewise, the 1753 transfer from Chapline to Shaff includes the following: ". . . by a straight line to the beginning tree containing and now laid out for seventy five acres be the same more or less together with all houses buildings fences improvements whatsoever . . ."[68]

Shaff sold 150 acres of the Resurvey on Exchange to Valentine Fidler in 1767.[69] The land then passed to George Fidler who sold 100 acres to Ludwick Layman in 1786. Peter

Layman sold the 100 acres to George Fox in 1805. Certainly, the Fox Inn must date to the time the land was owned by the only person named Fox who owned it. Daniel G. Fox indicated workmen found writings on the walls of the building during repairs. The writings mentioned the years of 1777 and later.

George Fox (Mar. 10, 1781 - June 14, 1847)[70] was the oldest son of Frederick Fox and the great, great, great grandfather of the author.[71] Records of the Zion Lutheran Church of Middletown indicate he was a member of that church.[72] He married Elizabeth Ann Link (Jan. 28, 1784 - Mar. 9, 1872) of Shepherdstown, on Aug. 9, 1807.[73] She was the daughter of John Adam Link II and Jane Ogle.[74] John Adam Link II was a descendant of Johan Jacob Link, an ancestor of Dwight D. Eisenhower.[75] Jane Ogle, daughter of Alexander Ogle, was a descendant of John Ogle of Delaware.[76]

Stanley F. Young to Richard and Helen Rudy

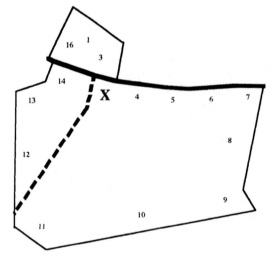

The location of the Fox Inn, at the intersection of Marker Road and Reno Monument Road, is marked by an **X**. The solid, heavy black line represents the old Sharpsburg Road. The dotted line represents the road to Burkittsville.

George Fox sold the inn and 100 acres to John Ringer in late 1807[77] when George and his wife Elizabeth, along with other members of the Fox family, moved to near what became Dayton, Ohio.[78] Sidney Ringer, widow of John, sold the property to Vincent Sanner.[79] The May 28, 1834, deed indicates line 4 was "to the middle of the main road." Line 5 of the same deed was "with said road" for 5 perches. These five perches are a short distance directly south of Betty's Good Will. Sanner sold the property to Samuel Ausherman in 1868.[80]

Mr. and Mrs. Richard Rudy obtained the Fox Inn from Stanley F. Young in 1958. The tract acquired by the Rudys in 1958 is very similar to the tract obtained by Samuel Ausherman from Vincent Sanner in 1868. Line 5 of the Sidney Ringer-Vincent Sanner deed is the same as line 15 of the Young-Rudy tract.

The following two land records identify tracts in the vicinity of the Fox Inn. Neighbor's Content, a resurvey for Andrew Smith, mentions the tracts of Middle Town, Youngest Brother, the Resurvey on Exchange, Widows Design, the Resurvey on Learning, and Loving Brother.[81] Also in the area is a tract transferred in a deed between Mathias Flook and George Butt, April 7, 1802. This tract mentions the Resurvey on Learning, the Resurvey on Oxford, and a point in "the middle of the main road."[82]

Fox's Gap

Fox's Gap includes the area in the immediate vicinity of the Reno Monument (see Appendix C - Land Tract Analysis, the Reno Monument).[83] Bowser's Addition,[84] surveyed in 1763, is contiguous to the north side of the Wise Tract[85] of Civil War fame. The ten acres of Bowser's Addition was "by the side of the wagon road leading from Sharpsburg to Frederick Town and on top of South Mountain." The Bowser's Addition tract offers proof the road through Fox's Gap crossed the mountain at the same point in 1763 as it does today.

The Reno Monument stands on a 40 foot square portion of the Wise Tract.[86] The Wise tract is part of Addition to Friendship, patented by Frederick Fox in 1805.[87] Addition to Friendship consisted of 202 acres. Approximately 65 acres were at Fox's Gap on the south side of the road. Approximately 125 acres were on the east and north sides of Turner's Gap. The remaining 12 acres or so ran from Fox's Gap to Turner's Gap, connecting the two larger sections.

A deed from Susan Miller et al. to John Miller for 13 and 1/4 acres, recorded in 1845, included Bowser's Addition and 3 and 1/4 acres of Addition to Friendship.[88] The Wise Tract (i. e., John Wise to Jonas Gross) consists of only 4 and 3/4 acres. The Miller deed and Wise deed both include the two courses, "with said road, East 7 perches" and "North 86 degrees East, 16 perches." Lines 6 and 7 of the Miller - Miller deed are the same as lines 1 and 2 of the Wise Tract.

Frederick Fox's 1792 survey for Fredericksburg identifies lines 8, 9, and 10, a total of 144 perches or 2376 feet, along "the main road."[89] Line 10 went "to the bounded tree of a tract of land called Bowser's Addition." Fredericksburg was on the east side of Fox's Gap and primarily on the north side of the road. Also in the vicinity of Fox' Gap are David's Will[90] of David Bowser and the Cool Spring Resurvey[91] in 1801 of Samuel Shoup. The Shoup tract is not a resurvey on the Cool Spring patented by James Wardrop in 1750.

The deed for Grim's Fancy is the only proof John Fox lived in the vicinity of Fox's Gap. There are no land records for John Fox except for lots in Sharpsburg. A deed between John Fox of Frederick Town and Elias Bruner, farmer, recorded May 22, 1766, transfered lot 269 in Frederick Town "being the lot where the said John Fox now lives."[92] Daniel G. Fox refers to this deed in *The Fox Genealogy.* John Fox acquired Lot 269 from Daniel Dulany on May 16, 1764.[93] This author believes the John Fox of Frederick Town was not the same John Fox who lived at Fox's Gap. Church records of the period indicate there was a John George Fox and wife Christina at Frederick Town.[94]

It is possible John Fox owned a tract named Friendship at Fox's Gap. Whatever tract John Frederick Fox owned at Fox's Gap may have passed to Frederick Fox sometime after John Fox died in 1784. The will of John Fox indicates, "I give and Bequeath unto my beloved Wife Christina all that I do possess of during her Natural life . . ." Perhaps she gave the land at Fox's Gap to Frederick Fox about 1792. Christina died August 6, 1812.[95]

Addition to Friendship

202 acres

Beginning at the end of the first line of a tract of land called David's Will

1. to the beginning of said land it being also the beginning of Friendship the present original

2. to the end of the last line of David's Will

3. to the 3rd line of Jacob Hess's Resurvey called Security

7. to the end of the 1st line of a tract of land called Flonham

8. to the bounded Tree of said land

10. to the end of 21 perches on the 3rd line of said Flonham

12. to the end of the 7th line of a tract of land called Knaves Good Will

20. to the 14th line of a tract of land called Turkey Ramble

27. to the end of the 3rd line of a tract of land called Bowsers Addition

30. to the bounded tree of said Bowsers Addition it being the end of the tenth line of a tract of land called Friendship

34. to a rock marked FF

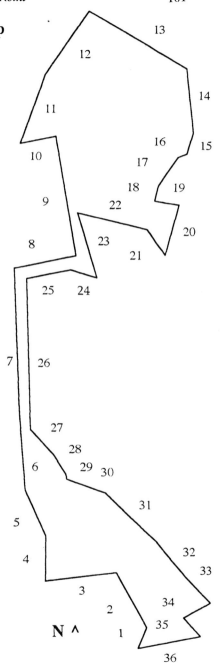

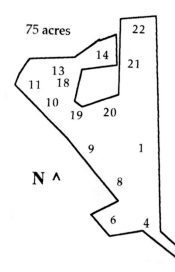

75 acres

Fredericksburg

Beginning at the end of the 12th line of a tract of land called Pickall

6. to a stone marked FF
7. to the main road, then with said road 3 courses
10. to the bounded tree of a tract of land called Bowser's Addition

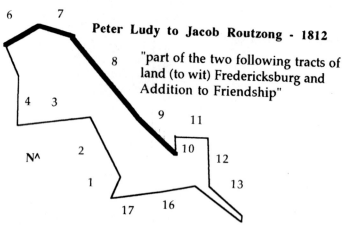

Peter Ludy to Jacob Routzong - 1812

"part of the two following tracts of land (to wit) Fredericksburg and Addition to Friendship"

6. N 60 degrees East 35 perches to the top of the mountain in the said road then with it three following courses
7. S 75 degrees East 31 perches to the bounded tree of a tract of land called Bowser's Addition
8. S 43 degrees East 88 perches
9. S 35 degrees East 47 perches to the end of the seventh line of the aforesaid land called Fredericksburg
(**Note:** bold line - along road)

Fox's Gap

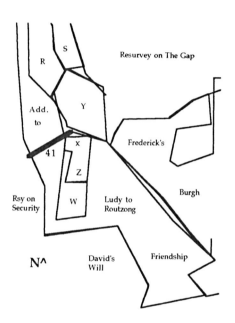

R   = Resurvey on The Gap
S   = Apple Brandy
Z   = The Wise Tract
X   = The Reno Monument
W   = The Kefauver Tract
Y   = Bowser's Addition and Susan Miller et al. to John Miller
4 1 = Last line of 1792 Map - *Road from Swearingen's Ferry to Fox's Gap*

The last line given on the *Map of the Road from Swearingen's Ferry to Fox's Gap* ends at the end of line 5 of Bowser's Addition.[96] Line 41 of the road was "North 60 degrees East 41 perches to a stone set up in the road on the top of the mountain at the county line." Line 6 of a deed from Peter Ludy to Jacob Routzong contained the following line: "North 60 degrees East 35 perches to the top of the mountain in the said road."[97] This deed was for part of Addition to Friendship and Fredericksburg. Line 6 of the Ludy-Routzong deed ends at the end of line 5 of Bowser's Addition. Line 7 of the Ludy-Routzong deed went "to the bounded tree of a tract of land called Bowser's Addition."

The Braddock Road and The Battle of South Mountain

Braddock's Gap appears in the writings of several generals who participated in the Battle of South Mountain. Let us turn first to General Jacob D. Cox, commander of the Kanawha Division at Fox's Gap during the Battle of South Mountain and one of the foremost military historians of the United States in the later part of the 1800s:

> The Sharpsburg Road is also called the Braddock Road, as it was the way by which Braddock and Washington had marched to Fort Duquesne (Pittsburgh, Pa.) in the old French war. For the same reason the gap is called Braddock's Gap. I have adopted that which seems to be in most common local use.[98]

General Cox included a map of the Battle of South Mountain in his book.[99] Cox labeled the road through Fox's Gap as the "old Sharpsburg or Braddock Road" on his map. If anyone had need of a time and place to know the facts concerning a region and its roads, it was at the Battle of South Mountain. The material previously presented indicates General Cox had perfect knowledge of the old Sharpsburg Road. Indeed, his success in the battle, in part, hinged on this knowledge.

General Cox proceeds to use the terms "Fox's Gap" and "the Sharpsburg Road" throughout the remainder of his book. In reading Cox's statement above, the key phrase is, "that which seems to be in most common local use." What did Cox mean by "local use?" Did he mean within Frederick County, within Election District #3, or what? Webster defines "local" as "serving a particular limited district." What was local? The answer is from the fork in the road at the Catoctin Creek to Sharpsburg. General Cox tells us the Braddock Road was called the Sharpsburg Road in the local area. This agrees with the 1781 Frederick County Court Minutes previously cited.

What did the 1781 court minutes mean by, "from the forks of the roads where the Sharpsburgh Road leads out of Braddock's Road"? Webster defines "lead" as "to guide on a way." He defines "out" as "in a direction away from the inside or center." Where is the center of the road? The center is where the yellow "no passing" lines are. The Sharpsburg Road led out of Braddock Road. The Braddock Road, designated by that name, ended at the fork in the road near the Catoctin creek.

One might ask, "Why didn't *The Fox Genealogy* mention the Braddock Road went through Fox's Gap?"[100] Did the author not want us to know this fact? This question and the one related to the road not being called the Braddock Road beyond the fork in the road may both be addressed by turning to *The Fox Genealogy*. Daniel Gebhart Fox was a lawyer and the author of *The Fox Genealogy*, which he compiled between 1911 and 1914 and published in 1924. He lived and grew up in Miamisburg, Ohio, were he was one-time mayor.[101] He was descended as follows from Frederick Fox: Daniel Booker Fox, Frederick Chrisman Fox, and Daniel Coffman Fox. How did Daniel G. Fox obtain his information about the old Sharpsburg Road he presented in his book? Where did Daniel G. Fox learn about the road that went by the Fox Inn?

The answer is on page 14 of his book:

"Why this house was built at this place seems to be a mystery, but by an examination of the records pertaining to the old roads, by Judge John C. Castle, (who was born and resides a quarter of a mile west of the old tavern, and has given the writer much valuable information) it has been found that this old Sharpsburg Road, (also known as Fox's Road) was a traders' pass as early as the State road was laid out, and traveling was very great through to Sharpsburg and on to the West Virginia mountains."

Therefore, Daniel G. Fox obtained his information about the old Sharpsburg Road from Judge John C. Castle.

The judge, born in 1855, lived a quarter of a mile west of the Fox Inn on the old Sharpsburg Road. John C. Castle was born November 25, 1855.[102] His home was approximately 2.1 miles west of the fork in the road at the Catoctin creek. According to Judge Castle, the road was called the old Sharpsburg Road or Fox's Road. He did not indicate it was called the Braddock Road. The judge lived within the "local" area referred to by General Cox. The statement of Judge Castle, as recorded by Daniel G. Fox in his book, confirms the statement of General Cox and the 1781 Frederick County Court Minutes.

We take another quotation from *The Fox Genealogy*, again concerning the name of the road through Fox's Gap. "From the Union tablets erected by the battlefield commission on the field of Antietam. On the morning of September 15, 1862, Sykes' division of the Fifth Corps, the Reserve Artillery and the Ninth Corps came west by Fox's or the old Sharpsburg Road." The road also was known as Fox's Road. Frederick Fox owned, at one time or another, most of the land from Fox's Gap to the area of the Fox Inn.

People in the local area never called the road through Fox's Gap the Braddock Road. They didn't refer to Fox's Gap as Braddock's Gap. The reason is simple. Many people living along the road were direct members of the Fox family or in-laws. Frederick Fox owned property at the gap to about two miles east of there until 1807. His in-laws, the Bookers, lived in the area that became the site of the present town of Bolivar. There also were Leiters (Lighters), Methards, and Benners in the area. All of these families were related to the Fox family.

The people living in the local area of Fox's Gap never accepted the name of Braddock's Gap or Braddock's Road. These families were all German. Frederick Fox served four years in the Revolutionary War, including the Valley Forge encampment. It is very doubtful Frederick Fox or other people in the area cared much for the British. It was always Fox's Gap and Fox's Road to them.

The people living outside the local area of Fox's Gap now accept the name "Fox's Gap." There is no longer any "local" area that limits the use of the term. The authors who wrote of the Civil War battle there called it Fox's Gap. Because of what happened on September 14, 1862, it will always be Fox's Gap to everyone.

Daniel Harvey Hill Jr., the son of Major General Daniel Harvey Hill, wrote *From Bethel to Sharpsburg* many years after the war. He included the following statement on page 365 of his book:

> Hill's reconnoissance had revealed that the Federal left was advancing on the old Sharpsburg, or Braddock Road, a road parallel to the National Road and passing through Fox's Gap, about a mile south of Boonsboro Gap.

Daniel Harvey Hill Jr. then used the terms "Fox's Gap" and "old Sharpsburg Road" throughout his discussion of the Battle of South Mountain. He also included a footnote that described Boonsboro or Turner's Gap, Fox's or Braddock's Gap, and Hamburg Pass.

From Bethel to Sharpsburg was published in 1926, two years after Daniel Jr.'s death. "His research was exhaustive and meticulous. For his writing he collected between five and six thousand volumes relating to the Civil War, an exceptionally fine working library on the subject, which was later turned over to the North Carolina Historical Commission."[103]

Three generals who participated in the Battle of South Mountain refer to Fox's Gap as Braddock's Gap and to the old Sharpsburg Road as Braddock's Road. General Jacob D. Cox, commanding the Kanawha Division of the Ninth Corps, wrote his *Military Reminiscences* long after the battle (1897-1900). Two generals writing much closer in time to the Battle of South Mountain were Major General James E. B. Stuart and Brigadier General Roswell S. Ripley. Stuart commanded the cavalry in the Army of Northern Virginia. Ripley commanded a regiment at Fox's Gap. It is obvious Stuart and Ripley referred to Fox's Gap when they used the term "Braddock's Gap," and that by the term "Braddock Road" they meant the old Sharpsburg Road.

Stuart identifies all three gaps in the Battle of South Mountain in his report:

> On reaching the vicinity of the gap near Boonsborough, finding General Hill's troops occupying the gap, I turned off General Hampton, with all his cavalry except the Jeff. Davis Legion, to re-enforce Munford, at Crampton's Gap, which was now the weakest point of the line. I remained myself at the gap near Boonsborough until night, but the enemy did not attack the position. This was obviously no place for cavalry operations, a single horseman passing from point to point on the mountain with difficulty. Leaving the Jeff. Davis Legion here, therefore, and directing Colonel Rosser, with a detachment of cavalry and the Stuart Horse Artillery, to occupy Braddock's Gap, I started on my way to join the main portion of my command at Crampton's Gap, stopping for the night near Boonsborough. I had not, up to this time, seen General D. H. Hill, but about midnight he sent General Ripley to me to get information concerning roads and gaps in a locality where General Hill had been lying for two days with his command. All the information I had was cheerfully given, and the situation of the gaps explained by map.[104]

Rosser and his cavalry unit fought dismounted in the battle at Fox's Gap. Stuart tells us he was the one who directed Rosser's unit there. We also learn from Stuart that he had a map of the area. His information was from, or confirmed by, a map in his possession. It is clear from his report and corroborating information that Stuart referred to Fox's Gap as Braddock's Gap. Why Stuart waited till February 13, 1864, to file his report we do not know.

The report of General Ripley bears a date of September 21, 1862, one week after the Battle of South Mountain. Here is what Ripley reported, in part:

At about 9 o'clock I received orders to send forward my artillery, and, soon after, to move with the whole force to the main pass east of Boonsborough. Upon arriving, I was directed to follow the road leading to Braddock's Gap, and place myself in communication with Brigadier-General Anderson, who had preceded me in that direction. Upon coming up and communicating with that officer, it was arranged that he should extend along the Braddock Road and make room for the troops of my command, and that an attack should be made upon the enemy, then occupying the heights to the south.[105]

Ripley refers to the Braddock Road a number of times in his report. General Ripley's troops fought at Fox's Gap. The *History of the First North Carolina Regiment* also mentions the Braddock Road.[106] The First North Carolina Regiment was part of General Ripley's Brigade.

Ripley's use of the term "Braddock Road" obviously was a reference to the old Sharpsburg Road. It is likely Ripley received his information about the roads and gaps in the area of South Mountain solely from General Stuart. We do not know what other sources of information were available to Ripley or Stuart. At a minimum, we know Stuart had a map of the area in his possession. Stonewall Jackson and his chief cartographer, Jedediah Hotchkiss, passed through "Braddock's Gap" on Wednesday, September 10, 1862, on their way from Middletown to Sharpsburg.[107] Without question, both Stuart and Ripley identified Fox's Gap as Braddock's Gap. They, as well as the mapmaker, were not from the local area. It is for this reason they did not use the term Fox's Gap at the time of the battle.

Mention also should be made that General Braddock traveled from Frederick Town to Winchester in a coach he purchased from Governor Sharpe. The use of the coach supports the idea that the road from Frederick Town to Swearingen's Ferry must have been more than a path or narrow trail in 1755.

A letter from General Braddock to Governor Sharpe included the following:

> . . . as I find impracticable to take my Chariot with me if you will send for it & the Harness for the six

Horses I shall be much oblig'd to you & you will make
use of it till I want it. I shall be still more so as I am sure
it will be less damag'd by good usage than by lying still.
It will also save you the trouble of sending for another to
England as it shall be at your service at your own price
when I leave this part of the World. Let your servants
take care of the harness & have it oiled if you don't use
it. I shall leave directions to Col. Innes to deliver
Chariot Harness spare axle trees & pole to your
order.[108]

Also, in a letter written July 28, 1755, to Captain Orme, Governor
Dinwiddie mentions the "Gen'l's Chariot." "I presume the
Gen'l's Chariot is at the Fort; in it You may come here, and my
House is heartily at Y'r Com'd."[109]

A final question remains. Does the same route of the road
taken by Braddock and Washington in 1755 exist today? We can
read from the 1792 map of the road that the road commissioners
made minor modifications in "the old road" in 1792. They made
no modifications coming down the mountain from Fox's Gap, at
the Orndorff Bridge, or through the town of Sharpsburg. They
made only fairly minor modifications in other places, except
near the Potomac. There is no reason to believe the route changed
much before 1792. The 1792 road appears to be similar to the
route of the road indicated by land records prior to 1792 (see
Appendix A - Maps).

In his book, General Cox gives the route of the old
Sharpsburg Road from Fox's Gap to Sharpsburg. "The Ninth
Corps was ordered to follow the old Sharpsburg Road through
Fox's Gap, our line of march being thus parallel to the others till
we should reach the road from Boonsboro to Sharpsburg . . . Our
road led through a little hamlet called Springvale, and thence
to another, Porterstown, near the left bank of the Antietam,
where it runs into the Boonsboro and Sharpsburg turnpike." This
description agrees with the Antietam and South Mountain
battlefield maps prepared by the U. S. Government and included
in the *Atlas* that accompanies the *Official Records*. Springvale
was just beyond the home of G. Shiffler.

The route of the road from Swearingen's Ferry to Fox's Gap in 1792 appears to be the same as the route of the old Sharpsburg Road as shown on the battlefield maps of 1862. The battlefield maps of 1862 appear quite similar to 1995 maps of Washington County. In Frederick County, the fork in the roads is near the Catoctin Creek. Today, the Fox Inn stands along Marker Road. Fox's Gap itself is on the county line. The route of the old Sharpsburg Road in Frederick County apparently changed little over the years.

The preceeding analysis leads this author to conclude the route of the old Sharpsburg Road through Fox's Gap changed very little, if at all, along most of the route, from the early 1700s to the present. There is no indication the following points, which are along the road today, were not along the route in 1755. These points are: the site of Swearingen's Ferry on the Potomac, the main street through Sharpsburg, the Orndorff (or Middle) Bridge over the Antietam, the Moses Chapline family cemetery, Fox's Gap, the Fox Inn, and the fork in the road near the Catoctin Creek. In order to retrace the old road from Middletown to Sharpsburg, one would take Marker Road off the old National Pike, just after crossing the Catoctin Creek north of Middletown. The route follows Reno Monument Road, Dog Street Road, and Geeting Street into Sharpsburg.

A pitcher said to have been used by George Washington at the Fox Inn remains with descendants of Daniel Booker Fox. Daniel Booker, son of Frederick, was born June 6, 1783. Robert H. Fox of Cincinnati, Ohio, is a descendant of Daniel Booker Fox. He visited with Daniel G. Fox, author of *The Fox Genealogy*, in the 1930s. He received one of Frederick Fox's long rifles as a gift at that time. Robert and his grandfather, Scott Fox, visited Will Hendrickson of south Dayton, Ohio, in the 1930s and was shown the pitcher. Robert took a photo of the glass pitcher at that time.

Perhaps Frederick Fox owned a tavern or inn that has long since been torn down. It is obvious George Washington did not visit the present Fox Inn during the period George Fox owned the building because Washington died in 1799. An article written in 1932 by Robert H. Fox discusses the possible visit by Washington. Robert indicates the Washington visit took place in 1788 when George took the road out of Frederick, Maryland, to visit his brother Charles at Charlestown, Virginia.[110] Perhaps the visit ocurred Aug. 6, 1785, when Washington was at Shepherdstown to witness the first successful steam-power boat, built by James Rumsey.

The State Roads Commission erected an historical marker on the main street in Sharpsburg to mark the Braddock route (see Appendix B - Photos). The location was correct, but the date was May 2, 1755, instead of April 1755 indicated by the Commission. The same State Roads Commission published "A History of Road Building in Maryland" in 1958. They placed Braddock in his chariot leading Dunbar's Regiment to present-day Williamsport.

The Frederick Chapter of the Daughters of the American Revolution erected a monument at Braddock Spring to commemorate the visit there of General Braddock and George Washington. A huge boulder and plaque was dedicated on Flag Day, June 14, 1924, only a few steps from the spring along the old National Highway.

The cabin in which George Washington stayed in Frederick on May 1, 1755, stood on All Saints Street until torn down about 1913. On April 30, 1955, a plaque was unveiled on the bridge over Carroll Creek on South Court Street in Frederick to call attention to the site where Washington stayed. The plaque includes the following information:

> 50 yards west of this point, near Carroll Creek, stood the Log Cabin Quarters used by Col. George Washington when he joined the Staff of Maj. Gen. Edward Braddock in this town April 30, 1755. Marked by the Historical Society of Frederick County, Inc., April 30, 1955.

A photograph of the boulder at Braddock Spring and a 1906 picture of the Frederick cabin in which Washington stayed in 1755 appear in *The News*, Frederick, Maryland, Saturday, May 12, 1973.

The Society of Colonial Wars and the Maryland Historical Society placed a marker about General Braddock near the front of the Maryland State Police Barrack B in Frederick on Route 40 (Patrick Street). The James Rumsey Bridge crosses the

Potomac near the former site of Swearingen's Ferry. An historical marker, placed by the Maryland Bicentennial Commission and the Maryland Historical Society, identifies the site of Swearingen's Ferry (see Appendix B - Photos).

Fox's and Turner's Gaps today are on the Appalachian Trail. The Potomac Appalachian Trail Club, with headquarters in Vienna, Virginia, is active in maintaining the trail. The Central Maryland Heritage League, Inc., Middletown, Maryland, plays an active role in preserving the Battlefield of South Mountain.

Conclusions about The Braddock and Washington Route

General Braddock, accompanied by George Washington and Gov. Horatio Sharpe, traveled by the main road from Frederick Town, Maryland, to Swearingen's Ferry at Shepherdstown, Virginia, on May 2, 1755. The route passed through Fox's Gap and was known for a number of years thereafter as the main road from Frederick Town to Swearingen's Ferry. There was no other direct route in 1755 by which General Braddock could travel by horse-drawn coach from Frederick Town to Swearingen's Ferry.

Accounts that indicate General Braddock accompanied Dunbar's Regiment to Conococheague, or traveled to Conococheague at any time, are not correct. John Fox arrived at Fox's Gap a number of years before the earliest records, those around 1763, indicate he lived there. Bartholomew Booker lived within the vicinity of Fox's Gap at the time of the Braddock Expedition.

Land tract records confirm the route of the old Sharpsburg Road through Fox's Gap remains substantially the same between the time of General Braddock's passage and today. George Washington probably visited a tavern or inn kept by Frederick Fox along the old Sharpsburg Road in the 1780s. Fox's Gap represents a page of American history worthy of preservation.

1995 Distances along the old Sharpsburg Road from Middletown to the Rumsey Bridge at Shepherdstown

the bridge at Catoctin Creek to the Fox Inn, about 1.8 miles
the Fox Inn to Reno Monument Road, about .8 miles
Reno Monument Road to Fox Gap Road, about .3 miles
Fox Gap Road to the Reno Monument, about .8 miles
the Reno Monument to the Moses Chapline Sr. cemetery, about 2
      miles
the Reno Monument to Moser Road, about .6 miles
Moser Road to Route 67, about 1.6 miles
Route 67 to Dog Street Road, about .3 miles
Dog Street Road to the Antietam (Middle) Bridge, about 3.4
      miles

Daniel Booker Fox, circa 1860. (retouched)
Photo courtesy of Robert H. Fox of Cincinnati, Ohio.

The Fox Inn. Photo by Susanne Flowers.

The Reno Monument. Photo by Susanne Flowers.

Braddock sign in Sharpsburg. Photo by Susanne Flowers.

Swearingen's Ferry Marker. Photo by Susanne Flowers.

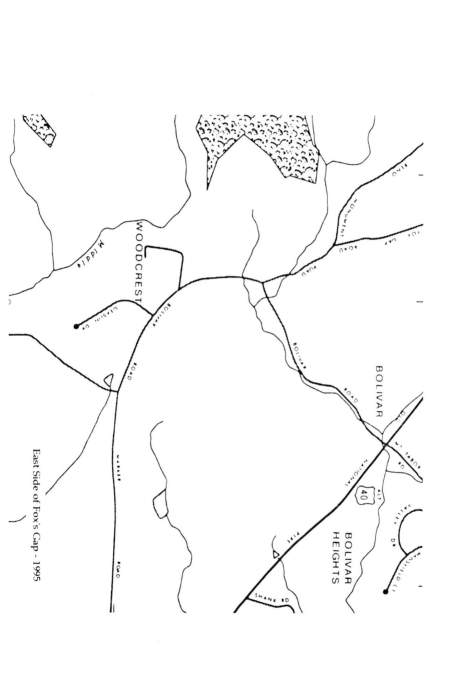

East Side of Fox's Gap - 1995

Chapter Four

The Dunbar Route From Frederick Town to Conococheague

A remaining question to be addressed is, "By what route did Dunbar's Regiment march to Conococheague from Frederick Town?" Various authors disagree on the route taken by Dunbar's Regiment. Since their destinations differed, Braddock's route and Dunbar's route must differ, either in whole or in part. Perhaps both routes began on the same road as they left Frederick Town towards the northwest. The Dunbar route might coincide with the Braddock route until beyond Middletown. At some point it veered off and headed north to Conococheague.

Two sources of material on the Dunbar route are books and maps. One also must consider documents such as land records and court minutes from the period surrounding 1755. Let us evaluate a number of specific areas related to the Dunbar route. These include Orr's, Turner's, and Crampton's Gaps, the creation of the road through Turner's Gap, the 1781 Frederick County Court Minutes, and the overnight stopping place of Dunbar's Regiment. The standard by which to judge all of these materials is their agreement with the writings of the participants to the events.

Writings about the Dunbar Route

Let us begin with the *History of Frederick County* by T. J. C. Williams:

> The first day's march was nearly over the line of the present turnpike road to South Mountain; the army camped at night near the foot of the mountain not far

from the present site of the village of Middletown. The next day the army crossed the mountain through Turner's Gap since rendered famous as the scene of the battle of South Mountain. The next morning the march was resumed and the route taken was over the "Devil's Back Bone" at Delemere Mill, and along the present Williamsport and Boonsboro Road.[1]

Williams's book includes a copy of "General Braddock's Orderly Book." Williams's version of the Dunbar route is from an unknown source. It does not come from General Braddock's Orderly Book.

Let us examine the propriety of Williams's statement as to when Dunbar's Regiment crossed the South Mountain. The date of crossing is critical to determine where Dunbar's troops stopped the first night out of Frederick Town. The location of the stopping place should indicate the route to Conococheague.

Williams's version does not agree with a participant in the march. The Morris (or Seaman's) Journal gives the following:

> On the 29th: - We began our march at 6, but found much difficulty in loading our baggage, so that we left several things behind us, particularly the men's hammocks. We arrived at 3 o'clock at one Walker's, 18 miles from Frederick, and encamped there on good ground; this day we passed the South Ridge or Shannandah Mountains, very easy in the ascent. We saw pleanty of Hares, Deer, and Partridges: This place is wanting of all refreshments (MR, 370).

Clearly, Dunbar's Regiment crossed the South Mountain the first day out of Frederick Town.

Helen Ashe Hays, in *The Antietam and Its Bridges*, includes a number of paragraphs related to the Braddock Expedition:

> But Braddock himself went to meet Franklin at Frederick and from that point a regiment under Colonel Dunbar passed over the South Mountain by Turner's Gap,

and crossed the Antietam twice, at Keedysville and at Delemere, on their way to the Potomac at Williamsport. At the Hitt bridge near Keedysville a road is pointed out, coming down to the water by a steep declivity, now almost abandoned in favor of one that approaches it by a more gentle slope. This abrupt and difficult track is Braddock's Road, and characteristic of his methods.

When he heard that the Antietam had to be crossed, he sent a detachment on with orders to seize all the boats and canoes on the river for the use of his army, taking it for granted that it was both wide and deep. When the troops reached it, they found good fords at both places.[2]

The statement to which Hays refers is the entry for Wednesday, April 23, in the Orderly Book of General Braddock:

You are to go immediately to that part of the Antietam that lies on the road to Connogogee and press such boats or canoes as you shall meet with upon the river agreeable to the orders you shall receive from Governor Sharpe. If you shall find any difficulty in the execution of his order you are to send an express to me and you shall be immediately supplied with a party of men to enforce it, sending word when they shall join you, and you are to collect all the boats, &c. at that pass by the 28th of this month.

The last part of the sentence from General Braddock's Orderly Book infers the General did not go to the Antietam, but expected a messenger be sent to him if there was a problem obtaining boats and canoes. Braddock indicates "at that pass" as if it were a single location.

T. C. Williams, who also comments on this order of General Braddock, feels it showed Braddock's lack of knowledge of the area since, "The Antietam is but a shallow stream at this place, a few yards wide and there was not a boat anywhere upon it."[3] Hays and T. C. Williams assume the boats or canoes would be used to cross Antietam Creek. The fact Braddock's troops built a bridge over the Antietam refutes their assumption.

There is a distinct possibility the boats and canoes on the Antietam, if found, went to Conococheague for use on the Potomac. We do not know the source of Williams's information that Braddock's men found no boats on the Antietam. No record of any orders given by Governor Sharpe at the Antietam exist. In his letter of May 9 to Governor Dinwiddie, Sharpe indicated supplies went up the Potomac from Conococheague to Wills's Creek. From where did the canoes used on the Potomac come?

The Bridge Over the Antietam

Hays makes no mention of perhaps the first bridge on the Antietam, the one built by Braddock's men. Amazingly, Hays includes in her book a poem entitled "Sir John St. Clair." The poem includes the following segment:

His were the bridges over the Opequan
And the Antietam in the morn of time,
Crossed by a multitude no man can reckon
To sceneries and destinies sublime.

Hays simply passes over the fact Braddock's troops built a bridge over the Antietam.

The refutation of her claim Dunbar's Regiment forded the Antietam, indeed twice by her account, is in the Orme Journal:

The General ordered a bridge to be built over the Antietum, which being furnished, and provision laid in on the road, Colonel Dunbar marched with his regiment from Frederick on the 28th of April, and about this time the bridge over the Opeccon was finished for the passage of the Artillery, and floats were built on all the rivers and creeks.[4]

Hays cites no references in her book.

A bridge probably was necessary or convenient for wagons. The bridge on the Antietam was for the use of Dunbar's Regiment and the transportation of supplies to Conococheague. It was not used by General Braddock on his way to Winchester. The Orme Journal implies Dunbar crossed the Antietam once and that they built only one bridge over the Antietam. In passing, we note the bridge over the Opequon in Virginia was for the use of Halkett's Regiment. "If the bridge should not be laid over the Opeckon canoes will be provided for the Troops."[5]

Governor Sharpe, in a letter to St. Clair, mentions the bridge built over the Antietam by Braddock's men. "I suppose it might be supported on triangular piers made with logs & filled with stones as is that which was made over Antieatum when General Braddock marched that way . . ."[6] Governor Sharpe met some of Braddock's troops at the Antietam. It seems most likely he met them at the bridge built over the Antietam. Did he go all the way up to the Hagerstown area from Frederick Town to meet these troops or did he meet them near Keedysville? Governor Sharpe undoubtedly was at this bridge on at least one occasion, probably more.

Rice includes the following from the court minutes of Frederick County for June, 1759:

> Unnamed inhabitants of the Andeatum area state to the Court that "ever since the march of General Braddock" there has been a bridge over Andeatum built by the inhabitants at the request of Governor Sharpe. The bridge, although slightly built, has been found of great convenience to the inhabitants and travelers. They request the Court to build a better bridge, and the Court grants the request.[7]

The most fascinating item presented by Hays appears on pages 66 and 67 of her book:

> Moses Chapline, whose log house with loopholes in the walls, built for defence, was a place of refuge for his neighbors, lived farther up the Antietam, on his tracts of "Bounded White Oak" and "Josiah's Bit." He had not the dominating personality of his brother, but was greatly respected, and made warm friends among gentle and simple. Both brothers entertained distinguished company on their estates.

Generals Washington, Braddock, and Gates visited them; and the Governor of Maryland, General Horatio Sharpe, was a great friend of Joseph Chapline, who named the town in his honor.

Hays's claim that General Braddock visited the homes of Moses and Joseph Chapline is a significant revelation if true. Unfortunately, she provides nothing to support her statement. However, that is not to say her statement is not true.

In summation, Hays presents some statements contradicted by the writings of participants to the events. She places Dunbar's Regiment crossing the Antietam at, or near, the Hitt (or Upper) Bridge at Keedysville and again at Delemere, where Beaver Creek meets the Antietam. Presumably her route for Dunbar led through Smoketown and Bakersville. The most difficult aspect to understand is why the troops went through Turner's Gap to reach the Keedysville area when the road through Fox's Gap was more reasonable. Hays provides material that may be correct, but without supporting evidence.

The most significant book on the routes of Halkett's and Dunbar's Regiments through Virginia is *Braddock's Road Through the Virginia Colony* by Walter S. Hough. The meticulous work of Dr. Hough indicates Dunbar's unit did not cross the Opequon after it entered Virginia from Conococheague.[8] Several statements in his book merit attention because they relate to the Maryland portion of the Braddock Expedition.

Many writers who have dealt with the Braddock Expedition come to the same conclusion as Hough concerning the use of the Potomac River. "The so-called Maryland route might have been chosen for political reasons, but somewhere along the way it was learned that a road through Maryland from Conococheague Creek to Wills Creek did not exist and that supplies already stored at the mouth of Conococheague Creek could not be transported by boat up the Potomac."[9] Both Governor Sharpe and the Morris Journal contradict this statement by Hough. Governor Sharpe indicates in his letter of May 9 to Governor Dinwiddie the use of the Potomac to transport some items to Wills's Creek. The Morris Journal mentions artillery stores going by water to Wills's Creek on April 30.

Hough indicates General Braddock did not travel with Dunbar's Regiment when it left Frederick Town, Maryland. The only indication Hough gives about the route of General Braddock is the following: "Apparently he was with the 48th Regiment between Alexandria and Frederick, then other business in connection with the Expedition necessitated his presence at various places including Winchester." While Hough goes to unbelievable lengths to trace the Braddock Road in Virginia, he appears to be unaware General Braddock traveled to Winchester by way of Swearingen's Ferry. The route from Swearingen's Ferry to Winchester does not appear in his book.

Hough appears confused as to why there are no entries in the Orderly Book of General Braddock from April 30 to May 9. "This Orderly Book now in the Library of Congress does not have a complete record of the Expedition, nor is there a daily entry of orders on the march of the 48th Regiment from April 29 through May 9."[10] He seems unaware General Braddock was not with any troops to whom he could give orders during this period. There are no missing orders for this period of time as Hough indicates.

Another author, Albert H. Heusser, seems to possess some knowledge of the Dunbar route:

> Back and forth over this old road Braddock and Washington marched with their soldiers. The fine spring a few miles out of town, which furnished water to the Indians, and later to Braddock's men, is known as Braddock's Spring, and is in existence to-day. Four miles west of the city is a range of hills of the Catoctin Mountains called Braddock's Heights, commanding beautiful views of the Frederick and Middletown valleys, while the Antietam battlefield is only a few miles distant and easily reached by carriage.[11]

This passage identifies the Antietam Battlefield as on the route of General Braddock, Dunbar's Regiment, or both. Huesser could mean either the old Sharpsburg Road taken by Braddock or the route to Williamsport through Fox's Gap, Keedysville, Smoketown, and Bakersville.

Heusser's book includes a picture of the house where Washington stayed in Frederick Town before leaving with the General for Winchester. The only problem found with Heusser is the propriety of the statement about the marching of the men back and forth along the road by Braddock and Washington. Washington was not in Frederick Town for more than one night. Also, George Washington held no rank, and therefore had no command authority during the Braddock Expedition. He was an aide-de-camp and found that arrangement suitable because General Braddock did not have authority to give him the rank he felt he should hold.

The State Roads Commission of Maryland, in *A History of Road Building in Maryland* published in 1959, makes the error of placing General Braddock on the road to Conococheague: "Dunbar's regiment, which was led by the general himself riding in a new chariot, took the road to Frederick, present-day Williamsport, Oldtown and Cumberland as here described." Elsewhere they state, "The army followed the wagon road from Frederick to Watkins Ferry (the general route of present-day Alternate US. 40 through Braddock Heights and Boonsboro and on to Williamsport by State Route 68." The State Roads Commission's route for Dunbar's Regiment passes through Turner's Gap.

Drums Along the Antietam by John W. Schildt includes the following passage: "The next morning, April 30, the rolling Antietam heard the beat of the British regimental drums as the troops formed to march at six o'clock. They forded the Antietam Creek near the Hitt Bridge or the Upper Bridge of Civil War fame. These soldiers were over one hundred years in advance of other who would wear not red coats, but blue tunics."[12]

General Bradley T. Johnson gives the following version:

On April 30th Braddock left Frederick in the chariot he had purchased from Governor Sharpe and escorted by his bodyguard, a troop of Virginia Light Horse--the only cavalry in his command--passed over the mountain north of Frederick, across Middletown Valley, through a gap in South Mountain, which still bears his name (over what, in subsequent years, became the battlefield of Antietam), to the mouth of the Conococheague, where he crossed the Potomac. The town of Williamsport is now at the ford where he crossed, and Williamsport long afterward became one of the principal competitors for the site of the federal city. In the order of the day of April 27th the route is published, providing for the march to Wills Creek, a total of one hundred and twenty-nine miles to be made by May 9th.[13]

A portion of an article by Arthur Tracey, in the Historical Society of Carroll County, follows:

> One of the branches of the Old Monocacy Road led to the foot of the Blue Ridge just east of the present Braddock Heights where the road forked; a branch leading in a north-westerly direction, crossing South Mountain at a place known as Braddock's Gap; being the place where General Braddock crossed with his army in the year 1755; thence to Stull's Mill. This Stull's Mill was an outstanding junction of paths as well as an important land mark, established in about the year 1733 by John Stull.[14]

Tracey places Braddock and Dunbar's Regiment on the old Hagerstown Road through Orr's Gap.

Another interesting statement about the Braddock Expedition is the following from a book about Christian Orndorff and his descendants:

> During the Revolution "Old Pack Horse Ford," one mile below Shepherdstown, was the only crossing E. or W. of Shepherdstown. The river was forded one mile S. of Shepherdstown or three miles from Sharpsburg. On April 30, 1755, British soldiers under Braddock, on the way from Frederick Town, Md., to Va., crossed the Potomac at the Old Pack Horse Ford. By way of this ford came the Germans from Pa. who found a gateway to the fertile land south of the Potomac. During the Civil War the ford was known as Blackford's Ford.[15]

These authors place Dunbar's Regiment, or at least some of his troops, on the Braddock and Washington's route. This indeed is a switch!

A book released in 1990, *The Old South Mountain Inn* by Byron Williams, contends Dunbar's Regiment, Braddock, and perhaps Washington, crossed South Mountain at Turner's Gap. This book bases the history of Turner's Gap and the Mountain House on the 1781 Frederick County Court Minutes:

> An entry in the 1781 Frederick County court minutes is of interest; it describes a road "from the forks of the roads where the Sharpsburgh Road leads out of Braddock's Road to the top of South Mountain, being the direct road from Frederick passing Robert Turner's old place to Fort Frederick".[16]

From this one document Williams marches Dunbar's Regiment by Robert Turner's old place, which he contends is today the Old South Mountain Inn at Turner's Gap:

> On April 29, 1755, Braddock's army marched out of Frederick with its drums rattling, fifes crying and flags waving everywhere. Turner's Gap had seen nothing like it. After the army passed, maybe it was the next morning, General Braddock followed in the coach that Governor Sharpe had loaned him. Maybe George Washington rode among the officers that escorted the General.[17]

The Historical Societies of Washington and Frederick Counties have sparse information on the Braddock Road. Two articles are of note. E. R. Goldsborough wrote an article dated December 4, 1936, entitled, "Route of General Braddock's Army." The other article lists neither the name of its author nor a date. However, from the contents of the article, the author probably lived in the mid to late 1800s.

The Goldsborough article includes the following statement:

The route lead from the camp at the south-western part of the town (where the Washington Street School now stands) to and across the present Harper's Ferry Road (US. 340), then due west by what is now locally called "Butter Fly" Lane to the Gap at Braddock Heights, down the western slope of Catoctin Mountain in the rear of the residences of Mrs. Charles Brane and Dr. Noah Kefauver, entering what is now Middletown about where the residence of the late Herman Routzahn now stands. From here it followed practically the same route as the old National Road (US. 40) through Turners Gap to where "one Walker's" tavern stood, about one mile east of the present Boonsboro; here the road turned left passing through the present Keedysville, across the Devil's back-bone (where Beaver Creek enters the Antietam) to Lappans Cross-roads and then to Conococheague (Williamsport).

Portions of the article by the anonymous author follow:

Keeping to the left of the pike (or what is now the pike) crossing the Catoctin about three hundred yards south of the bridge that now spans that stream, taking the bed of what is now the Sharpsburg Road, traveling West two miles and then leaving what is now the bed of the Sharpsburg Road, he turned north for about a half-mile. Here it is supposed he bivouacked for the night. He then marched West, keeping to the left of what is now the pike, and crossed the mountain at what is now known as the "Mountain House" or Dalgren's Home.

About a mile from the Catoctin stream, on the Sharpsburg Road, West, stood a large white oak tree that was marked by the pioneer's of Braddock's Army. This was a very large tree, and for some reason was left standing when the early settlers cleared the land. This tree was cut down about eighteen hundred and sixty-six and sawed into lumber for a house. A little farther on was another large White Oak which was marked . . . About a mile from this tree, in a dense forest, lived at that time, an old German, by the name of Casper Young, whose team was pressed into service to haul supplies for General Braddock's army. I do not know just how far they took this man, but when he finally returned home, there was a gun left in his wagon. This gun was in the possession of the Youngs until about ten years ago. I have tried hard to locate it, but up to this time have failed. Mr. Young's grand-son related this to me while standing near the tree when the one tree was being cut down, saying that it had been told him over and over again by his grand-father.

There is something a little singular as to why Braddock left the Indian trail that passes through Fox's Gap, which would have been several miles nearer. The Sharpsburg Road starts on that trail near where Braddock crossed the Antietam and runs thence East through Fox's Gap until it strikes the bed where Braddock left the Sharpsburg Road. This, at that time, was called the Great Road, and I find, in looking over the land records of Washington County, the Call is to the Great Road - the Sharpsburg and Frederick Town Road.

In summary, the writings reviewed represent most of the material available on the routes of Dunbar's Regiment and General Braddock when they left Frederick Town in Maryland. Most of the authors place General Braddock on the same route as Dunbar's Regiment. None of the writers specifically state General Braddock went to Swearingen's Ferry from Frederick Town.

Maps

One might hope maps would resolve the question of the Dunbar Route. What maps are available to assist us? The 1751 and 1775 *Jefferson and Fry Map of Virginia*, as well as related versions of these maps, identify roads from Winchester to Williamsport and Shepherdstown (see Appendix A - Maps).

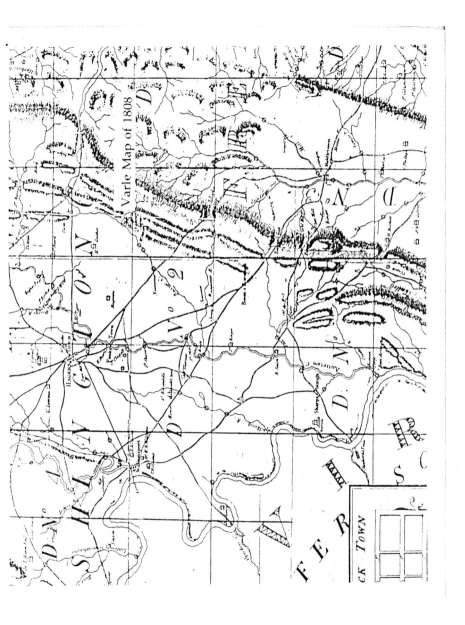

Varle Map of 1808

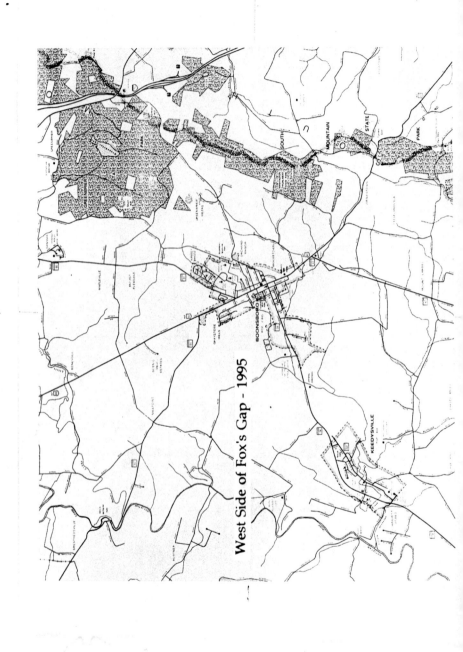

West Side of Fox's Gap - 1995

Both of these roads led to Philadelphia and are identified as such on the maps.

A map, dated April 5, 1791, of the *Road from Elizabethtown to Newcomber's Mill and Frederick County Line* is in the Maryland Archives.[18] This map identifies Orr's Gap as Braddock's Gap. Conrad Hogmire, Daniel Winder, and an unknown individual signed this map. It shows John Orr's house about one mile northwest of the gap in South Mountain. *Stull's* appears near a bridge, about one mile from the Market House in Elizabethtown [Hagerstown]. The map includes the courses of the route similar to a land tract record. However, these measurements are difficult to read.

Another map, recorded October 17, 1791, is the *Road Leading from Williamsport to Turner's Gap in the South Mountain,* also in the Maryland Archives.[19] The route shown on this map appears quite similar to present route 68 between Boonsboro and Williamsport. Points identified on the map include Booth's Bridge on Antietam Creek, the point where the road crosses Beaver Creek, John Ringer's land, Boon's land, Booke's Tavern, Aulabaugh's land, and Summers's land.

The map gives six courses of 300 perches, 4950 feet, "up through the gap . . . to where it is supposed to intersect the Frederick County line on the top of the mountain." Minor changes in the course of this road were made in 1791 by the road commissioners.

The 1794 *Dennis Griffith Map of Maryland* shows a road from Boonsboro towards South Mountain and the area of Turner's Gap. The map shows a location entitled *Orrs* just northwest of the gap in the mountain. It seems probable a traveler from Frederick Town to Conococheague passing through Orr's Gap would pass through the area that became Hagerstown. The Griffith map shows a route from Margaretsville [Boonsboro] to South Mountain where it abruptly ends. The road appears to end near the west side of Turner's Gap. Griffith did not assign names to any of the South Mountain gaps.

Daniel Harvey Hill Jr. indicates a gap called Hamburg Pass was on the old Hagerstown Road. "North of the main turnpike about two miles was another gap known as Hamburg Pass. The road to this pass branches off from the National Road at Bolivar, sweeps north by Mount Tabor Church. It is generally known as the old Hagerstown Road."[20]

Charles Varle, engineer, offered to publish by subscription a map of Washington County together with a plan of Hagerstown in the July 22, 1807, *Maryland Herald and Hagerstown Weekly*.[21] The Varle Map of 1808 shows Braddock's Gap on the old Hagerstown Road from Frederick Town. This gap also was known as Orr's Gap. Varle shows Fox's Gap and Turner's Gap on his map as well. The Varle Map identifies the Fox Inn, labeled as "Ringer." George Fox sold the Fox Inn to John Ringer in 1807. The map makes no note of an inn or other landmark at Turner's Gap.

The 1808 Varle Map shows the road from Boonsboro through Turner's Gap meeting the road through Fox's Gap a little east of the Fox Inn. These routes appear to meet in the same area on an 1840 map in the Tracey Collection. Only on the Civil War Battlefield Map of South Mountain and later maps do the old National Pike and the old Sharpsburg Road meet at the bridge over the Catoctin Creek just north of Middletown.

A map by Dr. Tracey, showing the *Old Monocacy Roads in Frederick County*, is in the Tracey Collection at the Historical Society of Carroll County. Dr. Tracey labels the gap on the old Hagerstown Road from Frederick Town [by way of Stull's Mill] as Braddock's Gap. He does not show a route through Turner's Gap on his map. Dr. Tracey shows one route passing through Fox's Gap, the road to Conococheague. He does not show a road through Fox's Gap to the Winchester or Sharpsburg areas.

The 1792 map in the Maryland Archives entitled *Road from Swearingen's Ferry on the Potomac River through Sharpsburg to Fox's Gap in South Mountain* also is significant. A discussion of this map appears in Chapter Three of this book.

There also is a 1757 map by Thomas Kitchin, *A Map of Maryland with the Delaware Counties*.[22] The Maryland Archives also has a map that is an attempt by the maker to portray the *Monocacy* roads in Maryland.[23] The source of this map is anonymous. The map shows the Braddock Road from Frederick Town through Turner's Gap to Conococheague and on to Winchester. The map shows the Fox Inn on the road through Turner's Gap.

Other Relevant Material

A question that at first seems to have an obvious answer may be much more complex. Why would a gap in the mountain or a road be named for General Braddock? At first thought, the obvious answer is that General Braddock traveled by that route. The answer may not be that simple. There are many possibilities. We can attempt to construct a list of reasons. The following seem plausible.

1. General Braddock traveled the route.

2. Dunbar's or Halkett's forces traveled the route.

3. Some of Braddock's men, in search of recruits, wagons, horses, or provisions, traveled the route.

4. It was a route of escape for settlers fleeing the Indians after Braddock's defeat.

5. The route was used during the French and Indian War.

6. A route or gap was named in General Braddock's honor although he or his forces never traveled the route.

7. The route was created as a war measure as a result of Braddock's defeat.

8. A combination of the above.

9. A source, indicating a road or gap named for General Braddock, is erroneous.

The following letter, written in 1756, at the height of the French and Indian War, exemplifies possibility number four:

> The whole settlement of Conococheague (the name given at that time to all the country between the mountains) in Maryland is fled, and there remains but only two families from thence to Frederick Town. That the Maryland settlements are all abandoned is certainly a fact, as I had the accounts transmitted to me by several hands and confirmed yesterday, the 28th, by Henry Brinker, who left Monocacy the day before, and who also affirms that 350 wagons passed that place to avoid the enemy within the space of three days.[24]

The preceding list of possibilities, if accepted, implies we cannot assume General Braddock traveled by way of a certain road or gap just because it bears his name. Likewise, we will never know if our list is complete.

An interesting account appears in "Mrs. Browne's Diary in Virginia and Maryland," edited by Fairfax Harrison. There were two roads in 1755 from Alexandria to Winchester. Halkett's Regiment and Mrs. Browne's driver took the same road from Alexandria to Winchester. The locations along the route noted both by Halkett and by Mrs. Browne prove which of the two roads they took.

Harrison makes the following observations while discussing the two routes from Alexandria through Virginia to the Valley [Winchester] in 1755.[25] Route A - "This was the route by which Sir Peter Halkett had marched his regiment a few weeks ahead of Mrs. Browne." This route was by way of Vestal's Gap. Route B - "This was the 'better road' which Mrs. Browne's driver wanted to take. It had been opened up as a through route only in 1754, but it was expected that Braddock would himself follow it to Winchester . . . On the principle of *lucus a non lucendo* it has been known in the Fairfax County tradition, even since 1755, as the 'Braddock Road'." The route known as the Braddock Road was by way of William's Gap.

Both Halkett's Regiment and Mrs. Browne's driver took the road NOT known as the "Braddock Road" between Alexandria and Winchester! The closest General Braddock got to these two Virginia routes was the city of Alexandria, since he went from Alexandria through Maryland to Winchester. It is clear General Braddock or Halkett's Regiment never used the road known as the Braddock Road in that part of Virginia. *Webster's Third New International Dictionary* defines *lucus a non lucendo* as, "an illogical explanation or absurd derivation: NON SEQUITUR."

The Routes from Frederick Town to Conococheague in 1755

Our task at this point is to break down the problem of the Dunbar route into specific issues we can study and resolve. Four primary routes have supporters among area residents and history buffs as the route of Dunbar's Regiment in April 1755. These routes are the roads through Crampton's, Fox's, Orr's, and Turner's Gaps.

Crampton's Gap

"Thomas Crampton was born on the ocean in 1735, where his father had just died. Crampton came to Pleasant Valley before 1759. He aided in building a road through the wilderness which led from the old pack horse ford below Shepherdstown, through Crampton's Gap, and on to Frederick Town."[26]

Two land records eliminate Crampton's Gap as a wagon road at the time of the Braddock Expedition. Stoney Ridge,[27] between Crampton's and Fox's Gaps according to Tracey Collection records, surveyed July 29, 1768, was "between the bridal road gap and the main road gap that leads from Sharpsburg to Frederick." Fox's Gap was the main road gap, as documented by the Grim's Fancy land record.

Wilyards Lot,[28] surveyed December 31, 1765, was "at the foot of the Blue Ridge Mountain where the bridal road crosses said Mountain about 2 or 3 perches north of said road." Dr. Tracey placed this tract about 1/2 mile east of Crampton's Gap. The Forest, patented or surveyed in 1734, was "on the north side of the Conococheague Road near the Shenandoah Mountain." The location of this tract, according to Dr. Tracey, is near Crampton's Gap.

The trail through Crampton's Gap to Conococheague crossed the wagon road through Fox's Gap to Shepherdstown, just south of Keedysville. The route through Fox's Gap was the shortest of the two routes from Frederick Town to the Keedysville area.

Crampton's Gap was not the primary route used to travel from Frederick Town to Swearingen's Ferry or Conococheague, either by horse or wagon. The main road from Frederick Town to the Sharpsburg area was through Fox's Gap, not Crampton's. Travelers through Crampton's Gap from Frederick Town probably went on to the area that became Harper's Ferry or perhaps the area at the mouth of the Antietam Creek on the Potomac.

This author rules out Crampton's Gap as a route used to transport supplies by wagon during the Braddock Expedition. The route through Crampton's Gap was only a horse trail as late as the late 1760s. The previous discussion leads this author to conclude Crampton's Gap was not the route of march for Dunbar's

Regiment.

Orr's Gap and The Old Hagerstown Road

Jonathan Hager Sr. founded Hagerstown in 1762.[29] He was accidentally killed November 6, 1775, at his new saw mill, where he was supervising the preparation of timber for building a German Reformed Church in Hagerstown. One of the earliest roads in western Maryland connected the areas that became Frederick Town, Middletown, and Hagerstown.[30] In the 1740s this was the road from Monocacy to Stull's Mill. "The road from Monocacy to John Stull's mill was made a public road by the November Court of 1739. John Stull had built his mill on 'Whiskey,' located where the Hagerstown power plant now stands."[31] The road crossed South Mountain through Orr's Gap, about three miles northeast of Fox's Gap. This route became the old Hagerstown Road from Frederick Town. Today Interstate 70 and Route 40 cross the Blue Ridge at Orr's Gap.

According to Tracey and Dern, "Monocacy" was an area, not a single town or location.[32] However, Nead cites page six of *First Settlements in Maryland* by Edward T. Schultz.[33] Schultz claims to have found the exact site, which he says is a little south of the present site of Creagerstown. Millard M. Rice, in *New Facts and Old Families*, disputes Schultz's conclusion.[34]

Just north of Middletown, before crossing the Catoctin Creek, a sign today identifies the old Hagerstown Road branching off to the right and passing through Orr's Gap. The 1808 Varle Map agrees with the currently posted sign. It indicates the road through Orr's Gap met the road through Fox's Gap at the Catoctin Creek just north of Middletown. Some records indicate the road branching off the old National Pike near Bolivar and passing through Orr's Gap by way of the Mount Tabor Church, also was known as the old Hagerstown Road.

The road from Frederick Town to Stull's Mill, near the area that became Hagerstown, was a wagon road by the time of the Braddock Expedition. Land records for Barron Hill (June 23, 1752), Mt. Pleasant (Aug. 24, 1747), John's Lot (Aug. 1, 1754), Terms Stool (May 13, 1745), and Gaming Alley (Aug. 27, 1744) support this conclusion. Gaming Alley was "on the great road that leads from Stulls Mill to the Monocacy. "

A road from the area of Stull's Mill to Conococheague existed by 1755. A tract named Contentment, in 1742, was "90 perches from a wagon road that goes from Bumgardners Mill to Feltygroves." This tract is between Hagerstown and Williamsport, according to records in the Tracey Collection. Jeffery Wyand cites the first session of the new Frederick County Court in March 1749. ". . . the road that Leads from Volgamots to Stulls." Wyand states, "Volgamot's or Wohlgemuth's mill was located not far above modern Williamsport."[35] Orr's Gap, therefore, was a viable route for the wagons of the Braddock Expedition as well as Dunbar's Regiment.

Dr. Tracey labeled Orr's Gap as Braddock's Gap on the map he created of the early roads in western Maryland. Dr. Tracey probably relied upon the 1808 Varle Map or the 1791 map of the *Road from Elizabethtown [Hagerstown] to Newcomber's Mill and Frederick County Line* as his source. An 1840 Maryland map in the Tracey Collection also shows Braddock's Gap at the location of Orr's Gap.

The following letter gives a possible explanation why Orr's Gap received the label of *Braddock's Gap:*

> I am also to inform your Excellency that one William Roberts (who is esteemed a Man of Credit) was with us Yesterday, and says he came through the South Mountain Thursday last, this side of which he saw four Houses burnt about four Miles from Major Ogles and that a Messenger came to him yesterday morning to give him an Account that four men were killed the same day he came through Mountain and at the same Gap he pass'd which is not above Sixty five Miles from this Place.[36]

Perhaps the gap to which the letter refers was Orr's Gap. The Orr family did not live at the gap but about one mile north. The label of Orr's Gap, for this reason, probably was not strong. An analogy seems appropriate at this point. Many streets across America have the name Washington. However, it is obvious George Washington never came near most of them. The same idea applies to Orr's Gap. General Braddock did not go through Orr's Gap to reach Swearingen's Ferry on May 2, 1755.

The Main Road from Frederick Town to Ft. Frederick

The earliest road from Frederick Town to the area that became Williamsport, passing through the general vicinity of Turner's Gap, was the main road from Frederick Town to Ft. Frederick. The name of this road describes both why it was built and when it was built. On May 14, 1756, the Maryland Assembly passed the Supply Bill. Entitled, "An Act for granting a Supply of Forty Thousand Pounds for his Majesty's Service and striking Thirty Four Thousand and Fifteen Pounds Six Shillings thereof, in Bills of Credit, and raising a Fund for sinking the same,"[37] the bill authorized the building of Ft. Frederick near the North Mountain. The bill allowed for the construction of one fort and up to four block-houses. The bill did not explicitly appropriate funds for the construction of a road to the fort, as indicated by the State Roads Commission quote that follows. However, the creation of a road to the fort does seem to be implicit in the act and an allowable expenditure under it:

> Following Braddock's ill-fated campaign, bands of Indians terrorized all Western Maryland and at least one group rampaged within 30 miles of Baltimore. The Maryland Legislature in 1755 took immediate action and appropriated money to build a huge stone fort and a road leading to it, twelve miles west of Williamsport. Called Fort Frederick, this massive edifice is still standing and is enshrined as a state park on the Potomac, south of present-day Clear Spring on U.S. 40 in Washington County. The road they built, leading to it from the east, can be identified as the course of State Routes 68 and 56.[38]

Later, the State Roads Commission indicates the following:

> Thus the French and Indian War advanced the opening of Western Maryland by many years. This new road, [connecting Ft. Frederick and Ft. Cumberland] together with Braddock's Road [through Turner's Gap

connecting Frederick Town and Ft. Frederick], both war measures, gave a direct if extremely rough connection between Baltimore, Annapolis and the far western parts of the province.[39]

Excerpts from the Supply Bill of 1756 follow:

And be it Enacted, That the said Sum of Forty Thousand Pounds be laid out and applied in Manner following, that is to say, in building and constructing one Fort, and any Number not exceeding four Block-Houses, on the Western Frontiers of this Province, accommodating and paying Workmen employed therein, in paying, arming and victualling, in Bounty-Money for enlisting, cloathing common Soldiers, transporting and conveying any Number not exceeding Two Hundred Men (Officers included), that shall be kept in Garrison in the same, and all other Necessaryies for the Support and Maintenance of the said Garrison, such Sum or Sums of Money as shall be necessary; not exceeding Eleven Thousand Pounds, including the Commissions of the Agents herein after appointed . . . Mr. William Murdock, Mr. James Dick, and Mr. Daniel Wolstenholme, shall be and are hereby appointed Agents . . . for the purchasing and procuring all such Tools, Cloaths, Provisions, Arms, and other Warlike Stores, and transporting and conveying the same, as shall be necessary and requite for the Officers and Soldiers in Garrison, in the said Fort and Block-Houses, to be built on such convenient Places on or near and not beyond the North-Mountain, and in such Form as his Excellency Horatio Sharpe, Esq; or the Governor or Commander in Chief, for the Time being, shall direct and appoint, and for the Payment of the Workmen, and the said Officers and Soldiers, that shall be in the same, or any others, that shall be enlisted or raised by Virtue of this Act for any Expedition, and for cloathing, providing for and arming the same, and for purchasing and contracting for any necessary Stores for his Majesty's Service for the Purposes in this Act mentioned.[40]

The new route crossed the South Mountain at Turner's or Curry's Gap. Frederick County court records support the creation of this road in the late 1750s. The following Frederick County Court Minutes are from records in the Tracey Collection:

> Nov. Court 1759: Road - The new road that goes through Currys Gap.
> Nov. Court 1759: The new road from Currys Gap to Beaver Creek.
> Nov. Court 1760: The new road that goes through Currys Gap (East Side) to Beaver Ck.
> Nov. Court 1761: The new road that goes through Currys Gap (East Side) to Beaver Ck.

A note on the card in the Tracey Collection indicates this route was along Old US 40, the route of the old National Pike through Turner's Gap. This is contradictory to other material by Arthur Tracey in the Tracey Collection that indicates Curry's Gap became Fox's Gap. Land records indicate Curry's Gap did not become Fox's Gap.

The following appear in *This Was the Life* by Millard M. Rice:

> Sundry inhabitants of the County, who are unnamed, petition the Court that they "conceive a better and nigher road might be made to Fort Frederick for the road to begin out of the road now leading thereto between the Mountains through Curry's Gap by Robert Turner's and by Joseph Holmes, by Dr. Neal's and so into the road by Joseph Volgamot's." The Court appointed Capt. Moses Chapline, Mr. James Smith and Mr. Joseph Tomlinson to lay out the road.[41]

> Joseph Smith and Moses Chapline, who had been appointed by the Court to view a road desired through a gap in the Mountains called Curry's Gap, state that this road "is a better way from Frederick Town to Fort Frederick than any yet carried across said Mountain."[42]

... the new road that goes through Curry's Gap: John George Arnold Jr. ... .[43]

The first statement above indicates the new road to Ft. Frederick was to lead out of the current road to the fort.

Land tract records support a route through Turner's or Curry's Gap only after the 1750s. "The main road from Frederick Town to Ft. Frederick" appears in deeds for Pick All, Worse and Worse, Flonham, Fox's Last Shift, Kizer's Lowden, and Smithsburg.

Pick All, patented in 1764, began at "the beginning tree of a tract of land called John's Delight patented by James Wardrop which tree is a white oak standing by the side of the main road that leads from Frederick Town to Fort Frederick."[44] John's Delight, patented in 1750, began "at a bounded white oak standing about thirty feet from a small run called Curry's Branch nigh the foot of Shanondore Mountain near Curry's Gap."[45] This record is the earliest found by the author that mentions Curry's Gap.

The patent for John's Delight does not indicate the beginning tree of the tract was along a road in 1750. However, five later tracts that began at the beginning tree of John's Delight identify the beginning tree as being along a main road. The Pick All patent, Shidler's Dispute deeds of 1760[46] and 1767,[47] the Long Dispute[48] deed of 1767, and the 304 acre tract of the Bartholomew Booker Estate[49] in 1792[50] refer to "the main road." Both Shidler's Dispute deeds mention Curry's Gap.

The following newspaper notice appeared after Bartholomew Booker's death:

101. FTM Aug 28 1792/Margaret Booker, Frederick Fox, exec, to sell farm, late the prop of Bartholomew Booker, decd, 304 a., on road from Fred Town to Williamsport, and Hager's Town, about 3 miles above Middletown/[51]

Following Page - tracts identified:

V	Daniel's Race Ground (1793)
DW	David's Will (1763)
F	Flonham (1770)
FLS	Fox's Last Shift (1764)
FB	Frederick's Burgh (1792)
G	The Gap (1761)
GF	Grim's Fancy (1764)
JD	John's Delight (1750)
R	Racon (1762)
RCS	Resurvey on Cool Spring (1801)
RWD	Resurvey on Well Done (1764)
S	Shettle (1744)
SD	Shidler's Dispute (1760)
SW	Swearingen's Disappointment (1782)
W	Worse and Worse (1766)

Following Page - beginning trees identified:

1	Racon - south side of a road (1762)
2	Fox's Last Shift - on the north side of the main country road (1764)
C	Flonham - on the right hand side of the main road (1770)
4	Worse and Worse - south side of road (1766)
5	Pick All - by the side of the main road (1764)
5	John's Delight (1750 - no road mentioned)
5	Shidler's Dispute, Long Dispute, 1791 Booker Estate - along the main country road
H	The Gap (warrant in 1750, patent in 1761 - no road mentioned)
K	Bowser's Addition - at Fox's Gap (1763)

Following Page - points on road:

3	End of line 8 of Apple Brandy, 1791 - "to the main road"
5	Shidler's Dispute, Long Dispute, 1791 Booker Estate - "with the main road," and Pick All, patented in 1764 - "by the side of the main road"

Dotted Line - main road from Frederick Town to Ft. Frederick
Solid Line - the old Sharpsburg Road through Fox's Gap

The Main Road from Frederick Town to Ft. Frederick through Turner's or Curry's Gap

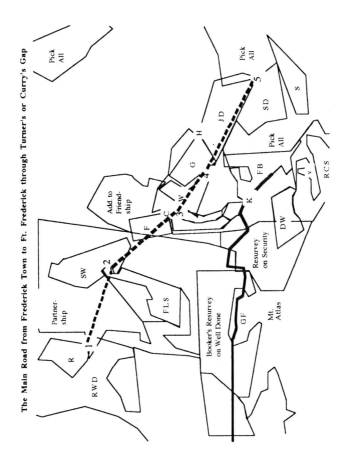

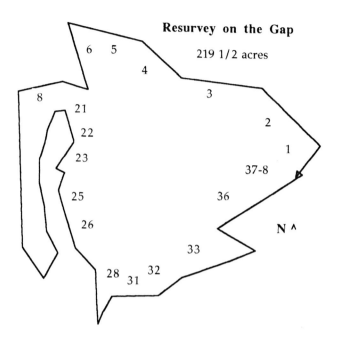

Beginning at the bounded tree of Turkey Ramble
3. to a stone planted at the end of the last line of The Gap, one of the originals
4. to the fifth line of Turkey Ramble one of the present originals
6. to a stone then leaving said land and running with the lines of a tract of land called Addition to Friendship
10. to the end of the third line of Bowser's Addition
12. to a tree on Apple Brandy and with said land 9 courses
21. to the 4th line of Worse and Worse one of the originals
23. to the 11th line of Apple Brandy and with said land
27. to the end of the first line of a tract of land called Bowsers Addition and with said line reverse
28. to the bounded tree of said land, then with the lines of a tract of land called Fredericks Burgh
33. to the end of the 12th line of a tract of land called Pick All
34. to the end of 38 perches on the given line of a tract called John's Delight and with said line reverse

**Overlay of Tracts in the Resurvey on the Gap, Apple
Brandy, and Bowser's Addition**

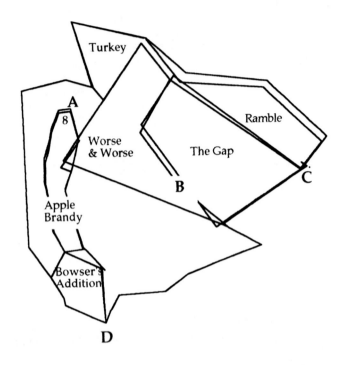

A = End of line 8 of Apple Brandy
B = Beginning tree of Worse and Worse
C = Beginning tree of The Gap and Turkey Ramble
D = Beginning tree of Bowser's Addition

The notice indicates a single road by Booker's led to both
Williamsport and Hagerstown in 1792.

   Worse and Worse, surveyed for John Teem on February 7,
1766, had its "beginning at a bounded white oak standing on the
east side of the South Mountain and on the south side of the main
road that leads from Frederick Town to Fort Frederick about
forty perches from the said John Teems dwelling house."[52] The
Worse and Worse tract eliminates Fox's Gap from possessing the
main road from Frederick Town to Ft. Frederick.

A tract named Its Bad Enough began "at a bounded white oak tree the beginning of a tract of land called Worse and Worse."[53] Its Bad Enough, a very narrow tract of 14 and 3/4 acres, was between the Worse and Worse tract and a tract called The Gap. The beginning of The Gap was "at the end of the third line of Wardrops Land called Curry's Old Place."[54] A deed from John Team to Joseph Chapline for The Gap, recorded December 27, 1766, had its "beginning at the end of the third line of Wardrops Land called Careys Old Place."[55] Perhaps Curry was Carey or Cary.

The tracts of It's Bad Enough, Worse and Worse, The Gap, and Turkey Ramble were part of the Resurvey on The Gap.[56] The Resurvey on The Gap was on the east side of South Mountain and ran from Fox's Gap to just south of Turner's Gap.

The Flonham tract, surveyed August 27, 1770, had its "beginning at a bounded white oak standing about a perch from the head of a spring on the south side of the Shannondore Mountain on the right hand of the main road leading from Frederick Town to Fort Frederick."[57] The Flonham tract is of rectangular shape. The Flonham survey in 1770 makes no mention of any buildings or appurtenances.

Fox's Last Shift was west of Flonham but extended farther north. It had its "beginning at a bounded white oak tree standing on the north side of the main country road that leads from Frederick Town to Fort Frederick in the South Mountain."[58] A deed in the early 1800s indicates the turnpike road crossed this tract.[59] A resurvey on Fox's Last Shift, called Newcomer's Purchase, is interesting.[60] Newcomer's Purchase, surveyed January 5, 1786, added 29 acres to the original 72 acres of Fox's Last Shift. The road to Williamsport, on the west side of Turner's Gap, appears to pass through these 29 acres. Partnership of John Mansberger encompassed 685 acres in 1795.[61] It surrounded the tracts of Fox's Last Shift, Newcomber's Purchase, and Swearingen's Disappointment.

The most interesting aspect of the tract named Fox's Last Shift is its name. No one named Fox owned the tract. This author feels the name derived from the fact a new route between Conococheague and Frederick Town came about in the late 1750s. The new road went through Turner's or Curry's Gap and Fox's Last Shift. This route was the main road from Frederick Town to

Ft. Frederick.

The 1791 map of the *Road Leading from Williamsport to Turner's Gap in the South Mountain* shows the road crossing the Antietam near the mouth of Beaver Creek. The area where the road crosses Beaver Creek is called the Devil's Backbone and is near Delemere. Beaver Creek, identified in the 1759-61 court minutes previously cited, must have meant the mouth of Beaver Creek on the Antietam Creek. Susanne Flowers indicates a large picture at the Washington County Court House in Hagerstown shows the Devil's Backbone Bridge over Little Beaver Creek on Maryland Highway 68. The picture indicates the bridge, built in 1824, was the "spot where Braddock and his Redcoats crossed the Little Beaver in 1755."

Farther west of Fox's Last Shift, Racon had its "beginning at a bounded white oak standing on the south side of a road near the south mountain."[62] Raccoon was a resurvey on Racon.[63] Raccoon was for 253 acres and began at the beginning tree of the original tract.

Kizer's Lowden lies northwest of Boonsboro according to Dr. Tracey. This is consistent with a route from the Boonsboro area to Williamsport. The tract had its "beginning at a bounded white oak standing on the north side of the main road leading from Frederick Town to Ft. Frederick between Robert Turner's plantation and Antietam Creek and by the side of a road that leads from Isaac Housers to Chaplines Mill."[64]

The road from Ft. Frederick to Ft. Cumberland was approved under Article XCV of an act that appropriated 250 pounds for building "a good wagon road" from Ft. Frederick to Ft. Cumberland.[65]

The 1781 Frederick County Court Minutes

Frederick court minutes from 1781 appear below:

> . . . from the forks of the roads where the Sharpsburgh Road leads out of Braddock's Road to the top of South Mountain, being the direct road from Frederick passing Robert Turner's old place to Fort Frederick.[66]

The court minutes contain at least five elements: 1) the road from Frederick to Ft. Frederick; 2) the location of Robert Turner's old place; 3) the "forks of the roads"; 4) the Sharpsburg Road and the Braddock Road met; and 5) the year, 1781. Elements four and five present statements of fact and need no further clarification. The first three elements require additional information to clarify them. The court minutes do not tell us where Robert Turner lived, the course of the road, or where the roads forked.

Court minutes in 1748 indicate, "Road that leads out from John Georges that leads via Robt. Evans to top of Shenandoah."[67] This author believes the 1748 court minutes refer to the fork in the roads just north of Middletown and very near the Catoctin Creek. John George's Road was the same as the road from Frederick Town to Stull's Mill [the old Hagerstown Road]. The road by Robert Evans was the same as the route of the old Sharpsburg Road from Frederick Town through Fox's Gap.

John George Arnold owned land near Orr's Gap. Tracts near Orr's Gap owned by John George Arnold include Ram's Horn[68] and Hog Yard.[69] However, a John George Arnold owned land near Conococheague, according to the Ash Swamp land record of February 19, 1739.[70]

Robert Evans[71] lived along the old Sharpsburg Road.[72] However, he owned other tracts, including Cuckhold's Horns,[73] near Orr's Gap. Early records tie Robert Evans to the old Sharpsburg Road:

> Beginning in 1741 and for several years thereafter, Mark and Thomas Whitaker were overseers for the road from "Shenandoah Mountain to Catoctin Mountain." Thomas Whitaker petitioned the March Court of 1745, "Having been appointed overseer of the main road and having marked and distinguished the Patomack Ferry [now Shepherdstown] Road extending to the city of Annapolis and several other remarkable places . . . to acquaint your honorable worships that a certain Robert Evans hath stopped the said road and will not suffer travellers to pass nor the road to extend through the inclosure as it formerly went but tumbles loggs into the road and hath turned the road where it is

mortally impossible to make it good. Pray further instructions..."[74]

The above records indicate the road through Fox's Gap was "the main road" and that it was extended to the city of Annapolis by Whitaker before 1745. The extension of the road to the city of Annapolis was approved in 1739 by the Maryland Assembly:

> Phillip Lee Esqr from the upper house delivers Mr. Speaker a petition of the inhabitants about monoccacy and about the mountains on Potomack River on the back part of Virginia. A petition of the inhabitants at and about monoccacy creek. A petition of the inhabitants to the northward of the blue ridge alias chenandore mountain, by which petition the several petitioners pray a road may be cleared through the country from the city of annapolis for the more easy carriage of their grain provisions and other commoditys which petitions by the upper house are indorsed recommended to a consideration of the lower house.[75]

Thomas Whitaker transferred a tract named Prevention to Nicholas Fink in 1750. Prevention had its "beginning at a bounded white oak standing at ye mouth of a run Called Mill run ye falls into Ketocktin Creek."[76] The fork of the old Sharpsburg Road and the old Hagerstown Road is just southeast of the mouth of Mill Creek on the Catoctin Creek (see the 1808 Varle Map). The fork of the roads is near the end of line three of a 66 acres tract, part of Goose Cap, from Nicholas Fink to Thomas Welch in 1771. "Beginning at a bounded Sycamore tree standing on the north west side of Mill Creek and about two perches from the said Creek." Line two went "South 29 degrees east 24 perches to the great road that leads from Frederick town to Hagers Town then by and with the said road the two following courses."[77]

An 1832 deed from John Stemple et ux to George Baltzell[78] included portions of the tracts of The Forrest, the Resurvey on Watson's Welfare,[79] Smithfield, Whiskey Alley,[80] Goose Cap, What Nots, and I Wish There Was More.[81]

Jacob Keefour deeded 50 acres of the Resurvey on Whiskey Alley to the "Trustees of the German Reformed Lutheran and Calvinist Congregations in and about Middletown" in 1783.[82]

Watson's Welfare had its "beginning at a bounded hickory tree standing on the east side of Kitocton Creek a draught of Potomac near a mile below the great Road that leads from John Stulls Mill to the mouth of Monocacy."[83] This author concludes "near a mile below the great Road that leads from John Stulls Mill to the mouth of Monocacy" meant one mile below the forks of the old Sharpsburg and old Hargerstown Roads (i.e., the roads through Fox's and Orr's Gaps).

The fork in the road identified by the 1781 Court Minutes was at the Catoctin Creek just north of Middletown, where the old Sharpsburg Road met the old Hagerstown Road (see Chapter Three, The Fox Inn Area to The Fork of the Roads). Middletown is about one mile south of the fork of the old Sharpsburg and old Hagerstown Roads. Millard M. Rice, in *New Facts and Old Famililes*, presents what is probably the most accurate history of the founding of Middletown.[84] His work includes land tract analysis and material on the road to Conococheague.

Some might argue the forks in the roads mentioned in the 1781 Court Minutes was where the main road from Frederick Town to Ft. Frederick, through Turner's or Curry's Gap, met the old Sharpsburg Road. This point, shown on the 1808 Varle Map just east of "Ringer," was between the Fox Inn and the bridge over the Catoctin Creek just north of Middletown. The intersection of these roads also appears on an 1840 map in the Tracey Collection. This fork in the roads was "by Casper Shaffs" in 1768.

Bartholomew Booker was "Overseer of road from the top of Kitoctin Mtn. that leads to Robert Turner's & to the top of South Mtn. from where the road forks by Casper Shaffs to the top of South Mtn" in 1768.[85] The beginning tree of the Bartholomew Booker Estate in 1791 was along the main road to Ft. Frederick. Casper Shaff owned Oxford, just east of the Fox Inn. The fork in the road at Casper Shaff's was where the roads through Fox's Gap and Turner's or Curry's Gap met in 1768.

Peter Beaver acquired Oxford from Casper Shaff on October 18, 1769. A portion of the Resurvey on Mend All from Jacob Smith Sr. to Bartholomew Booker, January 15, 1772, began "near a road that leads from Bartholomew Booker to Peter Beavers."[86] A 1760 deed from Bartholomew Booker to Michel Shepfell, for the same property as above, began "at a bounded red oak standing by the head of a little spring and near a road that leads from Bartholomew Bookers to Peter Beavers."[87] This material supports the conclusion the road from Frederick to Ft. Frederick met the road through Fox's Gap in the area between the Fox Inn and the Catoctin Creek at one time, as shown on the 1808 Varle Map.

The 1781 Frederick Court Minutes indicate the road from Frederick Town to Ft. Frederick went by Robert Turner's Old Place. Robert Turner did not live at Turner's Gap. He lived near the present site of Boonsboro.[88] The 1781 court minutes represent an accurate statement related to the roads in 1781. The biggest strike against them is that they are at a point in time 26 years after the Braddock Expedition. They cannot be used by themselves to conclude Dunbar's Regiment went through Turner's Gap. The 1781 Court Minutes refer to two roads built at different times. The road through Fox's Gap dates to before the Braddock Expedition. The road through Turner's or Curry's Gap dates only until after the Braddock Expedition.

Turner's or Curry's Gap

The main road from Frederick Town to Ft. Frederick passed through Turner's or Curry's Gap. The route of the turnpike road, built in the early 1800s, followed the roadbed of the main road from Frederick Town to Ft. Frederick except on the immediate near east side of the Mountain House at Turner's or Curry's Gap. The portion of the turnpike road coming up the mountain on the near east side of the Mountain House lies north of the roadbed of the main road from Frederick to Ft. Frederick.

Robert Turner patented Nelson's Folly, at the present site of Boonsboro, in 1750.[89] It is possible to trace lots in the town of Boonsboro to the Nelson's Folly tract.[90] Turner was "made overseer of roads in Antietam Hundred" in 1748.[91] The earliest mention of Robert Turner appears in a survey of Charlemount Pleasant for Samuel Ogle Esqr.[92] "Beginning at a bounded Black Oak standing on a small hill to the eastward of a spring that falls in Little Antieatom about half a mile to the southward of Robert Turners."

Nelson's Folly ran north and west from the present site of Boonsboro.[93] Related land records indicate Robert Turner did not live at Turner's Gap. Jacob's Brune had its "beginning at a bounded black oak standing on the east side of a tract of land called Lannafield near the foot of the south Mountain and on the west side thereof about 1 half a mile from Robert Turners House."[94] Martsome began "at a bounded white oak standing by the side of a branch falling from the end of the short hill mountain down to Robert Turners plantation being a draught of little anteatom."[95] There does not appear to be another Turner, other than Robert, for whom to name Turner's Gap.

Turner's Gap includes the area in the immediate vicinity of the Mountain House, now The Old South Mountain Inn (see Appendix C - Land Tract Analysis, The Mountain House). The 1791 map of the *Road Leading from Williamsport to Turner's Gap in the South Mountain* identifies almost one mile of road on the west side of the mountain as being "up through the gap." Byron L. Williams, author of *The Old South Mountain Inn, An Informal History,* was able to trace records from the present owners of the Mountain House, Russell and Judy Schwartz, back to the 1830s or 40s and the estate of Henry Miller. He was unable to trace land records for Robert Turner and his Nelson's Folly tract to the present owners of the Mountain House. He could not do this because Nelson's Folly is over one mile from The Old South Mountain Inn at Turner's Gap.

The Mountain House at Turner's Gap stands on the south side of the old National Pike and on the northern portion of a tract named Flonham (see Appendix C - Land Tract Analysis, The Mountain House). A portion of the ten acres that surround the Chapel, across the road from the Mountain House, is part of Addition to Friendship, patented by Frederick Fox in 1805 (see Appendix C - Land Tract Analysis, The Ten Acres Surrounding the Chapel at Turner's Gap).

The state of Maryland passed a law in November 1804 approving three turnpike companies. The Baltimore and Frederick Town Turnpike Company was to construct a turnpike from Baltimore through Frederick Town and Middletown to Boonsborough. Subscriptions for stock were taken in March, 1805.

In April of that year, a law passed providing for the extension of
the turnpike road to Williamsport and Hagerstown from
Boonsborough:[96]

>   Sec. 11. . . . and be it enacted, That the said roads
> shall be made in, over, and upon the beds of the present
> roads, as laid out and confirmed by the commissioners of
> review, and the several acts of Assembly relating to the
> same, and also upon every extension of the said roads as
> established by this law: Provided always, That, should
> it appear, on a resurvey of any part of the extension of
> said roads by sworn surveyors, that a considerable saving
> in distance would thence arise to the public, and in
> expense to the company or companies, that in all such
> cases it shall be lawful to depart from the tract of the
> road so originally laid down, and improve the shorter
> and less expensive route: Provided, also, That, in all
> such deviations, the road shall not be diverted or taken
> from any town or village through which it now passses . .
> .[97]

>   Sec. 17. . . . it shall in no place rise or fall more
> than will form an angle of four degrees, with a
> horizontal line, except over the Catoctin and South
> mountains, where it may rise or fall to an angle of six
> degrees, with a horizontal line . . .[98]

>   . . . and although the law authorizing this road
> admits of six degrees over the South mountain, still, as
> the same force will propel so much greater a load on a
> four degree hill than the same force would on an angle of
> six degrees, we shall rather submit to some loss of
> distance than exceed four degrees to the termination of
> the road.[99]

Election of a president, eight managers, and a treasurer
was held on May 13, 1805, by the Baltimore and Frederick Town
Turnpike Company. Notices for the letting of work appeared in
late May. An advertisement in June sought to hire a manager of

turnpike construction. The following newspaper notice ran October 2, 1805, and for a number of weeks thereafter:

Advertisement

I will sell a tract of land containing 105 acres in Washington County lying on the main road leading from Williamsport to Frederick Town and about two miles from Boonsborough - on this land are 2 never failing springs of excellent water, well calculated for a distillery - there is a dwelling house and out houses on the premises, also between two and three hundred bearing apple trees also a number of peach and cherry trees, - as the turnpike road is generally expected to pass on the present road, and near the dwelling house, presume it will make this property very valuable to a purchaser.   Peter Summers   living on the premises[100]

John Summers patented Raccoon in August 1770. As shown on the 1791 map of the *Road Leading from Williamsport to Turner's Gap in the South Mountain*, the course of the old road was just south of Summers' house. The new route was just north of Summers' house.

The report of the president and managers of the Baltimore and Frederick Town Turnpike Company on October 9, 1805, indicated ten miles through Baltimore County were to be completed by April 1, 1806, and three miles in Anne Arundel County were to be completed by August 1806. A January 2, 1807, notice by the turnpike company indicated sufficient money had been raised to complete the road at least as far as Boonsboro. A notice on August 22, 1807, indicated a Mr. Herbaugh had been hired by the company to oversee the building of a bridge over Monocacy, consisting of five arches of thirty feet each.[101]

Lewis Wampler, Secretary of the Baltimore and Frederick Town Turnpike Co. sent Governor Edward Lloyd a letter, dated January 28, 1811, requesting the appointment of a committee to inspect and approve ten miles, three furlongs, and twelve perches of the turnpike completed to Boonsboro. Fifty miles already had been approved from Baltimore. The Governor nominated John Schley, Stephen Stoner, and Lawrence Bringle on February 15. The three nominees sent a report to the Governor, indicating the road had been done in a workmanlike manner as far as Boonsboro on March 11, 1811.[102]

The road through Turner's Gap was destined to become part of a national road to the western part of the country. The House of Representatives of the United States approved a bill on March 27, 1806, previously passed in the Senate, for the construction of a road from Cumberland, Maryland, to Ohio. Discussion of the route of the road appears in articles in January and February 1807 in the *Maryland Herald and Hagerstown Weekly*. A January 13 article, discussing the route of the proposed road, mentions Braddock's Road and Dunbar's Run.

Four early land tracts lie in the vicinity of Turner's Gap.[103] These tracts are Addition to Friendship, Flonham, Partnership of John Mansberger, and Swearingen's Disappointment. The beginning tree of Flonham indicates the route of the turnpike road on the immediate near east side of the Mountain House was not the same route as the main road from Frederick to Ft. Frederick in that immediate area. The bounded tree of Flonham is about 1/4 mile south, southeast of the Mountain House. Two deeds in the 1800s substantiate the turnpike road was on the right hand side of the bounded tree of Flonham.

Flonham

36 acres

Beginning at a bounded white oak standing about a perche from the head of a spring on the south side of the Shannondore Mountain on the right hand of the main road leading from Frederick Town to Fort Frederick.

A deed from Susan Miller et al. to Daniel Beagley indicates the turnpike crossed the fourth line of Flonham at 84 purchases north of the beginning tree.[104] This tract is along the south and east sides of Flonham and consists entirely of land from the Addition to Friendship tract. A deed from George

Baltzell to Henry Miller[105] consisted of two tracts of land. The first tract consisted of 75 1/2 acres of Addition to Friendship lying south of the turnpike road. The second tract consisted of 114 acres of Addition to Friendship lying north of the turnpike road. Lines 14, 15, and 16 of the second tract are along the turnpike. In order for the beginning tree of Flonham to be on the right-hand side of a road through Turner's Gap, the road would need to run closer to and along the ridge of the mountain.

A tract named Apple Brandy also indicates the turnpike road on the immediate near east side of Turner's Gap did not lie on the roadbed of the main road from Frederick Town to Fort Frederick in that area. The beginning tree of Apple Brandy of Jacob Fulwiler was "a bounded Spanish oak near the top of the south mountain."[106] This tree is near the end of the second line of Bowser's Addition. Line 8 of Apple Brandy went "to the main road." The end of line eight is approximately 600 feet south of the beginning tree of Flonham. The beginning tree of Flonham was on the right-hand side of the point in the road identified in the Apple Brandy tract.

The Apple Brandy deed substantiates the main road from Frederick to Ft. Frederick was south of the turnpike on the near east side of the Mountain House. Line 20 of the Resurvey on The Gap, which is the same as line 8 of Apple Brandy, does not indicate "to the main road," but only "to the fourth line of Worse and Worse."[107]

The turnpike road through Turner's Gap ran in a southerly direction on the near east side of the mountain. At its closest point, the turnpike was approximately 460 feet from the beginning tree of Flonham. The turnpike road at Turner's Gap runs about 24 perches south of, and mostly parallel to, the North, or third, line of Flonham. The following information can be obtained from the deed from Phillip Sheffer to Henry Miller. The turnpike crosses the fourth line of Flonham 23 1/2 perches below the northeast corner of the tract and 82 1/2 perches north of the beginning tree of Flonham. Line 4 of 18 perches and line 5 of 20 3/4 perches were "by and in the middle of" the turnpike. Line 5 ended at the fourth or last line of Flonham. Line 6 went 23 1/2 perches with and to the end of line three of Flonham. The fourth, or last, line of Flonham was 108 perches.[108]

Road from Williamsport to Turner's Gap in the South Mountain - October 17, 1791

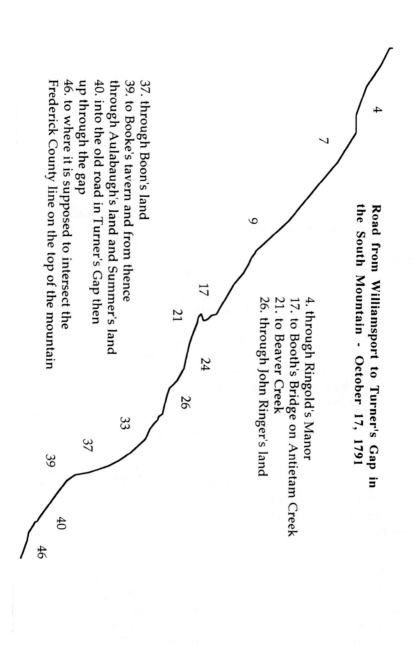

4. through Ringold's Manor
17. to Booth's Bridge on Antietam Creek
21. to Beaver Creek
26. through John Ringer's land

37. through Boon's land
39. to Booke's tavern and from thence through Aulabaugh's land and Summer's land
40. into the old road in Turner's Gap then up through the gap
46. to where it is supposed to intersect the Frederick County line on the top of the mountain

St. Mary's Academy of Notre Dame, St. Joseph's County, Indiana, to Charles M. Hewitt - 1925

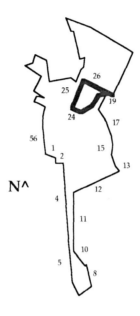

12. To the middle of the state road leading from Frederick to Hagerstown
15. To a white oak tree on the east side of the state road
19. Thence by lines now made to exclude the above mentioned 10 acres surrounding the chapel the 7 following courses
20. To a black oak tree on the west side of the public road
23. To the center line of the above mentioned state road

(**Note** - The public road is the Dahlgren road.)

Following Page - overlay of:
Addition to Friendship of Frederick Fox - surveyed 1797
Flonham of Philip Jacob Schafer - surveyed 1770
The Gap of Joseph Chapline Sr. - surveyed 1761
Worse and Worse of John Teem (Team) - surveyed 1766
Apple Brandy of Jacob Fulwiler - surveyed 1791
5 acres of Flonham - Henry Miller - recorded 1825
St. Mary's Academy of Notre Dame to Charles M. Hewitt - recorded 1925

Following Page - points identified:
1. 10 acres around the Chapel at Turner's Gap - 1925 - bold dotted line
2. The Mountain House at Turner's Gap
3. The turnpike road - 1800s - bold solid line
4. The beginning tree of Flonham - 1770
5. The end of line four of Apple Brandy - 1791
6. The beginning tree of Worse and Worse - 1766
7. The beginning tree of The Gap - 1761
8. The Reno Monument at Fox's Gap
9. Road through Fox's Gap - bold solid line

The turnpike continued almost due east at least 15 4/10 perches into Addition to Friendship. Line 6 of the Smith-Dahlgren deed went "to the middle of the aforesaid turnpike and with it." Lines 7 and 8 of this deed are the same as lines 4 and 5 of the Shaffer-Miller deed. Line 9 went "15 4/10 perches to a stake on the south side of said turnpike thence leaving it."[109] Part two of the Baltzell-Miller deed started at the end of the third line of Flonham.[110]

The end of line 12 of St. Mary's Academy of Notre Dame to Charles M. Hewitt was "to the middle of the state road leading from Frederick to Hagerstown" and line 15 was "to a white oak tree on the east side of the state road above mentioned."[111] Lines 13 and 14 probably were along the road. Deeds for Susan Miller et al. to Daniel Beagley[112] and John W. Derr et al. to Adam Koogle[113] place the turnpike and state road on the right-hand side of the beginning tree of Flonham.

Overlay of Tracts at Turner's or Curry's Gap and Fox's Gap

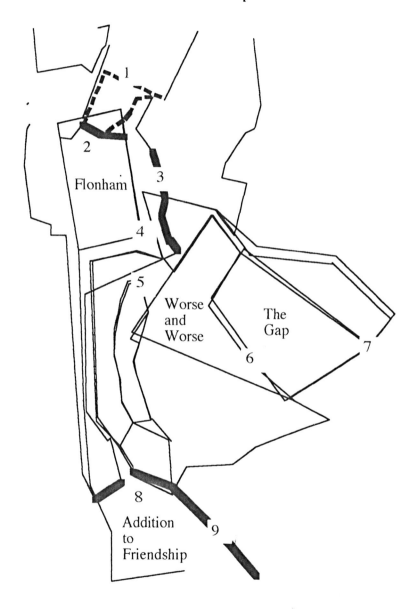

Philip Sheffer to Henry Miller
Flonham - Recorded July 6, 1825

Beginning at the end of the second line of the whole tract called Flonham and running thence with the second line of said land reversed
3. To the middle of the turnpike road then by and in the middle of said road
5. To intersect the given line of the whole tract called "Flonham" then by and with the given line thereof reversed
6. To the end of the third and last line of said land then by and with said third line reversed
7. To the first mentioned beginning containing five acres

Henry Miller acquired 67 acres that were part of Addition to Frendship and part of Fredericksburg under a writ of Fieri Facia from John Routzah.[114] Henry Miller acquired most of Addition to Friendship from the heirs of Joseph Swearingen.[115] George Baltzell, attorney, was Miller's agent for this acquisition. Swearingen acquired Addition to Friendship from Frederick Fox in 1807.[116] Frederick Fox patented Addition to Friendship May 27, 1805.[117] Joseph Swearingen was one of three individuals appointed by law in 1805 to take subscriptions for stock in the turnpike company at Middletown.[118]

Henry Miller acquired 5 acres of Flonham from Philip Jacob Shafer.[119] Shafer, or perhaps his father of the same name, acquired the patent to Flonham. A Philip Jacob Shafer was a witness to the will of Bartholomew Booker.[120]

Randolph Abott Shotwell, a Confederate soldier in the Battle of South Mountain, was a North Carolina newspaper editor after the war. The following statement about Turner's Gap appears in *The Papers of Randolph Abbot Shotwell*. "The present turnpike through the Gap is of modern construction; prior to it, the Gap was not used."[121]

Land records for Fox's Last Shift, Racon, and Raccoon, support the road through Turner's Gap on the west side of the mountain in the early 1760s. The 1791 map of the *Road Leading from Williamsport to Turner's Gap in the South Mountain* supports the use of the route on the west side of Turner's Gap prior to the creation of the turnpike, as does the advertisement by Peter Summers in 1805. The author has not determined precisely where the end of the last line of the 1791 map of the road meets the Frederick County line, but it appears to be in the vicinity of the Old South Mountain Inn at Turner's Gap.

The Road to Conococheague

A land tract near Keedysville identifies a road to Conococheague by the year 1740. This route is along the current road between Keedysville and Williamsport through Bakersville. The Vineyard had its "beginning at a bounded red oak standing on the west side of Antieatom Creek within ten poles of Conegochieg Road crosses the said creek."[122] The beginning tree of The Vineyard apparently is within 10 poles or perches of the Hitt (or Upper) Bridge over the Antietam, just northwest of Keedysville.[123] The author has not researched this point conclusively. The Vineyard is northwest of Fellfoot Enlarged. The tract became part of the Resurvey on The Vineyard[124] and The Resurvey on Hills and Dales and the Vineyard.[125] The Resurvey on The Vineyard was assigned to Benjamin Tasker Sr. and Benjamin Tasker Jr. by William Steuart on March 12, 1754.

A map drawn by Arthur Tracey in the Tracey Collection indicates the route through Fox's Gap to Conococheague was a "Public Road in 1733." Tracey and Dern indicate, "the first roads of present-day Frederick County to be made 'public roads' were identified in Prince George's County Court of November 1733."[126]

Material in the Tracey Collection also gives the following: "Nov. Court 1743 Overseer of road Monocacy to Conococheague - Robert Owings." Apparently there were two Robert Owings. One settled at Conewago and one at South Mountain. Tracey and Dern indicate: "One final resident who arrived in the upper Potomac area before 1743 should be noted. He was Robert Owings, who in that year was appointed overseer of the road from 'Monocacy to Conococheague' the road over Crampton's Gap."[127]

The following appears in the minutes of the August Court of 1764:

> A petition by sundry inhabitants of the County states that "there is a great want and need of a bridge to be made on the new road leading to Swearingen's Ferry and to the mouth of Connogojigue over Kittockton Creek between Samuel Magruder's and Philip Fink's as there has several people in great danger and almost lost at said fording these last freshes [freshets]." They ask that such a bridge be built.
>
> "The Court orders that Messrs. Joseph Smith and Peter Bainbridge agree with workmen to build a bridge over Kittockton Creek near Samuel Magruder's."[128]

These court minutes give clear evidence that one road over the Catoctin Creek led both to Swearingen's Ferry and to Conococheague.

The Overnight Stopping Place of Dunbar's Regiment

The last item of investigation is one of the most significant. Journals kept by participants to the events provide names associated with the stopping place between Frederick Town and Conococheague. They indicate the distances between the stopping place and Frederick Town as well as Conococheague. One must use both names and distances together to reach any conclusion.

The Orderly Book of General Braddock gives the distance from Frederick Town to the stopping place as 17 miles. From that halting place to Conococheague the orders indicate was 18 miles farther. These distances appear in both the orders of April 27 and April 28. The Morris Journal gives the distance from Frederick Town to the stopping place, "one Walkers," as 18 miles. The following entry in the Morris Journal relates to the distance from the stopping place to Conococheague:

"On the 30th: - At 6, marched in our way to Connecochieg, where we arrived at 2 o'clock, 16 miles from Walker's: This is a fine situation, close by the Potomack. We found the Artillery Stores going by water to Wills's Creek, and left 2 of our men here."

The following entry appears in the Orderly Book of General Braddock: "The Detachment of sailors and the Provost Marshalls Guard consisting of one Sergeant, one Corporal and 10 men to march with Colo. Dunbar's Regiment tomorrow morning and *to make the rear guard.*"[129] The seamen were at the end of the column, consisting of perhaps 700 men, during the march.

The Tracey Collection contains two cards which identify a land tract of a Thomas Walker on the route of the Conococheague Road near Bakersville. Dorsey's Resque had its beginning "at the beginning of a tract belonging to Thos. Walner."[130] This tract was surveyed for Edward Dorsey in 1754. Little Meadow of Thomas Walker was on the "wagon road that goes to Stulls Mill."[131] This tract is somewhat beyond the halfway point between Frederick and Williamsport. The two tracts are near the intersection of the Conococheague Road through Bakersville to Williamsport and the road from Sharpsburg to Hagerstown.

The 1762 will of Moses Chapline Sr. also might provide a clue. The names of John Perins, William Good, and John Waller appear as witnesses to the will. *Chapline's from Maryland and Virginia*, by Maria J. Liggett Dare, gives the third name as John Walter. There is a record of a Daniel Walter will of February 26, 1768.[132] The son's name was John. There is a record of a Zachariah Walker in Moses Chapline Sr.'s company during the French and Indian War.[133]

One of the two Commissaries for Provisions and Stores, appointed by Governor Dinwiddie, was Thomas Walker. It is possible the Morris Journal entries of April 29 and 30 refer to this Walker. Perhaps Commissary Walker provided supplies along the road for Dunbar's troops. The Morris Journal indicated, "This place is wanting of all refreshments." General Braddock's Orders also gave no name for the stopping place.

"The General ordered a bridge to be built over the Antietum, which being furnished, *and provision laid in on the road*, Colonel Dunbar marched with his regiment from Frederick on the 28th of April (OR, 308)." A letter from Governor Dinwiddie contains the following: "I am doing all I can to lay in a Qu'ty of Flour till the Fall of the Year. The Pork and Flour *to be lodged on the Road* is only for their Support on their March, and I think every private Soldier may carry four Day's Provision of Bread kind."[134]

The Orderly Book of General Braddock indicates, "as you will find Provisions very scarce on the Road you must take with you as many days of salt Provisions as the men can carry." On April 27 it states, "The men are to take from this place three Days provisions: at Conogogee they will have more."[135] The orders of General Braddock do not indicate supplies left along the route of march for the troops. Orme and Braddock contradict each other.

In conclusion, substantiation of the location of "one Walkers" remains elusive. The journalist infers "one Walkers" was an isolated and perhaps barren location. Nothing found by the author provides conclusive evidence for "one Walkers." For this reason, we turn to another possibility.

Another significant source of information concerning the stopping place the first night out of Frederick Town appears in a book by Charles Hamilton entitled, *Braddock's Defeat*. Hamilton first made known to historians, in 1959, a journal related to the Braddock Expedition. This journal survived the Braddock Expedition but remained unknown to historians for over 200 years. "It is the only known diary kept throughout the entire expedition in which entries were made at the time of the events described."[136]

Mr. Hamilton acquired the journal in 1958 at a London auction. The journal was described as "A Manuscript Diary of the events of the Campaign of 1755 against the French and the French Indians in America, written by a participant in the fighting." The auctioneer indicated the writer "appears to have been with the regiment commanded by Sir Peter Halkett or with that of Colonel Dunbar, and was possibly attached to Capt. Robert Cholmley."[137] "The Journal of Captain Robert Cholmley's Batman" is usually referred to as the Batman's Journal.

The Batman's Journal gives the following entries: "Tuesday April the 29th. We marched to Chapmans Oardianary, it being Nigh 18 miles." "Wednesday April the 30. We marched to Cunnecoejeg where we Incamped By the River

Portwomack, it being 18 miles and a pleasent Cuntry (BJ, 12)."[138] The term *nigh* means "nearly" or "almost." Thus, Chapmans Oardianary was 17 miles, almost 18, from Frederick Town. The distance to Conococheague from Chapman's was 18 miles.[139] The distances recorded in this journal are similar to those in General Braddock's Orderly Book.

Charles Hamilton confirmed to this author the original journal source stated "Chapmans Oardianary." The author of the Batman's Journal misspelled many words in his journal. Examples include: odared for ordered, indented servants for indentured servants, govener for governor, Widow Billingers for Widow Barringers, Potses Camp for Pott's Camp, etc. The probability a formal name was misspelled in the Batman's Journal is high. Perhaps the stopping place was not Chapmans but similar to Chapmans. Perhaps someone with a last name similar to Chapman lived along the line of march. One name that immediately comes to mind is Chapline.

Perhaps the journalist thought the stopping place was an ordinary, but in fact it was not. General Braddock's Orderly Book indicates the two stopping places from Rock Creek to Frederick were Owen's Ordinary and Dowden's Ordinary.[140] These locations were ordinaries. However, heading west from Frederick Town, civilization soon became very sparse. Since the journalist probably stopped at Owen's and Dowden's ordinaries, perhaps he felt the next stopping place also was an ordinary.

There was a Chapman with Braddock's troops. Major Russel Chapman was appointed major of the 44th, Halkett's Regiment, on March 7, 1751. He was with Halkett's Regiment during the Braddock Expedition. He arrived at Wills's Creek from Winchester on May 21.

The *Oxford English Dictionary* defines *chapman* as: "1. A man whose business is buying and selling; a merchant, trader, dealer. 2. An itinerant dealer who travels about from place to place selling or buying; one who keeps booths at markets, etc.; a hawker, pedlar. 3. An agent in a commercial transaction; a negotiator, broker. 4. A purchaser; a customer." The possibility exists the journalist used the term *chapman* in this context. Governor Sharpe used the term in a letter to Governor Dinwiddie. "Johnson complains that apprehending Gist was empowered to contract for the Government he reserved the

Cattle for him & has neglected & refused every other market or
Chapman whereby he must greatly suffer unless you will be
pleased to direct that the Beasts be accepted & payed for
according to his Agreement."[141]

The Tracey Collection lists several Chapman patent
owners. Three Chapmans, Nath., Luke, and Robert, acquired
land in the Woolery District. These tracts were Nathans Desire,
April 30, 1760; Buck's Forest, February 19, 1749; and Morgans Tent
Resurvey, September 17, 1756. These tracts are not near a possible
line of march. Of course, a Nathaniel Chapman was a member of
the Ohio Company.

The Moses Chapline Sr. property was on the west side of
the South Mountain. What distance was it from Frederick Town?
George Washington indicated Frederick Town was 15 miles
below the Blue Ridge. Undoubtedly he was giving the distance
from Fox's Gap to Frederick Town as 15 miles. It was
approximately two miles from Fox's Gap to the home of Moses
Chapline Sr. The distance from Frederick Town to Moses
Chapline Sr.'s home was very close to 17 miles, perhaps a little
farther. The land owned by Moses Chapline Sr. was along the
road from Frederick Town to Swearingen's Ferry.

Perhaps the journalist referred to Moses Chapline Sr.
when he recorded Chapman. Combining the name and distance
records, this author concludes the stopping place of Dunbar's
Regiment the first night out of Frederick Town was the property
of Moses Chapline Sr. The names of Chapman and Chapline
sound quite similar. The Moses Chapline Sr. property was along
the line of march and was in the 17 to 19 mile range from
Frederick Town. It was on the west side of South Mountain.
Helen Ashe Hays indicated General Braddock visited the home
of Moses Chapline Sr.

Conclusions about The Dunbar Route

Fox's Gap was on the main route between Frederick Town
and Conococheague in 1755. The Orderly Book of General
Braddock identifies the road between Frederick Town and
Conococheague as the "Road to Conococheague." The Vineyard
land tract, surveyed in 1739, identifies the intersection of the

"Conegochieg Road" and the Antietam Creek. This point is at, or near, the Upper Bridge, just northwest of Keedysville. The route was along the present route connecting Keedysville, Bakersville, and Williamsport. Braddock's men built one bridge over the Antietam.

Wagons transported supplies from Rock Creek to Conococheague during the Braddock Expedition. The roads through Fox's and Orr's Gaps both were wagon roads in 1755. These were the only two roads by which wagons could travel from Frederick Town to Conococheague. Crampton's Gap was suitable for horses but not wagons. There is no indication wagons accompanied Dunbar's Regiment to Conococheague. It seems certain, however, Dunbar's Regiment marched to Conococheague by the same route used by the wagons of the Braddock Expedition.

Dunbar's Regiment crossed South Mountain the first day out of Frederick Town. The stopping point, measured either by miles or by time, was half-way between Frederick Town and Conococheague. Chapman's Ordinary, identified in the Batman's Journal, referred to Moses Chapline Sr.'s property about two miles west of Fox's Gap. This was the stopping place for Dunbar's Troops the first day out of Frederick Town.

Accounts of Dunbar's Regiment marching on a road through Turner's or Curry's Gap and along present route 68 through Boonsboro to Williamsport are in error. General Braddock never went through Orr's Gap, nor did Dunbar's troops. The main route between the areas of Frederick and Williamsport never has been by way of Orr's Gap, Stull's Mill, and Hagerstown.

Legislative records, court minutes, and land tract records substantiate the main road from Frederick Town to Ft. Frederick was built after 1755. The road was built in conjunction with Ft. Frederick as a war measure. The land tract record for Worse and Worse eliminates Fox's Gap from possessing the the main road from Frederick Town to Ft. Frederick in 1766. The road crossed South Mountain through Turner's or Curry's Gap. Land tract records for Flonham and Apple Brandy indicate the turnpike road on the near east side of Turner's or Curry's Gap, in the immediate vicinity of the east side of the Mountain House, was not laid down on the bed of the main road from Frederick Town to

Ft. Frederick. Outside the immediate area on the east side of the Mountain House, the turnpike road and the main road from Frederick Town to Ft. Frederick appear to have followed the same roadbed from Middletown to Williamsport.

The following court minutes, cited by Millard M. Rice in *This Was the Life,* seem compelling:

> Sundry inhabitants of the County, who are unnamed, petition the Court that they "conceive a better and nigher road might be made to Fort Frederick for the road to begin out of the road now leading thereto between the Mountains through Curry's Gap by Robert Turner's and by Joseph Holmes, by Dr. Neal's and so into the road by Joseph Volgamot's."[142]

The main road from Frederick Town to Ft. Frederick did not lead out of the old Hagerstown Road through Orr's Gap. Land records, court minutes, and maps indicate the road through Turner's or Curry's Gap (i.e., the main road from Frederick Town to Ft. Frederick) led out of the road through Fox's Gap.

The 1808 Varle Map and an 1840 map in the Historical Society of Carroll County show the juncture of these routes between the Fox Inn and the Catoctin Creek north of Middletown. Court minutes and land records indicate the main road from Frederick Town to Ft. Frederick met the old Sharpsburg Road through Fox's Gap near a tract named Oxford. The juncture of these two roads was near property owned by Casper Shaff and Peter Beaver. It was only after 1840 that the road through Turner's or Curry's Gap met the road through Fox's Gap near the bridge over the Catoctin Creek north of Middletown. The 1791 map of the *Road from Williamsport to Turner's Gap* and the Fox's Last Shift tract of 1762 support the conclusion the main road from Frederick Town to Ft. Frederick came near the west side of the Mountain House at Turner's Gap.

Perhaps the land tract called Fox's Last Shift received its name because it was on the new route from Frederick Town to Ft. Frederick. The new road through Turner's or Curry's Gap replaced the road through Fox's Gap as the route of the main road between Frederick Town and Conococheague. The new route was more direct than the prior route through Fox's Gap and the present areas of Keedysville and the Upper Bridge over the Antietam. The land tract named Fox's Last Shift indicates Fox's Gap was the main route between Frederick Town and Conococheague prior to the completion of the new road through Curry's Gap in the late 1750s. The previous duty seen by Fox's Gap, particularly with respect to the settlers fleeing the Indians, was over.

The is no other Turner for whom to name Turner's Gap, other than Robert, who lived in the mid-1700s in the area now known as Boonsboro. There was no wagon road through Curry's or Turner's Gap in 1755. The road shown on the 1791 map of the *Road from Williamsport to Turner's Gap* is substantially the same road as present State Route 68 from Boonsboro to Williamsport.

Fox's Gap was on the Great Philadephia Wagon Road between Winchester and Philadelphia. This route also was known as the road from Conestoga to Opequon. The routes through Fox's Gap to Conococheague and Shepherdstown were the routes of Dunbar's Regiment and General Braddock, respectively, during the Braddock Expedition. These were the two most significant routes in western Maryland in the early to mid 1700s. Fox's Gap represents a page of American history worthy of preservation.

Ft. Frederick. Photo courtesy of Allan Powell.

Afterword

President Abraham Lincoln issued his Emancipation Proclamation on September 22, 1862, as a result of the Union victories in the Battle of South Mountain and the Battle of Antietam, known as Boonsboro and Sharpsburg in the South, September 14 and 17, 1862.

> . . . he remarked that he had made a vow, a covenant, that if God gave us the victory in the approaching battle, he would consider it an indication of Divine will . . .[1]
>
> Secretary of the Navy, Gideon Welles
> from his notes on the Cabinet meeting
> held September 22, 1862

President Lincoln met with Reverends William W. Patton and John Dempster on September 13, 1862. They presented the president with a memorial in favor of national emancipation:

> The subject presented in the memorial is one upon which I have thought much for weeks past, and I may even say for months . . . I hope it will not be irreverent for me to say that if it is probable that God would reveal his will to others, on a point so connected with my duty, it might be supposed he would reveal it directly to me; for, unless I am more deceived in myself than I often am, it is my earnest desire to know the will of Providence in this matter. *And if I can learn what it is I will do it!* These are not, however, the days of miracles, and I suppose it will be granted that I am not to expect a direct revelation. I must study the plain physical facts of the case, ascertain what is possible and learn what appears to be wise and right. The subject is difficult, and good men

do not agree . . . I admit that slavery is the root of the
rebellion, or at least its *sine qua non* . . . There are fifty
thousand bayonets in the Union armies from the Border
Slave States. It would be a serious matter if, in
consequence of a proclamation such as you desire, they
should go over to the rebels . . . I have not decided
against a proclamation of liberty to the slaves, but hold
the matter under advisement. And I can assure you that
the subject is on my mind, by day and night, more than
any other. *Whatever shall appear to be God's will I will
do.*[2]

President Abraham Lincoln

"The morning of Sunday the 14th - of September was a
bright one."[3]

General Jacob Dolson Cox

Confederate Major General Daniel Harvey Hill viewed
the approaching Union Army from the mountain top. "It was a
grand and glorious spectacle, and it was impossible to look at it
without admiration. I had never seen so tremendous an army
before, and did not see one like it afterwards. For though we
confronted greater forces at Yorktown, Sharpsburg,
Fredericksburg, and about Richmond under Grant, these were only
partly seen, at most a corps at a time. But here four corps were in
full view, one of which was on the mountain and almost within
rifle-range."[4]

"Hill's reconnoissance had revealed that the Federal
left was advancing on the old Sharpsburg, or Braddock Road, a
road parallel to the National Road and passing through Fox's
Gap, about a mile south of Boonsboro Gap."[5] "It was about half-
past seven when Crook's head of column filed off from the
turnpike upon the old Sharpsburg Road, and Scammon had
perhaps half an hour's start. We had fully two miles to go before
we should reach the place where our attack was actually
made."[6]

"When Scammon had got within half a mile of Fox's Gap
(the summit of the old Sharpsburg Road), the enemy opened upon
him with case-shot from the edge of the timber above the open

fields."[7] "The musketry fire, as described to me by officers wounded in the battle was the most continuous and sustained of the war. It rolled rapidly and fiercely from right to left, and back and forward, with irresistable fury."[8]

"It was a lovely September day-an ideal Sunday morning. Our regiment was quickly formed in the woods and charged over rocks and broken ground, through deep underbrush, under heavy fire of the enemy at short range, and after one of the hottest fights of the war, we drove them out of the woods into an open field near the hilltop."[9]

William McKinley

"Our men halted at a fence near the edge of the woods and kept up a brisk fire upon the enemy, who were sheltering themselves behind stone walls and fences near the top of the hill, beyond a cornfield in front of our position. Just as I gave the command to charge I felt a stunning blow and found a musket ball had struck my left arm just above the elbow."[10]

Rutherford Birchard Hayes

U. S. Major General George B. McClellan's Headquarters were between the Fox Inn and the turnpike:[11]

Headq's Army of the Potomac, 3 miles beyond Middletown, September 14, 9:40 P.M.
To Major General H. W. Halleck:
After a very severe engagement, the Corps of Hooker and Reno have carried the heights commanding the Hagerstown road.
The troops behaved magnificently! They never fought better.
Gen. Franklin has been hotly engaged on the extreme left. I do not yet know with what result, except that the firing indicates progress on his part.
The action continued until after dark and terminated in leaving us in possession of the entire crest!
It has been a glorious victory!

I cannot tell yet whether the enemy will retreat during the night or appear in increased force in the morning.

I regret to add that the gallant and able General Reno is killed.

G. B. McClellan. Major General.[12]

"I now consider it safe to say that Gen. McClellan has gained a great victory over the great rebel army in Maryland between Fredericktown and Hagerstown. He is now pursuing the flying foe."

President Lincoln to Col. Jesse K. Dubois
in Springfield, Illinois, 3 p.m., September 15

"Your despatch to Col. Dubois has filled our people with the wildest joy. Salutes are being fired & our citizens are relieved from a fearful state of suspense. We thank you for the welcome news."

Illinois Governor Richard Yates

"Such a picture of killed and wounded as the view presented next day was rarely seen during the whole war. This may be accounted for by the circumstances that both sides charged at the same time, and clashed together their intermingled host with about equal bravery for some minutes, until the stubborn Confederates gave way."[13] "In some parts of the field the enemy's dead lay in heaps and in a road for nearly a quarter of a mile they lay so thick that I had to pick my way carefully to avoid stepping on them."[14] "In the wooded slope of the mountain west of the gap, a good many of the confederate dead still lay where they had fallen in the fierce combats for the possession of the crest near Wise's house."[15]

After the Battle of South Mountain, the roads through Fox's and Turner's Gaps led the Confederate and Union Armies to the banks of the Antietam Creek and the village of Sharpsburg. September 17, 1862, became the single bloodiest day in American history.

"In the course of the discussion on this paper (Emancipation Proclamation), which was long, earnest, and, on the general principle involved, harmonious, he remarked that he had made a vow, a covenant, that if God gave us the victory in the approaching battle, he would consider it an indication of Divine will, and that it was his duty to move forward in the cause of emancipation. It might be thought strange, he said, that he had in this way submitted the disposal of matters when the way was not clear to his mind what he should do. God had decided this question in favor of the slaves. He was satisfied it was right, was confirmed and strengthened in his action by the vow and the results. His mind was fixed, his decison made, but he wished his paper announcing his course as correct in terms as i t could be made without any change in his determination."[16]

> Secretary of the Navy, Gideon Welles
> from his notes on the Cabinet meeting
> held September 22, 1862

". . . That on the first day of January, in the year of our Lord one thousand eight hundred and sixty-three, all persons held as slaves within any State or designated part of a State, the people whereof shall then be in rebellion against the United States, shall be then, thenceforward, and forever free . . ."[17]

> President Abraham Lincoln
> preliminary Emancipation Proclamation [18]
> September 22, 1862

On the evening of September 24, President Lincoln appeared before his fellow citizens outside the White House to acknowledge their support for the issuance of his Emancipation Proclamation.

"On the 14th and 17th days of the present month there have been battles bravely, skillfully and successfully fought. W e do not yet know the particulars. Let us be sure that in giving praise to particular individuals, we do no injustice to others. I only ask you, at the conclusion of these few remarks, to give three hearty cheers to all good and brave officers and men who fought those successful battles."[19]

"On the first day of October his Excellency the President honored the Army of the Potomac with a visit, and remained several days, during which he went through the different encampments, reviewed the troops, and went over the battle-fields of South Mountain and Antietam . . . During the visit we had many and long consultations alone. We parted on the field of South Mountain, whither I had accompanied him . . ."[20]

Figures given by Mathew Brady for the Battle of South Mountain.

U.S.: 1806 wounded, 443 killed, 0 captured, 0 missing
Confederate: 2343 wounded, 500 killed, 1500 captured

Appendix A

Maps

The following maps appear in this book or in other sources given below:

Post Map of New England, New York, New Jersey, and Pennsylvania, by Moll, dated 1730. It is probably the Monocacy Road that is shown on the map as the "Great Philadelphia Wagon Road." This map supports, in Pennsylvania to the Maryland line, the road from Conestoga to Opequon through Fox's Gap. This road also was known as the Great Philadelphia Wagon Road (to Winchester via Fox's Gap in Maryland). It was not the same road as the Great Wagon Road to Philadelphia (from Winchester through Conococheague).

Winslows Map of 1736. "Messrs. Wm. May, Robert Brook, --- Winslow, and --- Savage appointed surveyors in 1736. The party which performed this work consisted of the four surveyors with thirteen assistants, six of them chain-carriers, employed at three shillings per day. Among the names employed to describe features of Maryland territory may be noticed the following variations from present usage: Monokasy [Monocacy], Kittokton [Catoctin], Conigochego [Conococheague]."[1]

The "Mayo" Map of 1736-7. See Winslows Map of 1736.

Fry and Jefferson Map of 1751, 1755, and 1775. "The most important map of the Middle British Colonies published during the second half of the eighteenth century was the result of the joint labors of Professor Joshua Fry and Mr. Peter Jefferson. It is probable that the information represented on the map indicates the highest degree of knowledge of the country attainable at that time. The map apparently was completed in the year 1749, although it is dated 1751. The Maryland portion of the sheet does not adequately represent the high character of the map, since there is little indicated besides names and a few roads on the Maryland portion, while Virginia streams and roads are carefully delineated with their names attached. The roads are only such as were main thoroughfares connecting different portions of Virginia with Philadelphia."[2] Library of Congress: Fry, Joshua. A map of the inhabited part of Virginia . . . G3880 1751 .F7 (Negative No. 2802) [1755 ed].

Lewis Evans. See Henry M. Stevens, *Lewis Evans, His Map of the British Middle Colonies in America, A Comparative Account of 18 Different Editions Published between 1755 and 1814* (London: n.p., 1920). Also see Walter Klinefelter, *Lewis Evans and His Maps* (Philadelphia: American Philosophical Society, 1971).

Col. Thomas Cresap's Map of the Sources of the Potomac. June, 1754. This map appears in the Archives of Maryland, *Correspondence of Gov. Horatio Sharpe*, 6:72. The map shows "Conegocheig" along the course of the Potomac River.

Road from Elizabethtown [Hagerstown] to Newcomber's Mill and Frederick County Line. April 5, 1791. Maryland State Archives, Special Collections. MdHR G 1427 508 Maps.

Road from Swearingen's Ferry on the Potomac River Through Sharpsburg to the Top of the South Mountain at Fox's Gap. August 23, 1792. This map was recorded at one time in Washingon County Land Records, G, p. 867. Maryland State Archives, Special Collections. MdHR G 1427 507, B5-1-3.

Road from Williamsport to Turner's Gap in South Mountain. Recorded October 17, 1791. This map was recorded at one time in Washington County Land Records, G, p. 533. Maryland State Archives, Special Collections. MdHR G 1427 504, B5-1-3.

1794 Dennis Griffith Map of Maryland. Drawn by Dennis Griffith, a Philadelphian, and copyrighted June 20, 1794. "Map of the State of Maryland Laid down from an actual Survey of all the principal Waters, public Roads, and Divisions of the Counties therein; describing the Situation of the Cities, Towns, Villages, Houses of Worship and other public Buildings, Furnaces, Forges, Mills, and other remarkable Places."[3] Library of Congress: [G3840 1794.G72 Vault] Scale a:308,000. size 134 x 79 1/2 cm.

1808 Varle Map. The map shows Braddock's Gap at the location where today Interstate 70 and Main Route 40 pass over South Mountain. The map shows the name *Ringer* at the location of the Fox Inn. Library of Congress: A map of Frederick and Washington Counties, State of Maryland. 1808, by Charles Varle; engraved, Francis Shallus, Phila. G3843.F7 1808 .V3 1983. 84-691291.

1809 Map of Frederick, Berkeley, and Jefferson Counties in the state of Virginia. Executed AD 1809 by Charles Varle Engineer & Geographer. Engraved by Benjamin Jones Philadelphia. Berkeley County Historical Society.

Bond Map. Frederick County, Maryland. Prepared under the direction of Lieut. Col. J. N. Macomb, Chf. Topl. Engr. for the use of Maj. Gen. G. B. McClellan, Commanding US Army. Drawn from I. Bond's map by E. Hergesheimer. Based on Isaac Bond's map of Frederick County, Maryland, published 1858. Library of Congress G3843 .F7 1861 .H4

Battle-Fields of South Mountain. South Mountain, Md. September 14, 1862. *The Official Military Atlas of the Civil War*, Plate XXVII, 3. This map accompanies the report of Maj. Gen. Geo. B. McClellan, U.S. Army. See the *Official Records, Series 1*, Vol. XIX, Part 1, page 36. This map shows the old Sharpsburg Road from the "forks of the roads" at the Catoctin Creek to Moses Chapline Sr.'s homestead, indicated as "G. Shiffler" on the map.

Antietam. *The Official Military Atlas of the Civil War,* Plate XXIX, 2. Prepared by Bvt. Brig. Gen. N. Michler, Major of Engineers. Compiled and drawn by Major F. Weyss. Assisted by F. Theilkuhl, J. Strass, and G. Thompson. This map shows the old Sharpsburg Road from Moses Chapline Sr.'s homestead, indicated as "G. Shiffler" on the map, through Springvale, Porterstown, the square in Sharpsburg, and on to Shepherdstown.

Map of the Battle-Fields of Harper's Ferry and Antietam. September 13 to 17, 1862. *The Official Military Atlas of the Civil War,* Plate XXIX, 1. Prepared by S. Howell Brown, 1st Lt. Engineer Troops. This map shows the old Sharpsburg Road from Shepherdstown and Swearingen's Ferry on the Potomac through Sharpsburg, Porterstown, and east towards Fox's Gap.

200th Anniversary of Washington's Birthday - 1932. This map shows the routes traveled by George Washington in Maryland. Prepared for the Maryland Commision for the 200th Anniversary of George Washington's Birthday. This map is incorrect. It shows George Washington leading Braddock's troops to Williamsport. It does not indicate he visited Shepherdstown or the Fox Inn. [MdHR G 1427 528].

Monocacy Roads in Maryland. Maryland Archives Accession Number MSA G1427-1150 B5-2-1. The source of this map is listed as anonymous. The map is an attempt by the mapmaker to portray the "Monocacy" roads in Maryland.

Map accompanying the agreement between Lord Baltimore and T. & R. Penn. Pennsylvania Archives, 1760-1766, Volume 4.

The Johns Hopkins University Library in Baltimore has a special collection of early Maryland maps.

Appendix B

Photos

The following pictures appear in this book or in other sources as given below:

Society of Colonial Wars and Maryland Historical Society Marker. General Edward Braddock. This marker is near the front of the Maryland State Police Barrack B in Frederick on Route 40 (Patrick Street). Photo by Allan Powell.

Maryland Bicentennial Commission and Maryland Historical Society Marker. Swearingen's Ferry and Pack Horse Ford. This marker is at the Rumsey Bridge on the Potomac River at Shepherdstown. Photo by Susanne Flowers.

The Main Street of Sharpsburg, Maryland. September 1862, by Alexander Gardner. This photo appears in William A. Frassanito, *Antietam: The Photographic Legacy of America's Bloodiest Day* (New York: Scribner's, 1978), page 264.

State Roads Commission Marker. General Edward Braddock. This marker is on the square in Sharpsburg. Photo by Susanne Flowers.

The Orndorff (or Middle) Bridge on the Antietam. September 1862, by Alexander Gardner. This photo appears in William A. Frassanito, *Antietam: The Photographic Legacy of America's Bloodiest Day* (New York: Scribner's, 1978), page 83.

The Orndorff (or Middle) Bridge on the Antietam. Photo in 1972 by William Frassinito. This photo appears in William A. Frassanito, *Antietam: The Photographic Legacy of America's Bloodiest Day* (New York: Scribner's, 1978), page 83.

The Wise House on the old Sharpsburg Road at Fox's Gap. This photo appears in many Civil War books, including Ronald H. Bailey and the Editors of Time-Life Books, *The Bloodiest Day, The Battle of Antietam* (Alexandria, Va.: Time-Life Books, 1984), page 50.

Fox's Gap - The Approach to Wise's Field and Fox's Gap - Wise's Field as seen from the Pasture North of the Road. These drawings appear in *Battles and Leaders of the Civil War*, the Grant and Lee Edition. The two sketches were made from photographs in 1885. The editor's note indicates, "The old Sharpsburg or Braddock Road lies between the stone wall and the rail fence."

The Fox Inn. Photo in 1992 by Susan Flowers.

The Boulder at Braddock Spring. This photo appeared in *The News*, Frederick, Md., Saturday, March 12, 1973.

The Frederick Cabin Used by George Washington. This photo is as the Maryland Historical Society and appeared in *The News*, Frederick, Md., Saturday, March 12, 1973.

Appendix C

Land Tract Analysis

The Reno Monument

From Frederick Fox to the United States Government
Tract Name - Addition to Friendship

Reference	Date	Grantee of Deed
IC #P 672-3	5-9-1797	Frederick Fox - Addition to Friendship[1] - 202 acres
WR-32-26/8	9-21-1807	Joseph Swearingen from Frederick Fox - 202 acres of Addition to Friendship and 30 acres of Fredericksburg
WR-34-315	8-20-1808	Peter Ludy from Joseph Swearingen - part of Addition to Friendship and Fredericksburg - 58 acres
WR-42-550	7-9-1812	Jacob Routzong from Peter Ludy - part of Addition to Friendship and Fredericksburg - 68 acres[2]
JS-30-58/61	2-22-1828	Jacob Routzong to George Routzong - part of Addition to Friendship and Fredericksburg - 68 acres[3]
JS-38-194	2-18-1832	Henry Miller from Sheriff Peter Brengle - Writ of the state of Maryland of Fieri Facia issued out of the County Court in Frederick Town against Jacob Routzah[4] - 68 acres

Reference	Date	Grantee of Deed
Will-Henry Miller[5]	Date of Death	Estate of Henry Miller - 68 acres
Beneficiearies	Death of H. Miller	Estate of Henry Miller - 10 1/2 acres
Unknown	5-7-1844	Joel Keller from Susan Miller et al.[6] - 10 1/2 acres
BGF-6-216	5-7-1858	John and Matilda Wise from Joel Keller - 4 and 3/4 acres
WIP-9-149	6-9-1879	Jonas Gross from John W. Wise - 4 and 3/4 acres
WIP 11 fol. 8, 9, 10	11-23-1889	Trustees, Society of the Burnside Expedition from Jonas Gross[7] - 40 feet square
DHH-3-316	9-11-1898	United States Government - 40 feet square

Fredericksburg Deeds Related to Preceeding Transfers

Reference	Date	Grantee of Deed
HGO-1-564/5	6-11-1792	Frederick Fox - survey of Fredericksburg - 75 acres
WR-17-158/9	4-21-1798	George Methard from Frederick Fox - 10 acres
WR-31-478	9-12-1807	William Bottenberg from George Methard - 10 acres
WR-34-313	2-11-1809	Peter Ludy from William Bottenberg - 10 acres

The Wise Tract, upon which stands the Reno Monument, is contiguous to a 13 1/2 acre tract on the north side of the road, transferred from Susan Miller to John Miller, consisting of ten acres of Bowser's Addition and three and one-half acres Addition to Friendship.

The Fox Inn

From Daniel Dulany Sr. (1742) to Helen Rudy (1995)
Tract Name - The Exchange

(Note - The 1808 Varle Map identifies the Fox Inn by the name "Ringer")

Reference	Date	Grantee of Deed	Acres
MSA BC & GS #1, 177	10-5-1742	Daniel Dulany Esqr. - The Exchange - survey	100^8
MSA BY & GS #1, 177	4-29-1749	assignment to Robert Evans - The Exchange	100^9
MSA BY & GS #1, 177	5-20-1749	assignment to Joseph Chapline [Sr.] - The Exchange	100
FCLR, E-339	12-11-1753	Casper Shaff - The Exchange	75
MSA BY & GS 4, 585-6	5-9-1754	Joseph Chapline [Sr.] - Casper Shaff[11]	275^{10}
MSA BC & GS #27, 578	9-29-1765	Daniel [Jr.] and Walter Dulany - patent Resurvey on Exchange	100
K-1373	7-9--1767	Valentine Fidler Fidler's Purchase	150^{12}
Probably inherited from his father.		George Fidler	150^{13}
WR-7-48	11-8-1786	Ludwick Layman	100^{14}
WR-12-56	11-14-1793	Peter Layman	100^{15}
WR-27-543	10-7-1805	George Fox	100^{16}
WR-32-30	1807	John Ringer	100^{17}
JS-42-481	5-15-1833	Vincent Sanner	75^{18}
CM-1-582	4-14-1868	Samuel Ausherman[19]	194+
TG-3-298	5-10-1875	Eli Routzahn	192+
AF-9-90	4-2-1884	Simon D. Routzahn	192+
AF-9-91	4-2-1884	John H. Routzahn	192+
324/321	4-3-1918	Stanley J. Young	175+
388/316	8-21-1933	H. Noel Haller	175+
388/317	8-21-1933	Stanley F. Young	175+

Reference	Date	Grantee of Deed	Acres
605/469	9-25-1958	Richard & Helen Rudy[20]	173+

The Road from Swearingen's Ferry to Fox's Gap

Maryland State Archives, Special Collections (MSA Map Collection) 507 "Road from Swearingen's Ferry on the Potomac River through Sharpsburg to the top of the South Mountain at Fox's Gap." [MSA G1427-507, B5-1-3]

The old road shown by plain lines and is the distance of 11 1/4 miles - 56 pchs.

The alternations made by the commissioners is shown by dotted lines, and the road by them laid out is represented by lines numbered from 1 to 41 Difference 71 perches.

Note: The courses and boundaries above mentioned are to be taken for the middle of the road.

Washington County Sect.

By virtue of dower invested in an act of the assembly for the purpose we hereby certify that we laid out the road from Swearingen's Ferry on Potomac River through Sharpsburg to the top of the South Mountain in Fox's Gap agreeable to the courses and distances above expressed = As witness our hands and seals this 13th day of August 1792.

> William Good   (seal)
> Jacob   (seal)
> Christopher   (seal)

Beginning at the bank of the Potomac River at the said Ferry and running:

Crse No.	North South	Degrees East or West	Length
1	N	80 East	12 ps opposite the ferry house
2	S	49 East	56 ps to a post
3	S	62 East	62 ps to a post
4	N	44 East	43 ps to a marked poplar

Crse No.	North South	Degrees East or West	Length
5	N	62 East	264 ps to a marked white oak sapling
6	N	41 1/2 East	360 ps to a bounded white oak tree
7	N	69 1/2 East	320 ps to the square in Sharpsburg - still continuing the course
8	N	69 1/2 East	110 ps to a post
9	N	60 East	64 ps to a marked locust sapling
10	N	69 1/2 East	112 ps to a marked hickory sapling
11	S	76 East	20 ps to a marked white oak tree
12	N	65 East	84 ps to a marked apple tree
13	N	85 East	16 ps
14	S	54 East	14 ps to Orendorff's Bridge
15	S	77 East	8 ps
16	N	19 East	23 ps
17	N	3 West	26 ps to a bounded black oak
18	N	73 East	40 ps to a post
19	S	85 East	76 ps to a bounded Spanish oak
20	S	88 East	68 ps to a post
21	N	58 East	260 ps to a bounded black oak sapling
22	N	16 East	74 ps to a post
23	N	35 East	54 ps to a marked red oak & locust sapling
24	S	73 East	72 ps to a post
25	N	83 1/2 East	120 ps to a walnut tree at Conrad Snavely's house
26	S	89 1/2 East	161 ps to a bounded black oak sapling
27	S	66 1/2 East	170 ps to a post near a marked black oak sapling
28	S	74 East	71 ps to a post
29	S	85 East	84 ps to a post

Crse No.	North South	Degrees East or West	Length
30	N	69 East	62 ps to a post
31		E - - - - - - - - - -	324 perches to interesect the old road near top of Domer's Hill
32	S	69 1/2 East	30 ps along the old road
33	N	83 East	20 ps
34	S	86 1/2 East	54 ps
35	S	28 East	20 ps
36	S	84 East	50 ps
37	N	77 East	22 ps
38	N	5 1/2 East	44 ps
39	[estimate -	not given on the map - South 81 East 40-45 ps]	
40[21]	S	44 East	70 ps
41	N	60 East	41 perches to a stone set up in the road on the top of the mountain at the county line.

Two drawings of the road appear on this map, representing two measurement scales. The uppermost drawing is shown with the following indication: Scale 100P. The lower drawing is shown with the following indication: Scale 1/62,500 topographical map size.

The map identifies the following points along the road: Swearingen's Ferry on the Potomac River (starting point); the square in Sharpsburg (end of line 7); Orendorff's Bridge over the Antietam (end of line 15); Smith's shop (end of line 20); Jacob Russell (end of line 21); top of Red Hill (end of line 23); Conrad Snavely (end of line 25); Samuel Baker's (end of line 26); old road near top of Tomer's (or Domer's) Hill (line 31); Andrew Bash (end of line 36); top of the South Mountain at Fox's Gap (end of line 41)

The Vicinity of The Mountain House at Turner's Gap

Philip Jacob Shafer (1770) to Russell and Judy Schwartz (1995) - Tract Name - Flonham

Reference	Date	Grantee of Deed	Acres
BC & GS #47, pp. 496-497	6-15-1767	Philip Jacob Shafer[22] - Patent for Flonham	36

The following tracts are across the road from the Mountain House and include part of the ten acres around the Chapel:

Reference	Date	Grantee of Deed	Acres
FCLR, JS-25-372	1826-1827	Henry Miller - Flonham	5
WCLR, IN-9-595	5-25-1855	Edward L. Boteler[23]	58 1/8
WCLR, LBN-2-133	5-14-1867	George F. Smith[24]	60
WCLR, 74-264	4-19-1876	Madeleine V. Dahlgren[25]	60
Liber J. K. W. No. 2 fol. 304	11-30-1890	Ulrica Dahlgren Pierce[26]	60
WCLR, 163-294	5-31-1922	St. Mary's Academy[27]	60
WCLR, 172-524	9-28-1925	Charles M. Hewitt et ux[28]	60

The following deeds include the land on which the Mountain House stands:

Reference	Date	Grantee of Deed	Acres
WCLR, 227-454	9-18-1944	E. Stuart Bushong, Trustee	177
WCLR, 227-455	9-18-1944	Charles M. & Edna E. Hewitt	177
WCLR, 330-475	12-2-1957	Mitchell H. Dodson et ux[29]	3.7
WCLR, 527-627	7-19-1971	Charles F. Reichmuth et ux[30]	3.7
WCLR, 788-755	7-12-1985	Russell L. Schwartz et ux[31]	3.7

The Ten Acres Surrounding the Chapel at Turner's Gap
(Across the road from the Mountain House)

(from Addition to Friendship of Frederick Fox to the heirs of
Henry Miller)

Reference	Date	Grantee of Deed	Acres
MA IC #P 672-327	5-1805	Frederick Fox[32]	
		(Patent)	202
FCLR, WR-32-26/8	10-7-1807	Joseph Swearingen[33]	202
Will of Joseph	Date of Death	Heirs of Joseph	189 1/2
Swearingen	of Joseph	Swearingen[34]	
	Swearingen		
FCLR, JS-39-260/4	4-5-1832	George Baltzell[35]	189 1/2
FCLR, JS-39-264/8	5-31-1832	Henry Miller[36]	189 1/2
None[37]	Date of Death	Heirs at law of	
	of H. Miller	Henry Miller	189 1/2
Also see:			
WCLR, LBN-2-133	5-14-1867	George F. Smith[38]	60

According to FCLR, JS-39-264/8, George Baltzell, Atty, to Henry
Miller, recorded July 5, 1832, there were two portions of Addition
to Friendship transferred to Henry Miller from George Baltzell.
The first portion, consisting of 75 1/2 acres, was south of the
turnpike and the second portion, consisting of 114 acres was north
of the turnpike.

The Road from Williamsport to Turner's Gap in the South Mountain

Special Collections (Maps) No. 504 Road from Williamsport to Turner's Gap, 1791 [MdHR 1427-504, B5-1-3]

Persuant to an act entitled an act to straighten and amend the several roads, recorded October 17th 1791 to wit.

The plat and courses of the road leading from Williamsport to Turner's Gap in the South Mountain. Beginning for the said road at the south end of Artisans Street at Williamsport and running thence through Otho Holland Williams' land.

Line No.	North South	Degrees East or West	Length
1	S	5 East	15 perches
2	S	60 East	135
3	S	56 East	170
4	S	69 East	198 through Ringold's Manor
5	N	86 East	60
6	S	85 East	66
7	S	58 East	232 to the mouth of Ringold's Quarter Lane then through said plantation
8	S	50 East	506
9	S	42 East	315 to Iagnatious Simms his house
10	S	68 East	16
11	S	52 East	50
12	S	61 East	34
13	S	60 East	74
14	S	52 East	96
15	S	58 East	236
16	S	15 East	40
17	S	45 East	40 ps to Booth's Bridge on Antietam Creek
18	S	6 East	24
19	S	62 West	44

Line No.	North South	Degrees East or West	Length
20	S	52 East	22
21	S	72 East	44 to Beaver Creek
22	S	68 East	64
23	S	72 East	86
24	S	78 1/2 East	168 through Michael Taylor's land
25	S	58 East	96
26	S	45 East	74 through John Ringer's Land
27	S	72 East	48
28	S	78 East	122
29	S	40 East	32
30	S	53 East	26
31	S	59 East	28
32	S	49 East	54
33	S	70 East	72 through Scott's land
34	S	41 East	146
35	S	31 East	96
36	S	29 East	80
37	S	20 East	140 through Boon's land
38	S	9 East	100
39	S	35 East	66 to Booke's tavern and from thence through Aulabaugh's land and Summer's land
40	S	53 East	322 into the old road in Turner's Gap then up through the gap
41	S	58 East	14
42	S	32 East	22
43	S	54 East	20
44	S	57 East	68
45	S	86 East	48
46	S	70 East	128 ps to where it is supposed to intersect Frederick County line on the top of the mountain

Explanation   miles
Red line shows the straight course   13 & 27 ps
dotted line shows the new road and measures   14 miles

black lines show the old road measures 14 1/2 & 40 ps
new road shows and measures one half miles short & forty
perches

by a scale of 100 equal perches in the inch.

Commissioners

Wm VanLear   (seal)

Jonas Hogmire (seal)

Conrad Nicodemus (seal)

[The map also identifies the intersection of the road from
Williamsport to Turner's Gap and the road from Funkstown to
the gap. It also shows the road from Shafer's Mill to Turner's
Gap.]

Appendix D

The Fox Inn

Frederick Fox was an innkeeper, according to Daniel G. Fox, author of *The Fox Geneaology*.[1] Byron Williams, in *The Old South Mountain Inn, An Informal History*, quotes Lemoine Cree:

> Cree, in *A Brief History of South Mountain House*, identifies Jacob Young as an innkeeper, mentions "transactions" between Young and a Frederick Fox (also identified as an innkeeper) and records that in 1790, Frederick Fox "bought and 'possessed by special warrant' the land upon which the tavern now stands." Cree also states, on the basis of facts "gleaned from patents at the Land Office, Annapolis, Md.," that "it is certain that the tavern had been built by 1790." We do not dispute Cree's evidence; unfortunately, we have not been able to verify it independently.[2]

Ohio D.A.R. records describe Frederick Fox as a tavern owner.[3]

Land tract analysis by this author indicates Frederick Fox never owned the tract upon which stands the current building known as the Fox Inn. The present building known as the Fox Inn stands on The Exchange, surveyed for Daniel Dulany Sr. in 1742. George Fox, the oldest son of Frederick Fox, acquired the 100 acres of land from Peter Layman in 1805. George Fox was only 24 years old when he bought the land. Perhaps he received the money, £1800, from his father, Frederick, in order to start his own inn and continue in the tavern business like his father.

Daniel G. Fox talked with Judge Castle, who lived and grew up a quarter mile west of the building known today as the Fox Inn. A deed from Henry Derr to Daniel Castle for five acres began at the beginning tree of Betty's Good Will. This is consistent with the Civil War battlefield map of South Mountain that places a Daniel Castle about 1/4 mile west of the Fox Inn. It certainly seems the present Fox Inn along the old Sharpsburg Road has been known by that name since the time JudgeCastle grew up in the area. Why the name would last for such a long time when a member of the Fox family owned the building for only two years seems strange. Perhaps Frederick Fox ran the tavern but did not own it.

Daniel G. Fox indicates the Fox Inn was built on a tract named Turkeyfoot.[4] This is incorrect. Perhaps Daniel G. Fox had some other source of information, unknown to this author, regarding the location of the inn owned by Frederick Fox. Perhaps there was at one time an inn owned by Frederick Fox on the Turkeyfoot tract. The Turkeyfoot tract is contiguous on three sides to a tract called Mt. Pleasant.[5] Both of these tracts were patented by Frederick Fox and are just north of Betty's Good Will.

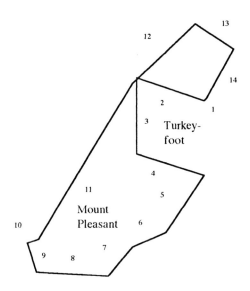

It would be easy to confuse the land transfers related to the Fox Inn property, especially if the tracts were not plotted on paper. Both Frederick Fox and his son George transfered land to

John Ringer in 1807.[6] It would be natural to think the Fox Inn was owned by Frederick, not his son George.

Cree is incorrect when he identifies Frederick Fox as the owner of the Mountain House at Turner's Gap. It is understandable how Cree concluded Frederick Fox owned the Mountain House, since Frederick Fox owned most of the ten acres surrounding the Chapel across the turnpike from the Mountain House. Both Daniel G. Fox and Lemoine Cree are very close to being correct in their analysis. However, they are both incorrect regarding what they say Frederick Fox owned.

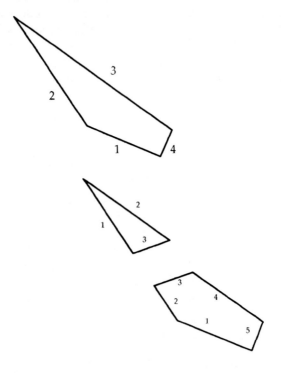

Shown above are: 1) The Exchange of Daniel Dulany Sr., surveyed October 5, 1742, 100 acres;[7] 2) Jacob Smith Sr. to Jacob Smith Jr., February 10, 1795, Exchange, 30 1/2 acres;[8] and 3) Exchange, Joseph Chapline Sr. to Casper Shaff, recorded December 11, 1753.[9] Tracts two and three, when joined, are identical to tract one.

Tracey and Dern indicate a tract named Exchange, patented to Daniel [Jr.] and Walter Dulaney in 1765, is in the area of the Fox Inn.[10] This tract was "by the side of a spring called Punch Spring it being a draught of Abrams Creek." The original survey was for Daniel Dulaney Esqr. in 1742. Daniel Sr. "assigned set over and transferred unto the said Robert Evans a tract of land called The Exchange containing one hundred acres," April 19, 1749. Robert Evans, for a valuable consideration, "received from Joseph Chapline of Frederick County have assigned set over and transferred unto the said Joseph Chapline a tract of land called The Exchange containing one hundred acres which was assigned me by Daniel Dulany Esqr."

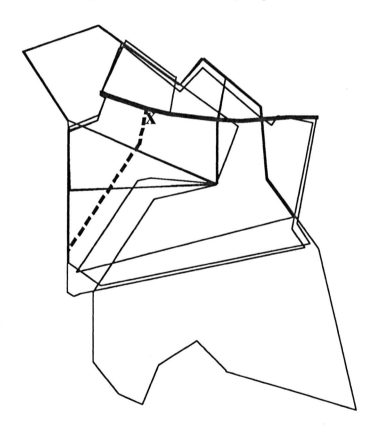

Daniel [Jr.] and Walter Dulaney were the "executors of the last Will and Testament of Daniel Dulany Esqr." They received the patent for The Exchange on September 29, 1765, originally surveyed October 5, 1742, in the amount of 100 acres for Daniel Dulany Sr.[11]

The diagram on the preceeding page is an overlay of the four tracts on the following page, as well as, 1) The Exchange, assigned by Daniel Dulany Sr. to Robert Evans and acquired in 1749 by Joseph Chapline Sr. (shown previously), and 2) the transfer from Stanley F. Young to Richard and Helen Rudy in 1958. The location of the Fox Inn, at the intersection of Marker Road and Reno Monument Road, is marked by an **X**. The solid, heavy black line represents the old Sharpsburg Road. The dotted line represents the road to Burkittsville.

Robert Evans also patented a tract named Exchange.[12] The patent states, "beginning at a bounded Red Oak standing by the head of a little spring a draft of Kitockton Creek." This tract had 11 courses and has not been located by the author.

There is an 1802 transfer from Joseph Chapline Jr. to Frederick Fox for 25 acres of a tract named Exchange "which was conveyed the said Joseph Chapline [Jr.] by a certain Jacob Smith by a deed bearing date on or about the thirteenth day of January Eighteen hundred and two".[13] This transfer was for the same tract as the 1795 transfer from Jacob Smith Sr. to Jacob Smith Jr. The tract appears to run afoul of Betty's Good Will.

A court case in the Chancery Records for Frederick County concerns the triangular portion of The Exchange tract.[14] Joseph Chapline Jr. sued William Williams Chapline and Jacob Smith for control of the tract. The case ran from 1791 until 1801 when the court decided in favor of Joseph Chapline Jr. The court records mention Frederick Fox.

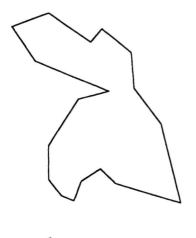

Resurvey on Exchange -
Casper Shaff

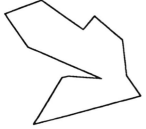

Fidler's Purchase - Casper
Shaff to Valentine Fidler

George Fidler to Ludwick
Layman; Peter Layman to
George Fox; and George Fox
to John Ringer

John Ringer to Vincent
Sanner

Appendix E

Research Sources

Mr. Doug Bast
Boonsborough Museum of
History
Boonsboro, Maryland

Catoctin Press
709 East Main Street
Middletown, Maryland

Charlotte Public Library
310 North Tryon Street
Charlotte, North Carolina

Davidson College Library
Davidson, North Carolina

Susanne F. Flowers
9144 Bethel Road
Frederick, Maryland

Robert H. Fox
3516 St. Charles Place
Cincinnati, Ohio

Frederick County Hist. Society
24 East Church Street
Frederick, Maryland

Gaston County Library
1555 East Garrison Blvd.
Gastonia, North Carolina

Hist. Society of Carroll County
210 East Main Street
Westminster, Maryland

Library of Congress
101 Independence Avenue
Washington, D. C.

Maryland Hall of Records
Maryland State Archives
350 Rowe Boulevard
Annapolis, Maryland

Maryland Historical Society
201 W. Monument St.
Baltimore, Maryland

Maryland State Law Library
361 Rowe Boulevard
Annapolis, Maryland

Potomac Appalachian Trail
Club
118 Park Street, Southeast
Vienna, Virginia

Washington County Hist.
Society
135 West Washington
Hagerstown, Maryland

Appendix F

Biographical Listing

(Unless otherwise noted, the following material is from the *Dictionary of American Biography,* edited by Allen Johnson and Dumas Malone, (New York: Charles Scribner's Sons, 1927).)

Booker, Bartholomew (Probably born in 1720. Died in 1791 or 1792.),[1] was age "71 years or thereabouts" on December 26, 1790.[2] Bartholomew and Peter Booker arrived in Philadelphia, September 3, 1739, on the Loyal Judith from Rotterdam.[3] Robert H. Fox of Cincinnati indicates the first land record for Bartholomew was August 1748 for 100 acres of land in Lancaster [now Franklin] county, Pennsylvania. Bartholomew married Margaret. They were the parents of 14 children. Bartholomew arrived in the Fox's Gap area by 1754, when he acquired a tract named Mendall (Mindall) from Joseph Chapline Sr. Bartholomew owned Pickall, patented February 22, 1764, a tract stretching from the forks of the roads at the Catoctin Creek just north of Middletown all the way to Orr's and Fox's Gaps. Bartholomew was the father-in-law of Frederick Fox. According to Robert H. Fox of Cincinnati, Ohio, a desk of Bartholomew Booker passed to his widow, Margaret, and then to Frederick Fox. Robert viewed the desk in the 1930s when he visited Daniel Gebhart Fox, author of *The Fox Genealogy,* who owned the desk at that time. Margaret Booker died in 1796.[4]

Boone, Daniel (Nov. 2, n.s., 1734 - Sept. 26, 1820), pioneer, Indian fighter, was born about eleven miles from Reading, Pa., the son of Squire and Sarah Morgan Boone. In the spring of 1750 most of the Boones started for North Carolina and arrived at Buffalo Lick, on the north fork of the Yadkin, in 1751.

Married Rebeccah Bryan, the seventeen-year-old daughter of a neighbor, on August 14, 1756. On April 1, 1775 he reached what was to become Boonesborough, Kentucky, where he at once began the erection of a fort. The seven stanzas that Lord Byron devoted to him in the eighth canto of Don Juan (1823) made him a world-wide celebrity, and he gradually became the one overshadowing figure of the frontier.

Braddock, Edward   (1695 - July 13, 1755), British general, entered the army in 1710 as ensign in the Coldstream Guards, the regiment of his father, Major-General Edward Braddock. Forty-three years' continuous service in one of the haughtiest regiments in the British army produced a man who was the sternest of disciplinarians, often brutal in dealing with civilians, and poor in purse, the butt of Fielding's satire and Walpole's wit. Selected by Cumberland to proceed to North America as commander-in-chief of all His Majesty's forces raised or to be raised there.

Carlyle, John "Of Scottish birth and immigrated to America early in life where he at once became a merchant on the Potomac. He was married twice, once to Sarah Fairfax, a daughter of William Fairfax. Before 1745 he was a merchant in Alexandria. It was in this town in a large stone house that he entertained Braddock in 1755. In 1754 Lieutenant-governor Dinwiddie appointed Carlyle to the position of commissary of provisions and stores for the Ohio expedition of that year.[5] Carlyle was a very close friend of Washington and with members of his family frequently visited at Mount Vernon. His connection with the Ohio company was brief as he withdrew in June, 1749, although he always remained friendly with its members."[6]

Carroll, Charles The name Charles Carroll is famous in Maryland History. An article by Calvin E. Schildknecht identifies eight Charles Carrolls of record in Maryland.[7]

The first Charles Carroll (1660-1720) was Attorney General and Land Agent of Lord Baltimore.[8] He gradually rose to the place of proprietary agent held by Darnall. A leading Catholic layman in the province, a lawyer and man of wealth, long connected with the Calverts while they were still Catholics. "It was in connection with the trial of his nephew that Charles Carroll produced a commission from the proprietor which gave him surprisingly large powers."9

A Dr. Charles Carroll of Annapolis lived from 1691 to 1755. His son lived from 1723 to 1783 and was Barrister of Annapolis. Dr. Charles Carroll was the owner of Fellowship, a land tract at Boonsboro, in 1753.

A Charles Carroll acquired Pile Grove, northwest of Fox's Gap, on July 9, 1753, from John Hepburn. He probably lived from 1703 to 1783. Known as Charles Carroll of Annapolis, but also sometimes known as Charles, the Landowner. He was the son of the first Charles Carroll of note in Maryland.

Cox, Jacob Dolson (Oct. 27, 1828 - Aug. 8, 1900) Elected to the state of Ohio Senate in 1859, he found there his friend James A. Garfield, and Governor-Elect Dennison, with whom he soon became intimate. This trio, together with Salmon P. Chase, then governor, formed a radical anti-slavery group. He was advanced to the rank of major-general on Oct. 6, 1862, but the following April was reduced to his former rank because the number of major-generals permitted by law had been inadvertently exceeded. Recommissioned major-general in 1864. Elected governor of Ohio after the war. Secretary of the Interior under Grant. Became president of the Wabash Railway in Toledo in 1873. Elected to Congress in 1876. Dean of the Cincinnati Law School for sixteen years. President of the University of Cincinnati from 1885-89. In 1897 he presented his library to Oberlin College and retired thither to write his *Military Reminiscences*. His work was barely completed and unpublished at his death. In his later years he devoted much time to the study of microscopy, in which field he won international distinction. Cox was tall, graceful, and well-proportioned, with erect, military bearing, and a frame denoting great physical strength. No small part of Cox's reputation rests upon his work as a writer. From 1874 until his death he was the *Nation's* military book critic. In general, he is recognized as an elegant and forceful writer, of fine critical ability and impartial judgment, one of the foremost military historians of the country.

Cressap, Thomas (c. 1702 - c. 1790), emigrated from Yorkshire, England, at the age of fifteen, and married at the age of thirty, near Havre de Grace, Maryland.10 Moved about 1742 to a farm near Old Town, which he called "Shipton," after the place of his nativity in England. It was on the north fork, a few miles above the north and south branches of the Potomac. Here he acquired a large landed estate. He renewed his intimacy with Washington, who always reposed confidence in him; employed in 1748 by the Ohio Company, he marked, with the aid of an Indian named Nemacolin, the road to their territory, which was the same route pursued by Braddock in his ill-fated expedition. Visited England at the age of 70, and whilst in London was commissioned by Lord Baltimore to run the western line of Maryland, in order to ascertain which of the two branches of the Potomac was in reality the fountain head of the stream. Commissary for the Maryland troops.[11]

Dinwiddie, Robert (1693 - July 27, 1770), colonial administrator, the son of Robert Dinwiddie, was born at "Germiston," near Glasgow. On July 20, 1751, he was appointed lieutenant-governor of Virginia. He left Virginia on Jan. 12, 1758, and was succeeded by Francis Fauquier. He died at Clifton, Bristol. His career as colonial administrator was marked by vision, strength, attention to detail, and untiring energy. As the man who precipitated the struggle which brought about the downfall of New France, he is a figure of first importance in the early history of the American continent.

Dobbs, Arthur (Apr. 2, 1689 - Mar. 28, 1765), colonial governor of North Carolina, was born at Castle Dobbs, County Antrim, Ireland. In 1745, Dobbs with John Selwyn purchased from the McCulloh estate 400,000 acres of land in North Carolina, lying in the present counties of Mecklenburg and Cabarrus, and was thereafter much interested in the affairs of the colony and increasingly dissatisfied with the administration of Gov. Gabriel Johnston. In 1754 he was selected as Johnston's successor and, sailing at once, was sworn in at New Bern on Oct. 31. He was a fanatical Protestant, obsessed by hatred of the French, a zealous servant of the Crown and an opponent of popular government, and very ignorant of conditions in the colony. Governor of North Carolina from November 1, 1754, till his death at Town Creek, N. C.

Dobbs, Edward Brice Son of the Governor of North Carolina, commanded the North Carolina militia. Major Dobbs was an officer of the British Regular Army. Since he was in North Carolina when the war broke out, he was given a company and sent into Virginia to aid the general defense of the colonies. Later, he was promoted major and placed in command of the entire force.[12]

Dunbar, Thomas "After thirty years in the army, most of them in the 18th (Royal Irish) regiment of which he became lieutenant colonel, was made colonel of the 48th in 1752. After his misguided retreat following Braddock's disaster, he was recalled, resigned his regiment, and became lieutenant governor of Gibraltar. He became major general in 1758 and lieutenant general in 1760 and died in 1767."[13]

Dulany Sr., Daniel (1685 - Dec. 5, 1753), lawyer, descended from a medieval Irish family, the O'Dulaneys, was born in Queen's County, Ireland, in the year 1685. Arrived at Port Tobacco, Md., about the year 1703. Admitted to the bar of Charles County in 1709. Having served for twenty years in the popular branch of the Legislative Assembly, he was sworn into the Governor's Council, September 25, 1742, and was a member of that body until his death in Annapolis eleven years later. He was married three times.[14]

Dulany Jr., Daniel (June 28, 1722 - Mar. 17, 1797), lawyer, was born in Annapolis, Md., the son of Daniel Dulany and his wife Rebecca (1696 - 1737). Educated in England at Eton College and at Clare Hall, Cambridge University, studied law at the Middle Temple, and was admitted to the bar in Maryland in 1747. Two years later he married Rebecca Tasker, daughter of Benjamin Tasker, who was a member of the Governor's Council and the proprietor's agent and receiver general. In 1751 Frederick County elected Dulany one of its representatives in the popular branch of the Maryland Legislative Assembly. Commissary general from 1759 to 1761 and secretary of the province from 1761 to 1774. His forceful arguments ranked foremost among the political writings of the period and were freely drawn upon by William Pitt when speaking for repeal of the stamp act. Having opposed radical factions from the beginning of his public career, he manifested no sympathy for the Revolution and at its outbreak retired to Hunting Ridge, near Baltimore. He resided there as a Loyalist, except during a brief visit to England, until

1781, when nearly all of his property was confiscated and he moved to Baltimore, where he died.[15]

Fairfax, Lord Thomas (1691 - Dec. 12, 1791), Thomas Fairfax, 6th Lord, and Baron of Cameron, the friend and patron of Washington in early life; died at his seat, "Greenway Court," Frederick County, Va. He was the son of Thomas, Lord Fairfax, and Catharine, daughter of Lord Culpeper. He was educated at Oxford. Succeeding to the title and estates in Virginia, (inherited from his mother,) between the Rappahannock and Potomac rivers, and a great portion of the Shenandoah Valley, known as the Northern Neck, and comprising 5,282,000 acres, he settled in Virginia in 1745, fixing his residence a few miles from Winchester. In 1748, impressed with the ability and energy of the youth George Washington, he employed him as a surveyor of his lands west of the Blue Ridge Mountains. He avowed himself a loyalist during the Revolution, but was never molested by the colonists on account of his sentiments. His estates, however, were confiscated at the close of the struggle.

Fox, Frederick (May 10, 1751 - Feb. 27, 1837), born at Hesse-Cassel, Germany.[16] Farmer[17] and probably a tavern owner or innkeeper.[18] Married Catharine Booker (1748 - Nov. 1, 1800),[19] oldest daughter of Bartholomew and Margaret Booker,[20] on March 1, 1773.[21] Father of Christiana, Rose, Mary Magdalena, George, Daniel Booker, Joseph, and Elizabeth.[22] Member of Joseph Chapline's Company of Militia, probably between 1775 and 1777.[23] Signed Patriot's Oath of Fidelity and Support in 1778.[24] Served as a drummer in the Lieutenant Colonel's Company of the 10th Regiment, Pennsylvania Continental Line from April 22, 1777, to January 1, 1781.[25] Survived the winter encampment at Valley Forge.[26] Probably fought in the battles of Brandywine, Paoli "Massacre," Germantown, and Monmouth. Served as an elder in the Zion Lutheran Church of Middletown, Md., from September 26, 1787, to November 21, 1790.[27] Sometime between 1800 and 1807 Frederick Fox married Susannah (Schutt) Young (Apr. 19, 1754 - Nov. 13, 1831), a widow. Mrs Young's former husband was accidently killed while hunting deer.[28] Moved to western Ohio in late 1807. ". . . of short and rather stout build, and wore his hair in the olden time cue style."[29] Played the violin, according to Robert H. Fox of Cincinnati, Ohio. Died near Miamisburg, Ohio. Buried at the St. John or Gebhart Church, Miamisburg, on the northeast side of the church yard.[30]

Fox, John Frederick (? - 1784), Johan Frederich Fuchs and his wife Christiana arrived at the port of Philadelphia on the ship Anderson, Captain Hugh Campbell, September 27, 1752.[31] John Fox appeared in the state house in Philadelphia the day of his arrival and "took and subscribed the usual Qualifications."[32] John and Christiana were the parents of Daniel, Frederick, Magdelin, Michael,[33] and Rachel.[34] John Fox was a skin-dresser by trade.[35]

The name of John Fox appears in the Moses Chapline Sr. Administration Account papers submitted by the executors of the estate, bearing a date of June 19, 1766.[36] A land record for a tract called Grims Fancy places John Fox's house at Fox's Gap between 1764 and 1769. The land record for the tract John Fox acquired at Fox's Gap is not on record. The name of his tract may have been Friendship. His house was along the Main Road from Swearingen's Ferry to Frederick Town. He acquired lots in Sharpsburg in 1767.[37]

It is possible John Fox and his family settled in the Pennsylvania German community before coming to Maryland. This author believes they may have settled at Fox's Gap shortly after arriving in Philadelphia. Christiana Fox died Aug. 6, 1812, probably in Sharpsburg.[38]

Fry, Joshua In 1745 he served with Peter Jefferson as Commissioners of the Crown for marking the line from the headsprings of the Potomac river, defining the western limit of the grant of the Northern Neck, and also with Jefferson completed the map of Virginia known as "Fry & Jefferson's." Commissioned as Colonel and entrusted with the command of the Virginia forces in the expedition against the French in 1754, he died May 31 while conducting it to the Ohio, and was buried near Wills' Creek, now Cumberland Creek.[39] Also see Kenneth Bailey, *The Ohio Company*, page 132, for a biography of Fry.

Gage, Thomas (1720 - Apr. 2, 1787), led British forces at battle of Boston in Revolutionary War.[40] Second son of the first Viscount Gage; entered the army in youth; Lt. Col. Forty Fourth Foot March 2, 1750; led the advance at Braddock's defeat and was wounded; married December 8, 1758, Margaret, daughter of Peter Kemble, President of the New Jersey Council; in the expedition under Amherst, against Ticonderoga; made Major-General May 1, 1761, and Governor of Montreal; succeeded Amherst in command of the British forces in America, 1763; Lieutenant-General, 1770; succeeded Hutchinson as Governor of Massachusetts Bay April, 1774; April 19, 1775, sent a detachment to destroy the cannon and ammunition at Concord, which caused the Battle of Lexington and the opening of the Revolutionary war; June 17th the battle of Bunker Hill was fought, and the royal army was shut up in Boston by the American militia. October 10, 1775, Gage resigned and returned to England.

  Gates, Horatio   (c. 1728/29 - Apr. 10, 1806), Revolutionary soldier, was born at Maldon, Essex, England, the son of Robert and Dortothy (Parker) Gates. On Sept. 30, 1754, commissioned captain in the "Independent Company of Foot doing duty in New York." In 1755, Gates's company joined Braddock's army in Virginia. He was severely wounded in the Battle of the Monongahela. Late in 1761, he joined General Monckton at New York, and he sailed with him on the conspicuously successful expedition for the conquest of Martinique. He returned to England and was living there until 1769. On receiving a letter from his old comrade in arms, Washington, advising him about land in Virginia, he and his wife and son, Robert Gates, sailed from Bristol in August 1772, and took up land in Berkeley County (now W. Va.). His first wife died in 1784. On July 31, 1786, he married Mary Vallance of Washington County, Md. Continued to reside in Virginia until about 1790, when he moved to New York. Served one term in N.Y. legislature. There can be no doubt he was exceedingly unpopular with many of the best officers in the army. "Spring of 1774 justice of the peace for Berkeley County," Horatio Gates. General Gates owned a plantation five or six miles beyond the Potomac River near Shenandoah, Virginia, according to Drake and Orndorff.

  Gist, Christopher   (c. 1706 - 1759), explorer, soldier, was born in Maryland, one of the three sons of Richard and Zipporah (Murray) Gist, who were married in 1705. Maryland surveyor's son employed by The Ohio Company. In 1750 he was living with his family near Daniel Boone, on the Yadkin, in northern North Carolina. Captain Christopher Gist, as the agent of the Ohio company, had explored the country for several hundred miles north of the Ohio and as far as the Falls, in 1750. In 1751, he continued his explorations up the south side of the Ohio to the Kanawha river, visiting the Twightwee Indians. He kept a journal of his explorations. He was at Wills's Creek, Md., in November 1753 when Major George Washington arrived on a mission from Governor Dinwiddie, and on November 15 the two started for Fort Duquesne on the celebrated journey in which Gist twice saved Washington's life. He was with Washington also in the defeat of Coullon de Jumonville, May 28, 1754, and in the surrender of Fort Necessity, July 4 following. Served as a guide to General Braddock and took part in the battle of July 9, 1755.

Gladwyn, Henry (Nov. 19, 1729 - June 22, 1791), British soldier, was the son of Henry and Mary (Dakeyne) Gladwin, of Stubbing Court, Derbyshire, England. Commissioned lieutenant in the 48th Regiment of Foot on Aug. 28, 1753, and thereafter sailed for America, where his regiment joined Braddock's force in the march to Fort Duquesne. Wounded in the Battle of the Monongahela, but managed to retreat with the defeated army. His conduct, however, had so commended itself to Colonel Thomas Gage, that when, in 1757, there was organized the new 80th Regiment, Gladwin was made captain therein and Gage became colonel. In the winter of 1762-63 he returned to the post a t Detroit, where he was stationed when Pontiac's War broke out in May. His brilliant defense of Detroit became the central theme of Francis Parkman's *History of the Conspiracy of Pontiac* (1851). Returned to England and died at his country seat, Stubbing Court, near Chesterfield in Derbyshire, and was buried at Wingerworth Church.

Halkett, Sir Peter of Pitferran, Fifeshire, a baronet of Nova Scotia, was the son of Sir Peter Wedderburne of Gosford, who, marrying the heiress of the ancient family of Halkett, assumed her name. On the February 26, 1751, he succeeded to the colonelcy of his regiment. One of his sons, James, a subaltern in his own regiment, died with him on July 9, 1755.[41]

Hill Jr., Daniel Harvey (Jan. 15, 1859 - July 31, 1924), college president, teacher, writer, and historian, was born at

Davidson College, the son of Isabella Morrison and Daniel
Harvey Hill. Served as president of North Carolina College of
Agriculture and Mechanic Arts (now North Carolina State
University) from 1908 until 1916. After serving the college for 29
years, Hill resigned as president to accept an offer by the N. C.
Historical Commission to write a history of N. C. troops in the
Civil War. The project was conceived and promoted by J. Bryan
Grimes. The two-volume work, entitled *Bethel to Sharpsburg:
North Carolina in the War Between the States,* was published
in 1926, two years after Hill's death. For his writing he
collected between five and six thousand volumes relating to the
Civil War, an exceptionally fine working library on the subject,
which was later turned over to the N. C. Historical Commission.

   Jefferson, Peter The father of the President, the son of
Thomas Jefferson, of Osborne's, Chesterfield county; born 1708;
married Jane, daughter of Isham Randolph, of "Dungenness,"
Goochland county, from which Albemarle was formed September
1744. Peter Jefferson and Joshua Fry seved as commissioners for
defining the western limits of the Northern Neck grant, and in
1749 as commissioners on the part of Virginia to continue the
boundary line between it and North Carolina. They also
prepared the map of Virginia, bearing their name. Peter
Jefferson was long County-Lieutenant or Commander-in-Chief of
Albemarle county.

   Keppel, Commodore (April 2, 1725 - 1786), The Hon.
Augustus, second son of William Anne Keppel, second Earl of
Albemarle; entered the navy as a midshipman and was wounded
at the capture of Paita; rapidly promoted, and distinguished
himself at Gorea and in the battle of Belle-Isle; Commodore in
1762, in the fleet sent out under Sir George Pocock to the
Havana.[42]

   Lee, Charles (1731 - Oct. 2, 1782), soldier of fortune,
Revolutionary general, born at Dernhall, Cheshire, England, the
son of John and Isabille (Bunbury) Lee. Commissioned lieutenant
in the 44th Regiment on May 2, 1751. Purchased a captaincy for
900 pounds in 1756. Adopted into a Mohawk tribe and married
the daughter of a Seneca chief. With the 44th during
Abercromby's disastrous attack on Fort Ticonderoga in July 1758.
Returned to America in 1773 and took up land in Berkeley

County, Virginia, now West Virginia, in 1775. Appointed second major-general of the Continental Army June 17, 1775.

At the age of fourteen he had received a commission in his father's regiment. While still in his early twenties, he served as lieutenant in one of two British regiments sent to America from Ireland in early 1755 under the command of Major General Edward Braddock. Lee was in the 44th Foot of Sir Peter Halket.[43]

Lewis, Andrew (1720 - Sept. 26, 1781), soldier, Revolutionary patriot, was born in Ireland. Surrendered with Washington at Fort Necessity. He was in Braddock's army but was not present at its defeat. However, see Sargent, *History of an Expedition,* 298, footnote 1. During General Forbes's campaign of 1758, Lewis was taken prisoner in Major Grant's unfortunate reconnaissance. He was later released and aided in making the Indian Treaty of Fort Stanwix (1768), one of the several important treaties which he helped to frame. Lewis' chief claim to fame was his victory over the Indians in the battle of Point Pleasant, the outstanding event of Lord Dunmore's War. Commissioned brigadier-general, March 1, 1776, though Washington wished a higher command for him. He assumed command of the American forces stationed at Williamsburg. Resigned from Continental Army April 15, 1777, but continued to serve his state in the military forces and in Governor Thomas Jefferson's executive council until his death.

Mercer, Dr. Hugh (c. 1725 - Jan. 12, 1777), soldier, was born in Aberdeenshire, Scotland, the son of the Rev. William Mercer and his wife, Anna Munro. Educated as a physician at Marischal College, University of Aberdeen (1740-1744), he joined the army of Prince Charles Edward as surgeon's mate, and was present at the Battle of Culloden. Emigrated to America about 1746 or 1747 and settled near the present site of Mercersburg, Pa. For about ten years he practised his profession in the Conococheague settlement, winning the esteem of the frontier community by his skill and courage. At the outbreak of the French and Indian War, he abandoned the lancet for the sword, becoming an officer of the Penn. Regiment, a provincial corps. It is said that he took part in Braddock's expedition in 1755 and was wounded in the action of July 9. During the course of the war he made the acquaintance of Washington, and at his suggestion, it is said, removed from Pennsylvania to Fredericksburg, Va. He attended the same Masonic lodge as Washington, and he was an occasional visitor at Mount Vernon. On June 5, he was elected brigadier-general by the Continetntal Congress. Died gloriously at Princeton, in 1777.

Morgan, Daniel (1736 - July 6, 1802), Revolutionary soldier, son of James and Eleanora Morgan, was of Welsh ancestry and born probably in Hunterdon County, N. J., though some authorities say just across the Delaware River in Bucks County, Pa. After quarreling with his father, he made his way to the Shenandoah Valley in Virginia, where he worked as a farm laborer and teamster until he had saved sufficient money to become an independent wagoner. He served as lieutenant in Pontiac's War and in 1774 accompanied Lord Dunmore's expedition to western Pennsylvania. Married Abigail Bailey. Won one of the most decisive battles of the Revolutionary War at the Cowpens in South Carolina. Served one term in Congress in 1797.

Apparently lived at Winchester, Virginia, at time of The Braddock Expedition. Drove a wagon under Dunbar's Regiment. No indication he ever went through Maryland as part of the Expedition.[44] In the battle, or on some occasion of the campaign, he was shot in the back of the neck, the ball passing through his mouth and teeth.[45] Emigrated to Virginia in 1755. For an excellent account of Daniel Morgan see pages 386-94, Volume I, *Memoirs of the War in the Southern Department of the United States* by Henry Lee. Buried at Winchester, Virginia.

Ogle, Samuel (c. 1702 - May 3, 1752), colonial governor of Maryland,[46] was born in Northumberland County, England, where the Ogle family had become prominent as early as the eleventh century.

While in England served with the British Army, and by the time of his departure for America in 1731, had advanced to the rank of Captain of Cavalry. After his arrival in Annapolis in December 1731, assumed office as Lieutenant Governor of Maryland, a position he held until December of 1732. Also served as lieutenant governor from July 1733 to August 1742, and from March 1747 until his death.

In 1741 he married Anne, the daughter of Benjamin Tasker, through whom he came into possession of "Belair," an estate of 3600 acres in Prince George's County twenty miles west of Annapolis. Brother of Thomas and perhaps others. Father of Anne (died young), Samuel (died young), Benjamin who was governor of Maryland from 1798 to 1801, Mary and Mellora.

Ogle defended Maryland's interests during a "border war" with Pennsylvania in 1736-37, a skirmish resulting from a boundary dispute between the two colonies. While still in office, Ogle died in Annapolis, Maryland, on May 3, 1752.[47]

Sharpe, Horatio (Nov. 15, 1718 - Nov. 9, 1790), Governor of colonial Maryland, was born near Hull, Yorkshire, England, one of a numerous and celebrated family.[48] Some historians credit him with first suggesting the Stamp Act; certain it is that in 1754 in a communication to Lord Baltimore he outlined concisely a plan that is a prototype of the famous act (Archives, post, VI, 99). Especially charged to determine the boundaries of his province, he set men at work surveying the line in dispute with Virginia and by 1760 arrived at an agreement that eventuated in the Mason and Dixon line.

Commissioned as Captain of Marines in 1745; later promoted to Lt. Col. of Foot in the West Indies. Appointed Lt. Gov. of Maryland, and arrived in the province in August 1753, to assume that office. Served as Commander-in-Chief of troops raised "to defend the frontiers of Virginia and the neighboring colonies, and to repel the unjustifiable invasion and encroachments of the French, on the river Ohio." Replaced by General Braddock as commander in 1755. In June 1769, replaced as Governor by Robert Eden. Sharpe retired to "Whitehall," his country estate near Annapolis. In 1773 he returned to England, where he remained until his death on November 9, 1790.[49]

St. Clair, Sir John On March 20, 1756, he was made a Lieutenant-Colonel of the Sixtieth regiment; in January, 1758, received the local rank of Colonel in America, and February 19, 1762, was made a full Colonel. He is said to have dwelt near Tarbot, Argyleshire.[50] Sir John's title was probably spurious. He was the son of Sir George St. Clair or Sinclair of Kinnaird, Fife. He served as deputy quartermaster general in North America from 1754 until his death in 1767, an efficient officer in that

important post. He married an American girl, Betsy Moland. His
will is in *New Jersey Archives*, 1st ser., 33:370. A sketch of him
by C. R. Hildeburn is in *Pennsylvania Magazine of History and
Biography* , IX (1885), 1-14.[51]

      Swearingen, Thomas   (The Elder of the Ferry) (1708
- 1760), Thomas Swearingen's Ferry began operation in early
1755 near the site of the present Rumsey Bridge at
Shepherdstown. It operated until 1849.[52] Two brothers in
Maryland, Thomas and Van Swearingen, crossed the Potomac
River and settled on the banks of the Virginia side in the 1740s.

      "Van Swearingen and his brother Thomas Swearingen
and his son Thomas (son of Thomas the Elder) were prominent
early settlers and played a big part in the settlement and
development of the area from north of Shepherdstown to the
Hard Scrabble (Jones Mill) area of present Berkeley County.
Thomas Swearingen the Elder established a Ferry that operated
on the Potomac River just north of Mecklenburg in 1755 at what
became known as Bellevue. The original dwelling on the place,
known as the Hip Roof House built in 1760 by Thomas the Elder,
was located on a 478 acre land grant from Lord Fairfax in 1750
and joined the 210 acre tract his brother Van had purchased from
Richard Morgan."[53]

      Tasker Sr., Benjamin Son of Captain Thomas Tasker,
Benjamin Tasker was President of the Council of Maryland for
thirty-two years, and as such was acting Governor of the
Province from the death of Governor Ogle, May 3, 1752, until the
arrival of Governor Horatio Sharpe, August 10, 1753.[54] He and
Charles Carroll (signer of the Declaration of Independence) were
the delegates from the Province to the famous Albany
Convention of 1754. He was on the Committee appointed to draw
up a Constituion for a perpetual Confederacy.

      He married Anne, daughter of the Hon. Wm. Bladen,
Commissary-General of the Province, They had five children,
one son and four daughters. Rebecca married Daniel Dulaney,
Counsellor of Maryland in 1776. Anne Tasker married Governor
Samuel Ogle of Maryland. The tomb of Governor Benjamin
Tasker is at Annapolis, Md.

      Walker, Dr. Thomas (Jan. 25, 1715 - Nov. 9, 1794),
physician, soldier, and explorer who had reached Kentucky in

1750. Principal commissary of the Braddock Expedition.[55] Lived at "Castle Hill," Albemarle County, where he was a neighbor of Peter Jefferson and later acted as a guardian for his son Thomas. He is believed to have been the first white man who explored Kentucky. In 1753, Colonel Joshua Fry recommended to the Virginia Assembly an exploration with the view of the discovery of a route to the Pacific coast, and according to the Rev. James Maury, his "worthy friend and neighbor, Dr. Thomas Walker, was to be the chief conductor of the whole affair." He was a member of the House of Burgesses, of the Virginia Convention of 1775, and the Council in 1777; one of the commissioners to treat with the Indians after the defeat of Andrew Lewis, and again, to run the boundary line between Virginia and North Carolina. He married twice, first in 1741, Mildred (Thornton), the widow of Nicholas Meriwether; second, Elizabeth Thornton, a cousin of General Washington. Buried at "Castle Hill."

Wardrop, James (? - 1760), Member of the Ohio Company who owned many land tracts in the Fox's Gap area from 1750 to 1760. "A wealthy merchant originally from Virginia who lived at Marlborough in lower Prince George's County, Maryland." "Although 'of Upper Marlboro,' Wardrop wrote his will in New York City. It was probated in Prince George's County in 1760, and in it he named his wife Lettice and his brother-in-law Alexander Symmer as executors. he devised to a nephew houses belonging to his father in Edinburgh, Scotland, and to his wife all his real estate in America."[56]

Washington, George (February 11/22, 1732 - Dec. 14, 1799), First president of the United States, was born in Westmoreland County, Va., on the estate of his father.." The eldest son of Augustine Washington and his second wife, Mary Ball (1708-89), of "Epping Fores," Va. Mt. Vernon was the home of his elder half-brother Lawrence, who had married Ann Fairfax. Elected a burgess from Frederick in 1758, after having been defeated in 1755 and 1757, and took his seat in the session of 1759, when he was thanked by the House for his military services. Chosen one of Virginia's delegates to the First Continental Congress, 1774. Elected to command the armies, June 15, 1775. He had assumed the presidency when the United States was little but a name, without power, prestige, or credit; when he retured from office the country was well on the road to international importance. First in war, first in peace, and first in the hearts of his countrymen.

Notes

In citing works in the notes, works frequently cited have been identified by the following abbreviations.

BJ   Charles Hamilton, "Journal of Captain Robert Chomley's Batman," *Braddock's Defeat* (Norman, OK: Univ. of Oklahoma Press, 1959). Hamilton's book also includes "The Orderly Book of Sir Peter Halkett.".

FCLR Frederick County (Maryland) Land Records.

GW   John C. Fitzpatrick, ed., *The Writings of George Washington from the Original Manuscript Sources 1744-1789, 39 vols.* (Washington, D.C.: U.S. Government Printing Office, 1933).

HS   Horatio Sharpe, *Correspondence of Governor Horatio Sharpe* ed. William Hand Browne, Archives of Maryland (Baltimore: Maryland Historical Society, 1888).

MdHR Maryland Hall of Records, Annapolis, Maryland.

MR   Winthrop Sargent, ed., "The Morris Journal," *The History of an Expedition Against Fort Duquesne in 1755; under Major General Braddock* (Philadelphia: Memoirs of the Historical Society of Pennsylvania, 1855).

OR   Winthrop Sargent, ed., "The Orme Journal," *The History of an Expedition Against Fort Duquesne in 1755; under Major General Braddock* (Philadelphia: Memoirs of the Historical Society of Pennsylvania, 1855).

RD   Virginia Historical Society, *The Official Records of Robert Dinwiddie*, 2 vols. (New York: AMS Press, 1884).

WCLR Washington County (Maryland) Land Records.

Introduction - Prelude to the Braddock Expedition

Pages 1 through 10.

[1] E. B. O'Callaghan and B. Fernow, eds., *Documents Relative to the Colonial History of New York*, 15 vols. (Albany: n.p., 1853-87), 6:853-97.

[2] Franklin T. Nichols, "The Braddock Expedition" (Ph. D. diss., Harvard University, 1947), 2.

[3] Kenneth P. Bailey, *The Ohio Company of Virginia: a chapter in the History of the Colonial Frontier, 1748-1792* (Glendale, Calif.: The Arthur H. Clark Company, 1939), 17-31.

[4] Kenneth P. Bailey, *Thomas Cresap* (Boston: The Christopher Publishing House, 1944), footnote six, chapter seven.

[5] Prince George's County, L.G.C., fol. 33.

[6] Land Office (Annapolis), LG-E, fol. 314.

[7] See Edward C. Papenfuse et al., *Biographical Dictionary of the Maryland Legislature, 1635 - 1789*, 2 vols. (Baltimore and London: The Johns Hopkins University Press, 1982), 1:244-5.

[8] T. J. C. Williams and Folger McKinsey, *History of Frederick County*, 2 vols. (Baltimore: Regional Publishing Company, 1967), 1:31 and 59.

[9] Sidney Methiot Culbertson, *The Hunter Family of Virginia and Connections* (Denver, Colorado: [n.p.], 1934), 171-9.

[10] Bailey, *Ohio Company*, 52. George Washington mentions a "Nathanl. Chapman" in his letter of May 2, 1792. See John C. Fitzpatrick, ed., *The Writings of George Washington from the Original Manuscript Sources 1744-1789*, 39 vols. (Washington, D.C.: U.S. Government Printing Office, 1933), 32:26-31.

[11] Petition of John Hanbury, 1748, P.R.O., C.O. 5: 1327/53 (Library of Congress transcript).

[12] William M. Darlington, ed., *Christopher Gist's Journals* (Pittsburgh: J.R. Weldin & Co., 1893), 235.

[13] Bailey, *Ohio Company*, 58.

[14] Karen Mauer Green, *The Maryland Gazette 1727-1761 Genealogical and Historical Abstracts* (Galveston: The Frontier Press, 1989), 117 and 129.

[15] See Papenfuse, *Biographical Dictionary*, 1:352-3.

[16] Petition of the Ohio company, April 2, 1754, P. R. O., C. O. 5: 1328/154-164 (Library of Congress transcript).

[17] Bailey, *Ohio Company*, 58.

[18] Green, *Maryland Gazette*, 274-5. Thursday, Oct 1, 1761.

[19] Calvin E. Schildknecht, "Which Charles Carroll?" *The News*, Frederick, Maryland, April 4, 1990. See MdHR 17,410, 1-23-3-4, Dr. Charles Carroll, survey for Fellowship, Dec. 2, 1752, 106 acres. This tract is at Boonsboro.

[20] Bailey, *Ohio Company*, 55-6.

[21] Aubrey C. Land, *The Dulanys of Maryland* (Baltimore: Maryland Historical Society, 1955), 180.

22 Maria J. Liggett Dare, *Chaplines from Maryland and Virginia* (Washington: The Franklin Print, 1902), 23.

23 Papenfuse, *Biographical Dictionary*, 1:210.

24 William Harrison Lowdermilk, *History of Cumberland, (Maryland) from the time of the Indian town Caiuctucuc, in 1728, up to the present day embracing an account of Washington's first campaign, and battle of Fort Necessity, together with a history of Braddock's Expedition* (Baltimore: Regional Publishing Co., 1976), 89.

25 Donald Jackson, ed., *The Diaries of George Washington*, 6 vols. (Charlottesville: University of Virginia Press, 1976), 1:12.

26 Bailey, *Thomas Cresap*, 96-7. See William Hand Browne, ed., *Correspondence of Governor Horatio Sharpe* Archives of Maryland (Baltimore: Maryland Historical Society, 1888), 6:78, for the Articles of Capitulation. For a summary of events leading up to the Braddock Expedition see HS to John Sharpe, April 19, 1755, *Correspondence*, 6:196-204.

Chapter One - Preparations are Made

Pages 11 through 38.

1 *The New Merriam-Webster Dictionary*, s.v. "expedition." A journey for a particular purpose. The *Monthly Bulletin of the Carnegie Library of Pittsburgh*, November 1906, contains a list of references on the Braddock Expedition, as does the Library of Congress.

2 Charles Hamilton, *Braddock's Defeat* (Norman: University of Oklahoma Press, 1959), Introduction.

3 Virginia Historical Society, *The Official Records of Robert Dinwiddie*, 2 vols. (New York: AMS Press, 1884), title page. Lt. Gov. from 1751 to 1758.

4 Louis K. Koontz, *The Virginia Frontier, 1754-1763* (Baltimore: Johns Hopkins Press, 1925), 30. Horatio Sharpe of Maryland, Governor from Aug. 10, 1753 to 1769; Arthur Dobbs of North Carolina, Governor from Nov. 1, 1754, until his death, Mar. 28, 1765; James De Lancey of New York, Lt. Gov. 1753-1755; Robert Hunter Morris of Pennsylvania, Lt. Gov. Oct., 1754 to Aug., 1756; William Shirley, Governor of Massachusetts, 1741 to 1756.

5 William Hand Browne, ed., *Correspondence of Governor Horatio Sharpe* Archives of Maryland (Baltimore: Maryland Historical Society, 1888), 6:73-4, for Commission to Sharpe. Also see Horatio Sharpe to Lord Baltimore, Oct. 25, 1754, *Correspondence*, 6:102. Lord Anson was responsible for Sharpe obtaining the appointment. See HS to Lord Anson, Nov. 5, 1754, *Correspondence*, 6:120. Most of Gov. Sharpe's papers from 1753 to 1771 are in Volumes 6, 9, 14, and 31.

6 Koontz, *Virginia Frontier*, 60. See also, William MacDonald, ed., *Select Charters and Other Documents Illustrative of American History, 1606 - 1775* (New York: The Macmillan Company, 1899), 11.

[7] Joshua Fry, "A Map of the Inhabited part of Virginia, containing the whole Province of Maryland, with part of Pensilvania, New Jersey and North Carolina," *The Fry and Jefferson map of Virginia and Maryland; facsimiles of the 1754 and 1794 printings with an index* 2nd ed. (Charlottesville: Univ. Press of Virginia, 1966).

[8] J. Thomas Scharf, *History of Western Maryland*, 2 vols. (Baltimore: Regional Publishing Co., 1968), 1:457.

[9] Stanley Pargellis, ed., *Military Affairs in North America 1748 - 1765* (New York: D. Appleton-Century Co., 1936), 84. Undated letter to Robert Napier by General Braddock, written sometime after May 17th from Ft. Cumberland.

[10] Pargellis, *Military Affairs*, 36-7.

[11] See *Colonial Records of North Carolina*, 10 vols. (Raleigh: Josephus Daniels, 1887), 5:251-5, for the plan of union.

[12] Leonard W. Labaree, et al, eds., *The Autobiography of Benjamin Franklin* (New Haven, Conn.: Yale Univ. Press, 1964), 130-1.

[13] Pargellis, *Military Affairs*, 34-5. Drafted as early as Oct. 22, 1754.

[14] Franklin T. Nichols, "The Braddock Expedition" (Ph.D. diss., Harvard University, 1947), 2.

[15] Letters of Sir John St. Clair, written during 1755 and 1756, were discovered in Scotland in 1987. See *Letterbook of Sir John St. Clair, Deputy Quartermaster General in North America January 12, 1755 - December 28, 1756*, Manuscript Dept., University of Virginia Library. See MdHR 16-3-3 1900 v2. Ross Netherton, *Braddock's Road and the Potomac Route to the West*, Winchester - Frederick Historical Society.

[16] Sir John St. Clair to HS, Feb. 22, 1755, *Correspondence*, 6:170.

[17] Pargellis, *Military Affairs*, 48.

[18] Pargellis, *Military Affairs*, 31.

[19] Parke Rouse, Jr., *The Great Wagon Road* (New York: McGraw-Hill Company, 1973).

[20] Col. Thomas Cresap's *Map of the Sources of the Potomac*, June, 1754, HS, *Correspondence*, 6:72.

[21] Daniel Wunderlich Nead, *The Pennsylvania-German in the Settlement of Maryland* (Lancaster, Pa.: The Pennsylvania-German Society, 1914), 45-9.

[22] Schlatter refers to "Lancaster in Conestoga." See William J. Hinke. *Ministers of the German Reformed Congregations in Pennsylvania and Other Colonies in the Eighteenth Century* (Lancaster: Rudisill and Co., Inc., 1951), 39.

[23] Grace L. Tracey and John P. Dern, *Pioneers of Old Monocacy* (Baltimore: Genealogical Publishing Company, 1987), 51.

[24] Pargellis, *Military Affairs*, 31.

[25] William J. Hinke, transl., "Report of the Journey of Francis Louis Michel, October 2, 1701 to December 1, 1702" *Virginia Magazine of History and Biography*, 24:1-43, 113-141, 275-303.

[26] Pargellis, *Military Affairs*, 45.

[27] HS, *Correspondence*, PREFACE, 6:5.

[28] "The Population of Maryland, 1755," *The Gentleman's Magazine*, 34 (1764). MdHR G 1213-449.

[29] HS to Cecilius Calvert, Nov. 29, 1753, *Correspondence*, 6:12.

[30] HS to Lord Frederick Baltimore, June 6, 1754, *Correspondence*, 6:68. See HS to John Sharpe, June 28, 1755, *Correspondence*, 6:235-6, for a discussion of the controversy between the Lord Proprietary and the Assembly.

[31] HS to Lord Frederick Baltimore, Aug. 8, 1754, *Correspondence*, 6:79-81.

[32] HS to Cecilius Calvert, Aug. 8, 1754, *Correspondence*, 6:89.

[33] James DeLancey to HS, Dec. 11, 1753, *Correspondence*, 6:16.

[34] Karen Mauer Green, *The Maryland Gazette, 1727-1761* (Galveston: The Frontier Press, 1989), 145. Thursday, Sept. 12, 1754.

[35] Green, *Maryland Gazette*, 146. Thursday, Oct. 3, 1754.

[36] Green, *Maryland Gazette*, 147. Thursday, Oct. 17, 1754.

[37] HS to Cecilius Calvert, Oct. 25, 1754, *Correspondence*, 6:103.

[38] Green, *Maryland Gazette*, 147. Thursday, Nov. 7, 1754.

[39] Green, *Maryland Gazette*, 148. Thursday, Nov. 14, 1754.

[40] HS to Cecilius Calvert, Nov. 5, 1754, *Correspondence*, 6:113.

[41] Green, *Maryland Gazette*, 149. Thursday, Dec. 5, 1754.

[42] Kenneth P. Bailey, *Thomas Cresap, Maryland Frontiersman* (Boston: The Christopher Publishing House, 1944), footnote 18, Chapter VIII.

[43] Dinwiddie, *Records*, 1:436.

[44] Green, *Maryland Gazette*, 151. Thursday, Jan. 23, 1755.

[45] RD to the Lords of Trade, Jan. 20, 1755, *Records*, 1: 475.

[46] Sir John St. Clair to General Braddock, Jan. 15, 1755, Pargellis, *Military Affairs*, 58.

[47] Green, *Maryland Gazette*, 150. Thursday, Jan. 16, 1755.

[48] HS to Robert Dinwiddie, Jan. 13, 1755, *Correspondence*, 6:167.

[49] HS to Braddock, from Williamsburg, Feb. 9, 1755, *Correspondence*, 6:168.

[50] Pargellis, *Military Affairs*, 59-60.

[51] Pargellis, *Military Affairs*, 61.

[52] A letter by Governor Dinwiddie to Governor Dobbs, on February 8, indicates, "Gov'r Sharpe and S'r J. St. Clair are now both with me from W. Creek." RD, *Records*, 1:486.

[53] HS to (William Sharpe?), Feb. ?, 1755, *Correspondence*, 6:174.

[54] Sir John St. Clair to Robert Napier, Jan. 15, 1755, Pargellis, *Military Affairs*, 60.

[55] Sir John St. Clair to General Braddock, Feb. 9, 1755, Pargellis, *Military Affairs*, 62-3.

[56] Variation of garavance: chickpea.

[57] HS to General Braddock, Feb. 9, 1755, *Correspondence*, 6:168.

[58] HS to John Sharpe, *Correspondence*, 6:202. Sharpe states 200 miles.

[59] HS to Lord Frederick Baltimore, Mar. 12, 1755, *Correspondence*, 6:186.

[60] RD, *Records*, 1: 418. Falmouth, on the Rappahannock river, opposite Fredericksburg, was erected into a town by Act of Assembly in 1727; *Virginia Magazine of History and Biography*, 14:337-8. "May 5, 1739, Samuel Earle & John Cobourne are appointed Inspectors at Falmouth

Warehouse." *Journals of the Council of Virginia in Executive Sessions 1737-1763.*

[61] Sir John St. Clair to Major General Braddock, Pargellis, *Military Affairs,* 63-4.

[62] RD to Lord Halifax, Feb. 24, 1755, *Records,* 1:512-3.

[63] Pargellis, *Military Affairs,* 63. Pennsylvania approved the flour Feb. 26.

[64] Sir John St. Clair to General Braddock, Feb. 9, 1755, Pargellis, *Military Affairs,* 61.

[65] Green, *Maryland Gazette,* 152. Thursday, Feb. 20, 1755; Sir John St. Clair to General Braddock, written before Apr. 14, 1755, Pargellis, *Military Affairs,* 65.

[66] Sir John St. Clair to General Braddock, Feb. 9, 1755, Pargellis, *Military Affairs,* 65.

[67] RD to Horatio Sharpe, Mar. 1, 1755, *Records,* 1:518.

[68] Green, *Maryland Gazette,* 152. Thursday, Mar. 6, 1755.

[69] Green, *Maryland Gazette,* 153. Thursday, Mar. 13, 1755. Last Saturday was the 8th.

[70] Winthrop Sargent, ed., *The History of An Expedition against Fort Duquesne, in 1755* (Philadelphia: J. B. Lippincott & Co., 1856), 283.

[71] Sargent, *History of An Expedition,* 283. Notes or quotations from the Orme Journal or from the Morris Journal will be cited in the text as follows.

      OR: "Captain Orme's Journal"
      MR: "The Morris Journal"

[72] Sargent, *History of An Expedition,* 359. Pargellis, *Military Affairs,* 104 indicates, "Archer Butler Hulbert, in *Braddock's Road and Three Relative Papers,* Volume IV of *Historic Highways of America* (1903), Chapter IV, printed the original version of the 'Seaman's Journal' which in an expanded form is printed in Sargent. Hulbert argues that the latter version was written by Harry Gordon from the original."

[73] RD to Arthur Dobbs, Feb. 27, 1755, *Records,* 1:515.

[74] RD to HS, Mar. 10, 1755, *Records,* 1:521.

[75] RD to Governor Morris, Mar. 10, 1755, *Records,* 1:522.

[76] RD to Governor Morris, Mar. 10, 1755, *Records,* 1:522.

[77] RD to William Allen, Mar. 10, 1755, *Records,* 1:523.

[78] General Braddock to Robert Napier, Mar. 17, 1755, Pargellis, *Military Affairs,* 77-8.

[79] General Braddock to Robert Napier, Mar. 17, 1755, Pargellis, *Military Affairs,* 77-8.

[80] General Braddock to Robert Napier, at Alexandria, Apr. 19, 1755, Pargellis, *Military Affairs,* 84.

[81] John C. Fitzpatrick, ed., *The Writings of George Washington from the Original Manuscript Sources 1744-1789,* 39 vols. (Washington, D.C.: U.S. Government Printing Office, 1933), 1:110.

[82] Sir John St. Clair to Robert Napier, June 13, 1755, Pargellis, *Military Affairs,* 93.

[83] Sir John St. Clair to Robert Napier, June 13, 1755, Pargellis, *Military Affairs,* 93.

[84] Sir John St. Clair to Robert Napier, June 13, 1755, Pargellis, *Military Affairs*, 93.

[85] Sargent, "Capt. Orme's Journal," *History of An Expedition*, 290; RD to Sharpe, from Alexandria, Mar. 29, 1755, *Records*, 2:5.

[86] Sargent, "Capt. Orme's Journal," *History of An Expedition*, 297; Pennsylvania Gazette, No. 1373.

[87] HS to Cecilius Calvert, Apr. 10, 1755, *Correspondence*, 6:189.

[88] Sargent, "Capt. Orme's Journal," *History of An Expedition*, 300. The minutes of this Council are in Doc. Hist. New York, 2:376 and Pennsylvania Colonial Records, 6:365. Also see Johnson MSS; Admiralty In-letters, 480, by Keppel and Keppel to Cleveland, Sec. of Admiralty, Apr. 20, 1755.

[89] John Kennedy Lacock, *Braddock Road* (n.p.: self-published, 1912), 3.

[90] Sargent, *History of An Expedition*, 158-9.

[91] HS to John Sharpe, Apr. 19, 1755, *Correspondence*, 6:203-4.

[92] Green, *Maryland Gazette*, 155.

[93] HS to Lord Frederick Baltimore, Apr. 19, 1755, *Correspondence*, 6:194.

[94] HS to Sir Thomas Robinson, Apr. 19, 1755, *Correspondence*, 6:196.

[95] Green, *Maryland Gazette*, 98. Thursday, Feb. 20, 1752. "Alexander Beall regarding the new town named George Town, adjacent to the Warehouse at the mouth of Rock Creek in Frederick County. Lots will be sold on Monday, 4 March, at the house of Joseph Belt, living in George Town."

[96] Green, *Maryland Gazette*, 231. Thursday, Aug. 16, 1759. "Thomas Daviss, living near the place where Lawrence Owen kept tavern in Frederick County, has 408 acres for sale near Seneca in Frederick County. Thursday, Apr. 27, 1758. "Lawrence Owen has a stray horse at his plantation at the head of Capt. John Creek in Frederick County."

[97] Green, *Maryland Gazette*, 205. Thursday, Jan. 19, 1758. Perhaps Michael Dowden's. "Richard Watts, living near Michael Dowden's, in Frederick County, has a stray horse at his plantation."

[98] Archives of Maryland, *Proceedings and Acts of the General Assembly, 1755-1756*, vol. 52, Mar. 11, 1756. MdHR M2764.

[99] The following book may be of interest to the reader: Lucy L. Bowie, *The Ancient Barracks at Fredericktown* (Frederick, Md.: Maryland State School for the Deaf, 1939).

[100] Daniel Dulany, Jr. "Military and Political Affairs in The Middle Colonies in 1755," *Pennsylvania Magazine of History and Biography* (1879), 3:14.

[101] T. J. C. Williams and Folger McKinsey, "Orderly Book of General Braddock," *History of Frederick County* (Baltimore: Regional Publishing Company, 1967), 1:53.

[102] HS to RD, May 9, 1755, *Correspondence*, 6:205.

[103] Green, *Maryland Gazette*, 155.

[104] Charles Hamilton, "Journal of Captain Robert Chomley's Batman," *Braddock's Defeat* (Norman, Ok.: Univ. of Oklahoma Press, 1959), 12.

[105] HS, *Correspondence*, 6:203. See Maryland Archives, *Acts of Assembly, 1737-1740*, 19:220, 307-8, for consideration of a road between Annapolis and Monocacy. Also, Tracey and Dern, *Pioneers of Old Monocacy*, 245.

[106] *Votes and Proceedings of the House of Representatives, 1754-1755* (Philadelphia: n.p., 1755), 73.

[107] Labaree, *Autobiography of Benjamin Franklin*, 130. See William B. Willcox, ed., *The Papers of Benjamin Franklin*, 30 vols. (New Haven: Yale University Press, 1986), 6:19-22, for advertisements by Franklin to raise wagons and horses.

[108] Archives of Maryland, *Proceedings and Acts of the General Assembly, 1755-1756*, 52:369. MdHR M 2764.

[109] Charles Henry Lincoln, ed., *William Shirley, Governor of Massachusetts and Military Commander in America, Correpsondence, 1731-1760*, 2 vols. (New York: [n.p.], 1912), 2:173. Also see Herbert L. Osgood, *The American Colonies in the Eighteenth Century*, 4 vols. (Gloucester, Mass.: P. Smith, 1958), 4:348.

[110] Albert H. Heusser, *In the Footsteps of Washington (Pope's Creek to Princeton)* (Paterson, N. J.: Privately Published, 1921), 110.

[111] Benjamin Franklin to Susanna Wright, April 28, 1755, Willcox, *Papers of Benjamin Franklin*, 6:23.

[112] Benjamin Franklin advertisement, Lancaster, May 6, 1755, Willcox, *Papers of Benjamin Franklin*, 6:27.

[113] Nead, *Settlement of Maryland*, 48.

[114] Nead, *Settlement of Maryland*, 46.

[115] Willcox, *Papers of Benjamin Franklin*, 6:60, May 28, 1755. See Lincoln, *William Shirley, Correspondence*, 2:99 and 2:13-17, 59.

[116] See William L. Iscrupe and Shirley G. M. Iscrupe, *Early History of Western Pennsylvania and the Western Campaigns 1754-1833* (Laughlintown, Pa.: Southwest Pennsylvania Genealogical Services, 1989), Appendix IX, 61-75.

[117] Nichols, *Braddock Expedition*, 200.

[118] Nichols, *Braddock Expedition*, 198.

[119] "Proposals for a Contract," May 24, *Pennsylvania Colonial Records*, 6:401: "Bread or flower and beeves, or in want of them salt beef, pork or fish, sufficient to subsist three thousand men for three months, to be laid in at Shippensburg." See Lily Lee Nixon, *James Burd, Frontier Defender, 1726-1793* (Philadelphia: [n.p.], 1941), 21-34; *Pennsylvania Colonial Records*, 6:376-7; I Pennsylvania Archives, 2:293, 317; Lincoln, *William Shirley, Correspondence*, 2:368-9; Thomas Balch, *Letters and Papers relating chiefly to the Provincial History of Pennsylvania* (Philadelphia: Privately Printed, 1855), 34-45. See the letters of Edward Shippen, James Burd, and Gov. Robert Morris.

[120] Lady [Matilda Ridout] Edgar, *A Colonial Governor in Maryland: Horatio Sharpe and his Times, 1753-1773* (New York: Longmans, Green, and Co., 1912), 45.

Chapter Two - Journey to the Monongahela

Pages 39 through 68.

[1] T. J. C. Williams and Folger McKinsey, "Orderly Book of General Braddock," *History of Frederick County*, 2 vols. (Baltimore: Regional Publishing Company, 1967), 1:59.

[2] Winthrop Sargent, ed., "The Morris Journal," *The History of an Expedition Against Fort Duquesne in 1755; under Major General Braddock* (Philadelphia: Memoirs of the Historical Society of Pennsylvania, 1855), 370.

[3] Letter from Charles Hamilton to the author.

[4] Charles Hamilton, "Journal of Captain Robert Chomley's Batman," *Braddock's Defeat* (Norman, Ok.: Univ. of Oklahoma Press, 1959), 12. Hamilton's book also includes "The Orderly Book of Sir Peter Halkett."

[5] Charles Hamilton, *Braddock's Defeat*, 12.

[6] Williams and McKinsey, "Orderly Book of General Braddock," *Frederick County*, 1:59-60.

[7] Robert Dinwiddie to Charles Dick, Jan. 25, 1755, *The Official Records of Robert Dinwiddie*, 2 vols. (New York: AMS Press, 1884), 1:479.

[8] C. Hamilton, "Journal of Capt. Robert Chomley's Batman," *Braddock's Defeat*, 12.

[9] Williams and McKinsey, "Orderly Book of General Braddock," *Frederick County*, 1:60.

[10] Williams and McKinsey, "Orderly Book of General Braddock," *Frederick County*, 1:60.

[11] William Hand Browne ed., *Procedings and Acts of the Asssembly, 1755-1756*, Archives of Maryland (Baltimore: Maryland Historical Society, 1888), 52:85-6.

[12] Horatio Sharpe to Robert Dinwiddie, May 9, 1755, William Hand Browne ed., *Correspondence of Gov. Horatio Sharpe*, Archives of Maryland (Baltimore: Maryland Historical Society, 1888), 6:205.

[13] Kenneth P. Bailey, *Thomas Cresap, Maryland Frontiersman* (Boston: The Christopher Publishing House, 1944), 98.

[14] Williams and McKinsey, "Orderly Book of General Braddock," *Frederick County*, 1:60.

[15] Maria J. Liggett Dare, *Chaplines from Maryland and Virginia* (Washington: The Franklin Print, 1902), 32.

[16] Albert H. Heusser, *In the Footsteps of Washington (Pope's Creek to Princeton)* (Paterson, N. J.: Privately Published, 1921), 113.

[17] HS to Gov. Robert Dinwiddie, May 9, 1755, *Correspondence*, 6:205.

[18] Sargent, *History of an Expedition*, 194.

[19] FCLR, WR 9-607, Batholowmew Booker et al. to Christian Koogle, Dec. 26, 1790. The agreement regarding the Resurvey on Wooden Platter includes a Deposition of Bartholomew Booker. ". . . and the said tract of land was surveyed by Thomas Prather about forty years or thereabout past. And that they came past said tree and it was then marked . . ."

232   Notes   (Chapter Two)

20 Tracey Collection records, Joseph Chapline to Bartholomew Booker, Dec. 4, 1754, Mindall, 66 acres. See MSA Y & S #7, 160, Mindall, Joseph Chapline, certificate of survey, examined and passed Dec. 9, 1751; patented by Joseph Chapline Dec. 12, 1750, 50 acres.

21 Maryland Historical Magazine, Dec. 1914, 9:370. "To Bartholomew Booker of Fredk. County as per Account 22..13.. 6."

22 HS to Sir John St. Clair, Mar. 27, 1758, Correspondence, 9:163-4. ". . . when he was writing to me to get a quantity of Forage laid in at the mouth of Conegochiegh that it will be impossible to get any thing in those Parts without ready money there being more than £2000 still due to the People of Frederick County on Account of General Braddock's Expedition."

23 Maryland Geological Survey, Report on the Highways of Maryland (Baltimore: The Johns Hopkins Press, 1899), 128. Also see William Waller Hening, ed., Hening's Statutes at Large of Virginia, 13 vols. (Richmond: Samuel Pleasants, 1809-23), 6:18. "1755 - From land of Thos. Swearingen in Frederick Co., Va." Includes the Ferry Act of 1748.

24 John Walter Wayland, The German Element of the Shenandoah Valley of Virginia (Bridgewater, Va.: C. J. Carrier Company, 1964), 84. Wayland cites Hening's Statutes, 6:494.

25 Millard M. Rice, This Was The Life (Redwood City, Calif.: Monocacy Book Company, 1979), 149. Excerpts from the Judgement Records of Frederick County, Maryland, 1748-1765, November Court of 1754.

26 Lee and Barbara Barron, The History of Sharpsburg, Maryland (Sharpsburgh, Md.: Barrons, 1972).

27 John W. Schildt, Drums Along the Antietam (Parson, W.Va.: McClain, 1972), 19.

28 John C. Fitzpatrick, ed., The Writings of George Washington from the Original Manuscript Sources 1744-1789, 39 vols. (Washington, D.C.: U.S. Government Printing Office, 1933), 1:119-20.

29 Sir John St. Clair to General Braddock, undated letter, Pargellis, Military Affairs, 64.

30 See Dieter Cunz, The Maryland Germans, a history (Princeton: Princeton University Press, 1948), for a study of the Germans in Maryland.

31 St. Clair to General Braddock, not dated, Pergallis, Military Affairs, 64.

32 HS to W. and J. Sharpe, Nov. 3, 1754, Correspondence, 6:110-1.

33 General Braddock to Robert Napier, Apr. 19, 1755, Pargellis, Military Affairs, 82.

34 RD to Sir Thomas Robinson, Mar. 17, 1755, Records, 1:524-6.

35 HS to RD, Dec. 10, 1754, Correspondence, 6:140.

36 HS to RD, Dec. 26, 1754, Correspondence, 6:150.

37 RD to HS, Sept. 5, 1754, Correspondence, 6:97.

38 Lewis Evans, Geographical, historical, political, philosophical and mechanical essays, the first containing an analysis of a general map of the middle British colonies in America, and of the country of the confederate Indians; a description of the face of the country; the boundaries of the confederates; and the maritime and inland navigations of the several rivers and lakes contained therein (Philadelphia: Franklin & Hall, 1755). Includes a discussion of the navigation possibilities on the Potomac River in 1755.

[39] Gov. Morris to HS, Nov. 14, 1754, *Correspondence*, 6:125-6.

[40] General Forbes to HS, Mar. 21, 1758, *Correspondence*, 9:158 and HS to General Forbes, *Correspondence*, 9:163.

[41] RD to Robert Morris, Jan. 14, 1755, *Records*, 1:454.

[42] RD to Robert Morris, Feb. 28, 1755, *Records*, 1:516.

[43] RD to William Allen, Feb. 28, 1755, *Records*, 1:517.

[44] RD to Colonel Innes, Mar. 7, 1755, *Records*, 1:519.

[45] RD to Dr. Alexander Colhoun, Mar. 7, 1755, *Records*, 1:520-1.

[46] Walter S. Hough, *Braddock's Road Through the Virginia Colony* (Winchester, Virginia: Winchester-Frederick County Historical Society, 1970).

[47] Maryland Geological Survey, *Report on the Highways of Maryland* (Baltimore: The Johns Hopkins Press, 1899), 128. See Hening's Statues at Large for ferries across the Potomac. "1744 - Evan Watkins, opposite mouth of Canagochego."

[48] RD to Sharpe, June 13, 1755, *Records*, 2:58.

[49] RD to HS, July 31, 1754, *Correspondence*, 6:77.

[50] RD to HS, Dec. 17, 1754, *Correspondence*, 6:145.

[51] St. Clair to Robert Napier, June 13, 1755, Pargellis, *Military Affairs*, 93.

[52] C. Hamilton, "Journal of Capt. Robert Chomley's Batman," *Braddock's Defeat*, 13.

[53] C. Hamilton, "Journal of Capt. Robert Chomley's Batman," *Braddock's Defeat*, 13.

[54] RD to Robert Orme, May 16, 1755, *Records*, 2:37.

[55] Sargent, *History of an Expedition*, 195.

[56] General Braddock to Robert Napier, June 8, 1755, at Ft. Cumberland, Pargellis, *Military Affairs*, 84.

[57] John Bakeless, *Daniel Boone* (Harrisburg, Pennsylvania: Stackpole Company, 1939), 21.

[58] Doug Bast, "William, George Boone Lay Out Boone's Berry," *Maryland Cracker Barrel, Inc.*, Vol. 20, No. 6, Boonsboro, Maryland.

[59] Bakeless, *Daniel Boone*, 21.

[60] North Callahan, *Daniel Morgan, Ranger of the Revolution* (New York: Holt, Rinehart and Winston, 1961), 3-17.

[61] Sargent, "The Morris Journal," *History of an Expedition*, 362-3. See Pargellis, *Military Affairs*, 86-8.

[62] Pargellis, *Military Affairs*, 86.

[63] See Appendix F - Biographical Listing. Also, see Sargent, *History of an Expedition*, 298, footnote 1.

[64] Pennsylvania, *Minutes of the Provincial Council, from the organization to the termination of the proprietary government [March 10, 1683 to September 27, 1775]* (Harrisburg: [n.p.], 1831-1840), 6:400. The first ten volumes are commonly known as the Pennsylvania Colonial Records.

[65] RD to HS, June 2, 1755, *Records*, 2: 47.

[66] Sargent, *History of an Expedition*, 302, footnote 1. Also see Colonial Records, 6:400, 409, 413, 405, 465; also see II Pennsylvania Archives, 347.

[67] RD to Braddock, June 3, 1755, *Records*, 2:49.

[68] RD to Shirley, June 24, 1755, *Records*, 2:74.

[69] RD to HS, July 5, 1755, *Records*, 2:85-6.

[70] RD to the several county Lieutenants upon the frontiers of the colony, June 17, 1755, *Records*, 2:67.

[71] RD to HS, June 18, 1755, *Records*, 2:67.

[72] RD to the Lords of Trade, June 23, 1755, *Records*, 2:71.

[73] Orme to HS, July 18, 1755, Sharpe, *Correspondence*, 6:253.

[74] Sargent, *History of an Expedition*, 388-9.

[75] *Scribner's Magazine*, 13:529-37. "An Unpublished Autograph Narrative by Washington," submitted by Henry G. Pickering.

[76] RD to the Earl of Halifax, Oct. 1, 1755, *Records*, 2:220-7.

[77] Pargellis, *Military Affairs*, 98-100. Also see Robert Orme to Gov. Morris, July 18, 1755, in *Early History of Western Pennsylvania* (Southwestern Pennsylvania Genealogical Services, Laughlintown, Pa. 1989), 106.

[78] Robert Orme to HS, July 18, 1755, *Correspondence*, 6: 252-4.

[79] Colonel Thomas Dunbar to Robert Napier, July 24, 1755, Pargellis, *Military Affairs*, 109-11.

[80] See Pargellis, *Military Affairs*, 125, for *A Return of the Troops Encamp'd at Wills' Creek, distinguishing the fit for duty, sick and wounded, July 25th 1755.*

[81] Williams and McKinsey, *History of Frederick County*, 1:30.

[82] Sir Bernard Burke, *Burke's American Families with British Ancestry* (Baltimore: Genealogical Publishing Company, 1975), 2847.

[83] RD to Robert Orme, July 28, 1755, *Records*, 2:121.

[84] RD to Gov. Dobbs, July 28, 1755, *Records*, 2:123-4.

[85] Lady Edgar, *Horatio Sharpe and His Times*, 60.

[86] HS to Thomas Robinson, Aug. 11, 1755, *Correspondence*, 6:264-5.

[87] Karen Mauer Green, *The Maryland Gazette, 1727-1761* (Galveston: The Frontier Press, 1989), 161. Thursday, Aug. 7, 1755.

[88] HS to RD, Aug. 11, 1755, *Correspondence*, 6:266.

[89] HS to John Sharpe, Apr. 2, 1756, *Correspondence*, 6:388.

[90] Sargent, *History of an Expedition*, 389.

[91] Dinwiddie confirms the route by way of Shippensburg in a Sept. 7, 1755, letter to Governor Shirley.

[92] Sept. 9, 1755, Robert Dinwiddie to William Shirley, *The Colonial Records of North Carolina* (Raleigh: Josephus Daniels, 1887), 5:430. Also see the *Pennsylvania Gazette* of Aug. 17, 1755, for a Dunbar letter from Shippensburg; Morris to Braddock, July 3, Pennsylvania Archives, 2:372; to Innes, July 14, PA, 2:377. "I have already sent to Shippensburgh 213 barrells of as good pork as ever was cut, etc."

[93] James Burd to Gov. Morris, July 25, *Pennsylvania Colonial Records*, 6:500.

[94] Nichols, *Braddock Expedition*, 397.

95 Robert Hunter Morris to William Shirley, Sept. 5, 1755, Pennsylvania Archives, 2:400; also see the *Pennsylvania Gazette*, Sept., 4, 1755.

96 RD to HS, Aug 25, 1755, *Records*, 2:169.

97 RD, *Records*, 2:184.

98 RD, *Records*, 2:184-5.

99 Fairfax Harrison, ed., "Mrs. Browne's Diary in Virginia and Maryland," *The Viriginia Magazine of History and Biography*, XXXII, No. 4, (October, 1924). The footnotes to this article contain information about the roads, ferries, and people along the route followed by Mrs. Browne.

100 See Tracey and Dern, *Pioneers of Old Monocacy*, 47. Also MdHR 5715, 1-20-6-13, Robert DeButts to Michael Thomas, Mar. 27, 1745. Also, see FCLR, B-172, Phillemon Church, schoolmaster, to John Berg, blacksmith, Bill of Sale, recorded May 18, 1750. Signed by Ths. Beatty and Robt DeButts.

101 HS to RD, Aug. 23, 1755, *Correspondence*, 6:270-1.

102 Louis K. Koontz, *The Virginia Frontier, 1754-1763* (Baltimore: Johns Hopkins Press, 1925), 90-1.

103 Herbert L. Osgood, *The American Colonies in the Eighteenth Century*, 4 vols. (Gloucester, Mass.: P. Smith, 1958).

104 Braddock to Robert Napier, June 8, 1755, Pargellis, *Military Affairs*, 92.

105 St. Clair to Robert Napier, June 13, 1755, Pargellis, *Military Affairs*, 94.

106 For a thorough analysis of the Braddock Expedition see, Franklin B. Nichols, "The Braddock Expedition" (Ph.D. diss., Harvard University, 1947). Probably the most significant study of the Braddock Expedition. Unfortunately, Nichols has both Braddock and Dunbar's Regiment crossing the Potomac at Swearingen's Ferry.

Chapter Three - Documentation of the Braddock Road through Fox's Gap

Pages 69 through 118.

1 T. J. C. Williams and Folger McKinsey, "The Orderly Book of General Braddock," *History of Frederick County*, 2 vols. (Baltimore: Regional Publishing Company, 1967), 1:53-67.

2 Winthrop Sargent, ed., "Captain Orme's Journal," *The History of An Expedition against Fort Duquesne, in 1755* (Philadelphia: J. B. Lippincott & Co, 1856), 309.

3 See MdHR G 1427 528 for a map prepared for the Maryland Commission for the 200th Anniversary of George Washington's Birthday, showing the routes traveled by George Washington in Maryland. The map does not include the route traveled by Washington from Frederick Town to Swearingen's Ferry on May 2, 1755. The map shows Washington leading Braddock's troops to Conococheague at that time.

[4] George Washington to William Fairfax, April 23, 1755, John C. Fitzpatrick, ed., *Writings of Washington*, 39 vols. (Washington, D.C.: U.S. Government Printing Office, 1933), 1:116-7.

[5] GW to Mrs. George William Fairfax, April 30, 1755, *Writings*, 1:117-8.

[6] GW to William Fairfax, May 5, 1755, *Writings*, 1:118-9.

[7] GW to John Augustine Washington, May 6, 1755, *Writings*, 1:119-20.

[8] GW to Major John Carlyle, May 14, 1755, *Writings*, 1:121-2.

[9] Horatio Sharpe to Gov. Robert Dinwiddie, May 9, 17 , William Hand Browne, ed., *The Correspondence of Gov. Horatio Sh e* Archives of Maryland (Baltimore: Maryland Historical Society, 1888, :205.

[10] Robert Dinwiddie, *The Official Records of Robert Din ddie*, 2 vols. (New York: Virginia Historical Society, 1884), 2:58-9.

[11] Karen Mauer Green, *The Maryland Gazette 1727-1761 Genealogical and Historical Abstracts* (Galveston: The Frontier Press, 1989 155.

[12] HS, *Correspondence*, 6:207.

[13] HS, *Correspondence*, 6:208.

[14] Frederick County, Maryland, A-1-182, will of Moses Ch apline [Sr.], Aug. 13, 1762.

[15] Maria J. Liggett Dare, *Chaplines from Maryland nd Virginia* (Washington: The Franklin Print, 1902), 32.

[16] Dare, *Chaplines from Maryland and Virginia*, 32.

[17] Dare, *Chaplines from Maryland and Virginia*, 32.

[18] George B. Davis, Leslie J. Perry, and Joseph W. Kirk ey, *Atlas to Accompany the Official Records of the Union and Confed rate Armies* (Washington: Government Printing Office, 1891-5), Plate XXV I, #3, Battle of South Mountain.

[19] John W. Schildt, *Drums Along the Antietam* (Parson, W.\ a.: McClain, 1972), 27.

[20] MdHR 17,451, 1-23-4-5, Alexander Grim, survey for Grim' Fancy, June 5, 1765, 50 acres. MSA BC & GS 40, 114.

[21] I. Daniel Rupp, *Thirty-Thousand Names of Immigrant* (Baltimore: Genealogical Publishing Co., 1971), 280-1.

[22] R. B. Strassburger and W. J. Hinke, *Pennsylvania German P oneers, Lists of Arrivals* (Norristown, Pa.: Pennsylvania German Society, 934), 488-9.

[23] Washington County, Maryland, Book A Liber 102, will f John Fox, Jan. 17, 1784.

[24] Daniel Gebhart Fox, *The Fox Genealogy including the Met erd, Benner and Leiter Descendants* (n.p., 1914), 12. A copy of *The Fox Ge ealogy* is at The Genealogical Society of the Church of Jesus Christ Latte -day Saints, Salt Lake City, Utah.

[25] Fox, *Fox Genealogy*, 12.

[26] Frederick County, Maryland, the Account of Joseph nd Jennett Chapline, Executors of Moses Chapline late of Frederick County Deceased. First Account, A-1-374; Second Account, A-1-414.

[27] Frederick County, Maryland, A-1-182, will of Moses Chapline [Sr.], Aug. 13, 1762.

[28] Maryland State Archives, Special Collections, MSA G1427-507, B5-1-3, *Road from Swearingen's Ferry on the Potomac River Through Sharpsburg to the Top of the South Mountain at Fox's Gap*, Aug. 13, 1792.

[29] Julia Angeline Drake and James Ridgely Orndorff, *From Mill Wheel to Plowshare, The Story of the Contribution of the Christian Orndorff Family to the Social and Industrial History of the United States* (Cedar Rapids, Iowa: Reprinted by the Maryland Historical Society, 1971). Spelled *Orendorff* on the August 23, 1792, map.

[30] Dare, *Chaplines*, 34.

[31] Drake and Orndorff, *From Mill Wheel to Plowshare*, 30.

[32] John W. Schildt, *Drums Along the Antietam* (Parson, W.Va.: McClain, 1972), 26-9.

[33] Byron L. Williams, *The Old South Mountain Inn* (Shippensburg, Pa.: Beidel Printing House, Inc., 1990), 70.

[34] GW to Robert Dinwiddie, from Winchester, June 25, 1756, *Writings*, 1:394.

[35] Berkeley County Historical Society, *The Berkeley Journal*, Issue Thirteen, 1989, 9-21.

[36] Joshua Fry, "A Map of the Inhabited part of Virginia, containing the whole Province of Maryland, with part of Pensilvania, New Jersey and North Carolina," *The Fry and Jefferson map of Virginia and Maryland; facsimiles of the 1754 and 1794 printings with an index* 2nd ed. (Charlottesville: Univ. Press of Virginia, 1966).

[37] MdHR 17,396, 1-23-2-30, James Smith, patent for Smith's Hills, Dec. 27, 1739, 208 acres. MSA PT #1, 261-3.

[38] MdHR 17,388, 1-23-2-20, Thomas Swearingen, patent for Fellfoot, Nov. 10, 1737, 115 acres. MSA EI #2, 623-4.

[39] MdHR 17,400, 1-23-2-34, Joseph Chapline, patent for Mountain, Apr. 9, 1745, 50 acres.

[40] MdHR 17,395-2, 1-23-2-29, Mount Pleasant, surveyed Mar. 11, 1744/5. MSA LG #E, 559-60.

[41] MdHR 17, 388, 1-23-2-20, Richard Sprigg, survey for Piles's Grove, Aug. 14, 1736, 560 acres. MSA EI #5, 106.

[42] FCLR, BD-1-535, Moses Chapline [Jr.] to John Cary and Christopher Edelen, Resurvey on Mt. Pleasant and Josiah's Bit, Oct. 18, 1775, 471 and 50 acres, except Old Purchase of 77 acres. Also see MdHR 17,410, 1-23-3-4. The Resurvey on Mt. Pleasant, surveyed Oct. 23, 1751. MSA GS #1, 101-2.

[43] [near to MdHR 17,438, 1-23-3-38], Moses Chapline, his certificate for Josiah's Last Bit, patented to William Good, April 20, 1786, 67 acres. Maryland State Archives, IC #B, 481.

[44] FCLR, BD-1, Moses Chapline [Jr.] to William Good, May 18, 1775, Old Purchase, 77 acres.

[45] MdHR 17,465, 1-23-4-19, William Good, survey for Pastures Green, Dec. 11, 1784, 290 acres. MSA IC #B, 480-1.

[46] MdHR 17,490, 1-23-5-3, John Miller, survey for Miller's Hills, Dec. 4, 1813, 180 acres. MSA IB #G, 303-4.

[47] MdHR 17,476, 1-23-4-32, Jacob Hess, survey for Security, May 10, 1791, 85 acres. MSA IC #N, 6-7.

[48] Jacob Hess, resurvey for Security, Sept. 11, 1792, 175 acres.

[49] Patent date of May 2, 1782.

[50] WCLR, G 7, 621-6, Jacob Hess et al., survey for Fellfoot Enlarged, March 19, 1792, 2100 acres.

[51] MdHR 17,745, 1-23-4-31, John Booth and Jonas Hogmire, patent for Mt. Atlas, 1798. MSA S11 IC #M, 470-1.

[52] MdHR 17,458, 1-23-4-12, Philip Booker, survey for Booker's Resurvey on Well Done, Apr. 2, 1772, 332 acres. MSA BC & GS #47, 39-40.

[53] MdHR 17,386, 1-23-2-18, John Magrudar, survey for The Forrest, Oct. 2, 1733, 300 acres. MSA AM #1, 365-6. Also see, MdHR 17,390, 1-23-2-22, John Magrudar, patent for The Forrest, Apr. 9, 1734, 300 acres. MSA El 4, 60-1.

[54] Maryland Geological Survey, *Report on the Highways of Maryland* (Baltimore: The Johns Hopkins Press, 1899), 128. See John Gibson, ed., *History of York Co., Pennsylvania* (Baltimore: Genealogical Publishing Company, 1975), 514. This book discusses the Post Map of New England, New York, New Jersey, and Pennsylvania, by Moll, dated 1730.

[55] MdHR 17,406-3, 1-23-2-44, James Wardrop, survey for Oxford, July 23, 1751, 54 acres. MSA BY & GS #5, 594.

[56] MdHR 17,406-3, 1-23-2-44, James Wardrop, survey for The Cool Spring, July 23, 1751, 75 acres. MSA BY & GS #5, 608-9.

[57] MdHR 17,415, 1-23-3-9, Robert Evans, survey for Betty's Good Will, Oct. 16, 1747, 50 acres. MSA BC & GS 4, 195-6.

[58] MdHR 17,415, 1-23-3-9, Edward Grimes, patent for Betty's Good Will, Sept. 29, 1754. MSA GS #2, 12-3. The Grimes patent gives a survey date of Oct. 20, 1727, in the name of Robert Evans.

[59] FCLR, WR-7, Bartholomew Booker to Frederick Fox, April 4, 1787, 92 acres. Part of I Hope It Is Well Done and Pegging Awl.

[60] FCLR, CM-1-582, Vincent Sanner to Samuel Ausherman, recorded April 14, 1868, 194 1/2 acres. Part of Fidler's Purchase, part of the Resurvey on Exchange, part of Bubble, and Deefer Snay.

[61] FCLR, THO-1-220, Jacob Smith Jr., resurvey called Now I Know It, Dec. 17, 1802, 198 acres.

[62] Patricia Abelard Andersen, "Jacob Fluck of Middletown, Frederick County, Maryland, and his Flook and Fluke Descendants," *National Genealogical Society Quarterly*, September 1984, Volume 72, Number 3, page 163. Tracts shown on page 179 include Blooming Month of May, Resurvey on Learning, No Matter What, Apple Brandy, Flook's Content, Resurvey on Oxford, Younger Brother, Neighbor's Content, Resurvey on Toms Gift, Dundalk, Peach Brandy, and the Resurvey on Whiskey Alley.

[63] MdHR 17,430-1, 1-23-3-26, Turkey Foot, Frederick Fox, patent of Mar. 13, 1794, 6 acres. MSA IC #G, 361. Surveyed March 13, 1788.

[64] MdHR 17,471, 1-23-4-27, Mt. Pleasant, Frederick Fox, patent of May 27, 1793, 23 acres.

[65] MSA BY & GS #1, 177. Also see MdHR 17,405-2, 1-23-2-43, Casper Shaff's patent for the Resurvey on Exchange, 1754.

[66] FCLR, E-339, Joseph Chapline [Sr.] to Casper Shaff, Dec. 11, 1753, Exchange, 75 acres.

[67] MdHR 17-405-2, 1-23-2-43, Casper Shaff, patent for the Resurvey on Exchange, Sept. 1, 1751, 1754. MSA BY & GS #4, 585-6. Shaff's Purchase began "at a bounded white oak the beginning tree of a tract of land called Betty's Good Will." See FCLR, O-112, Casper Shaff to Peter Ruble, recorded March 26, 1771, 93 acres.

[68] Exchange, E-339, Dec. 11, 1753, Joseph Chapline [Sr.] to Casper Shaff.

[69] FCLR, K-1373, July 9, 1767, Casper Shaff to Valentine Fidler.

[70] Warren County Genealogical Society, Lebanon, Ohio, Estate Papers of George Fox.

[71] Curtis L. Older, *Documentation Related to Frederick Fox including material on his Descendants* (unpublished manuscript).

[72] Frederick S.Weiser, ed., *Zion Lutheran Church 1781-1826*, Maryland German Church Records, Vol. 2, (Manchester, Md.: Noodle-Doosey Press, 1987), 25. "Samuel, son of Jacob and Magdelena Benner was born April 14, 1801. Baptised June 21, 1801. Sponsored by George Fox, a single person." (Mary) Magdelena Benner was the daughter of Frederick Fox and sister of George.

[73] Jefferson County, West Virginia, Marriage Records, 1807, page 286.

[74] *Index to Marriage Licenses, Frederick County, 1778-1810*. Married April 14, 1783.

[75] Paxson Link, *The Link Family* (Paris, Illinois: [n.p.], 1951).

[76] Francis Hamilton Hibbard, assisted by Stephen Parks, *The English origin of John Ogle, first of the name in Delaware* (Pittsburgh: n.p., 1967); Sir Henry Asgill Ogle, *Ogle and Bothal* (Newcastle-upon-Tyne: Andrew Reid & Company, 1902). Alexander Ogle, father of Jane Ogle, provided wheat and flour from his mills to the Maryland troops during the American Revolution. See Maryland State Papers, Series A, MdHR 6636-23-29/7 1/7/5 and related papers. Adam Link I, the grandfather of Elizabeth Ann Link , supplied bacon during the American Revolution. See Maryland State Papers, Series A, MdHR 4586-15 1/6/4/18. John Adam Link II, the father of Elizabeth Ann Link, was an officer during the American Revolution. See Paxson Link, *The Link Family*, 78.

[77] FCLR, WR-32-30, George Fox to John Ringer, 1807, 100 acres.

[78] Fox, *Fox Genealogy*, 15-6.

[79] FCLR, JS-42-481, Sidney Ringer to Vincent Sanner, recorded May 15, 1833. This deed transferred 31+ acres being part of I Hope Its Well Done, part of Peggin All, part of Turkey Foot, and part of Mount Pleasant; also 75 acres being part of Fidler's Purchase, part of the Resurvey on Exchange, and part of Bubble.

[80] FCLR, CM-1-582, Vincent Sanner to Samuel Ausherman, recorded Apr. 14, 1868, 194 1/2 acres.

[81] FCLR, HGO-1-466, Neighbor's Content, Andrew Smith, resurveyed Nov. 25, 1790.

[82] FCLR, WR-22-480, George Butt to Mathias Flook, recorded April 22, 1802.

[83] Maryland Historical Society, PAM 3326, *The Reno Memorial, South Mountain, Maryland*. Program at the dedication of the Reno Monument.

84 MdHR 17,448, 1-23-4-2, Bowser's Addition, surveyed April 10, 1765, 10 acres. MSA BC & GS #37, 138-9.

85 FCLR, BGF-6-216, Joel Keller to John Wise, recorded Oct. 17, 1860, "part of the same land which the said Joel Keller obtained from Susan Miller, John W. Derr, Elizabeth Derr and others heirs at law of the late Henry Miller deceased by deed dated the 7th day of May 1844." Also, FCLR, WIP-9-149, John W. Wise et ux to Jonas Gross, recorded Apr. 5, 1889, 4 3/4 acres. ". . . which is more particularly described in a deed from Joel Keller and wife to the said John Wise and Matilda Wise, dated on the seventh day of May in the year eighteen hundred and fifty eight . . . "

86 FCLR, WIP 11, folios 8, 9, and 10, Jonas Gross to Society of the Burnside Expedition, Nov. 23, 1889, 40 feet square.

87 MdHR 17,478, 1-23-4-34, Frederick Fox, patent for Addition to Friendship, May 27, 1805, 202 acres. MSA IC #P, 672-3.

88 FCLR, WBT-1-100, Susan Miller et al. to John Miller, recorded Apr. 1, 1845, 13 and 1/4 acres. Bowser's Addition and part of Addition to Friendship.

89 FCLR, HGO-1-156, Frederick Fox, survey for Fredericksburg, July 6, 1792, 75 acres.

90 MdHR 17,438, 1-23-3-38, David Bowser, patent for David's Will, Dec. 24, 1763, 49 acres. MSA BC & GS, 396.

91 FCLR, THO-1-194, Samuel Shoup, resurvey called The Cool Spring, Jan. 18, 1801, 266 1/2 acres. This is a resurvey of The Case Is At End.

92 FCLR, K-499-500, John Fox to Elias Bruner, Lot #269 in Frederick Town, May 22, 1766.

93 FCLR J-504-5, Daniel Dulany to John Fox, Lot #269 in Frederick Town, June 2, 1764.

94 Frederick S. Weiser, ed., *Evangelical Reformed Church, Frederick, Frederick County, 1746-1789,* Maryland German Church Records, Vol. 5, (Manchester, Md.: Noodle-Doosey Press, 1987), 23. "Christina, dau. of Philipp and Elisabetha Casper, b. 20 Oct. 1766, bp. 19 Dec. 1766. Sponsors: Johann Georg and Christina Fux [sic]."

95 Letter, dated "Aug 9, 1812," from "Sharpsburg," that was "received and forwarded from Lebanon, Warren County, Ohio, Sept. 8, 1812, addressed to Msrs. Fredric(k) & Michael Fox, Franklin Township, Warren Co. Ohio," from Jacob Reel. Robert H. Fox of Cincinnati, Ohio, provided the author with a copy of this letter.

96 Maryland State Archives, Special Collections, MSA G1427-507, B5-1-3, *Road from Swearingen's Ferry on the Potomac River Through Sharpsburg to the Top of the South Mountain at Fox's Gap,* Aug. 13, 1792.

97 FCLR, WR-42-550, Peter Ludy to Jacob Routzong, recorded July 9, 1812, 68 acres. Part of Addition to Friendship and part of Fredericksburg.

98 Jacob D. Cox, *Military Reminiscences* (New York: Charles Scribner's Sons, 1900), 1:287.

99 Cox, *Military Reminiscences,* 1:279.

100 Fox, *Fox Genealogy* (n.p., 1914), 15.

101 Robert H. Fox, Cinicinnati, Ohio.

102 Betty J. Mason, "Castle Bible Records," *Western Maryland Genealogy* (Middletown, Md., 1986), 2:153.

103 Source unknown, pages 132-3.
104 United States War Department, *The War of the Rebellion: A Compilation of the Official Records of the Union and Confederate Armies. including Atlas*, 70 vols. (Washington, D.C.: U. S. Government, 1880-1891), Series 1, Vol. 19, Part I, 817.
105 U. S. War Dept., *War of the Rebellion*, Series 1, Vol. 19, Part I, 1031-2.
106 Walter Clark, ed., *Histories of the Several Regiments and Battalions from North Carolina in the Great War 1861-1865*, 5 vols. (Raleigh: State of North Carolina, 1901), 1:140.
107 Jedediah Hotchkiss, *Make Me a Map of the Valley, The Civil War Journal of Stonewall Jackson's Topographer* Archie P. McDonald, ed. (Dallas: Southern Methodist Press, 1973), 80. See the *Civil War Writings of General Robert E. Lee* for his order instructing Jackson to proceed from Middletown to Sharpsburg.
108 HS, *Correspondence*, 6:210.
109 RD to Robert Orme, July 28, 1755, *Records*, 2:121.
110 See article by Robert H. Fox in the *Middletown Valley Register*, Aug. 19, 1932.

Chapter Four - The Dunbar Route from Frederick Town to Conococheague

Pages 119 through 176.

1 T. J. C. Williams and Folger McKinsey, *History of Frederick County*, 2 vols. (Baltimore: Regional Publishing Company, 1967), 1:30.
2 Helen Ashe Hays, *The Antietam and Its Bridges* (New York: The Knickerbocker Press, 1910), 13.
3 Williams and McKinsey, *Frederick County*, 1:30.
4 Winthrop Sargent, ed., "Captain Orme's Journal," *The History of An Expedition against Fort Duquesne, in 1755* (Philadelphia: J. B. Lippincott & Co., 1856), 308.
5 Williams and McKinsey, *Frederick County*, 1:59. "Orderly Book of General Braddock," orders of Friday, April 11, 1755, march route of Sir Peter Halkett's Regiment from Alexandria to Winchester.
6 Horatio Sharpe to Sir John St. Clair, June 25, 1758, from Ft. Frederick, William Hand Browne, ed., *Correspondence of Governor Horatio Sharpe* Archives of Maryland (Baltimore: Maryland Historical Society, 1888), 9:210-1.
7 Millard M. Rice, *This Was the Life excerpts from the judgment records of Frederick County, Maryland 1748-1765* (Redwood City, California: Monocacy Book Company, 1979), 193.
8 Walter S. Hough, *Braddock's Road Through the Virginia Colony* (Winchester, Va.: Frederick County Historical Society, 1970).

[9] Hough,*Braddock's Road through Virginia*, 2-3.

[10] Hough,*Braddock's Road through Virginia*, 59.

[11] Albert H. Heusser, *In the Footsteps of Washington (Pope's Creek to Princeton)* (Paterson, N. J.: Privately Published, 1921), 110.

[12] John W. Schildt, *Drums Along the Antietam* (Parson, W.Va.: McClain, 1972), 11.

[13] Bradley T. Johnson, *General Washington* (New York: D. Appleton & Co., 1898), 44-5.

[14] Arthur Tracey, "The Old Monocacy Road," Historical Society of Carroll County, Westminster, Maryland, 2.

[15] Julia A. Drake and James R. Orndorff, *From Mill Wheel to Plowshare* (Cedar Rapids, Iowa: The Torch Press, 1938), 57. Also see, D. Dandridge. *Historic Shepherdstown* (Charlottesville: Michie, c1910), 73.

[16] Byron L. Williams, *The Old South Mountain Inn, An Informal History* (Shippensburg, Pa.: Beidel Printing House, Inc., 1990), 70.

[17] B. Williams, *Old South Mountain Inn*, 16-7.

[18] MdHR G 1427 508, *Road from Elizabethtown to Newcomber's Mill and Frederick County Line*, April 5, 1791. WCLR G. f. 549.

[19] MdHR G 1427 504, B5-1-3, *Road Leading from Williamsport to Turner's Gap in the South Mountain*, October 17, 1791. WCLR G. p. 533.

[20] Daniel Harvey Hill Jr., *Bethel to Sharpsburg*, 2 vols. (Raleigh: Edwards & Broughton Co., 1926), 1:366.

[21] MSA Special Collections, *Maryland Herald and Hagerstown Weekly*, July 22, 1807. Microfilm MSA M 8099, 1805-1809.

[22] MdHR G 1213-437.

[23] MSA G1427-1150 B5-2-1.

[24] George Washington to Lord Fairfax, Winchester, August 29, 1756, John C. Fitzpatrick, ed., *The Writings of George Washington from the Original Manuscript Sources 1744-1789*, 39 vols. (Washington, D.C.: U.S. Government Printing Office, 1933), 1:447.

[25] Fairfax Harrison, ed. "Mrs. Browne's Diary in Virginia and Maryland" *The Virginia Magazine of History and Biography*, No. 4, Oct., 1924, 32:310-1.

[26] T. J. C. Williams, *History of Washington County, Maryland*, 2 vols. (Baltimore: Regional Publishing Company, 1968), 1:27-8.

[27] MdHR 17,448, 1-23-4-2, Stoney Ridge, surveyed July 29, 1768. MSA BC & GS #37, 144-5.

[28] MdHR 17,458, 1-23-4-12, Wilyard's Lot, surveyed Dec. 31, 1765. MSA BC & GS #30, 259-61.

[29] Dieter Cunz, *The Maryland Germans, a history* (Princeton: Princeton University Press, 1948), 81-3.

[30] Drake and Orndorff, *From Mill Wheel to Plow Share*, 41.

[31] Grace L. Tracey and John P. Dern, *Pioneers of Old Monocacy* (Baltimore: Genealogical Publishing Company, 1987), 55-6.

[32] Tracy and Dern, *Pioneers of Old Monocacy*, 45.

[33] Daniel Wunderlich Nead, *The Pennsylvania-German in the Settlement of Maryland* (Lancaster, Pa.: The Pennslvania-German Society, 1914), 51.

[34] Millard M. Rice, *New Facts and Old Families From the Records of Frederick County, Maryland* (Baltimore: Genealogical Publishing Company, 1984), 161-73.

[35] Jeffrey A. Wyand, *Maryland Historical Magazine*, Vol. 67, No. 3, Fall, 1972, 303-4.

[36] John Hall to HS, from Baltimore Town, Sept. 5, 1756, *Correspondence*, 6:479.

[37] Archives of Maryland, *Proceedings and Acts of the General Assembly, 1755-1756*, May 14, 1756, 52:480-521, Chapter 5, 1756. MSA SC 2908, MdHR 2764.

[38] State Roads Commisision of Maryland, *A History of Road Building in Maryland* (n. p., 1958), 16.

[39] State Roads Commisision of Maryland, *A History of Road Building in Maryland*, 17.

[40] Archives of Maryland, *Proceedings and Acts of the General Assembly, 1755-1756*, May 14, 1756, 52:487-8.

[41] Rice, *This Was the Life*, 186.

[42] Rice, *This Was the Life*, 189.

[43] Rice, *This Was the Life*, 200.

[44] MdHR 17,441, 1-23-3-41, Bartholomew Booker, patent for Pick All, Feb. 22, 1764, 1224 acres. MSA BC & GS #30, 214-6.

[45] MdHR 17,406, 1-23-2-44, James Wardrop, patent for John's Delight, May 17, 1750, 104 acres. MSA BY & GS #5, 59.

[46] FCLR, F-1064, Bartholomew Booker to George Shidler, June 25, 1760, 100 acres. Shidler's Dispute, being part of Mend All, and a tract called Small All.

[47] FCLR, L-69, George Shidler to Bartholomew Booker, Oct. 15, 1767, 100 acres. Shidler's Dispute, being part of Mend All, and a tract called Small All.

[48] FCLR, L-71, Bartholomew Booker to George Shidler, Oct. 15, 1767, 200 acres. Long Dispute, being all of Shidler's Dispute and part of Pick All.

[49] FCLR, WR-12, 358-64, Frederick Fox and Margaret Booker to John Routzahn, April 19, 1794, 304 acres. Part of five tracts of land: the Resurvey on Mend All, Pick All, I Hope Its Well Done, Shettle, and Martitany.

[50] Frederick County, Md., Register of Wills Records, GM-2-431, will of Bartholomew Booker, Oct. 21, 1791.

[51] F. Edward Wright, *Western Maryland Newspaper Abstracts 1786-1798* (Silver Spring, Md.: Family Line Publications, 1985), 1:14.

[52] MdHR 17,448, 1-23-4-2, John Teem, survey for Worse and Worse, Feb. 7, 1766, 41 1/2 acres. MSA BC & GS #37, 218-9. Also see FCLR, P-632, John Team to Adam Coil, recorded Mar. 22, 1773.

[53] FCLR, THO 1, Henry Beagley, survey for Its Bad Enough, June 8 , 1795, 14 3/4 acres.

[54] MdHR 17,435, 1-23-3-35, Joseph Chapline, survey for The Gap, Mar. 29, 1761, 50 acres. MSA BC & GS #24, 270.

[55] FCLR, K-917, Joseph Chapline to John Team, The Gap, Jan. 9, 1767, 50 acres.

[56] MdHR 17,476, 1-23-4-32, Henry Beakley, Resurvey on The Gap, May 1, 1798, 219 1/2 acres. MSA IC #N, 467-8.

[57] MdHR 17,458, 1-23-4-12, Philip Jacob Shafer, survey for Flonham, Aug. 27, 1770, 36 acres. MSA BC & BS #47, 496-7. MdHR 17,455, 1-23-4-9, Philip Jacob Shafer, patent for Flonham, April 20, 1774, 36 acres. MSA BC & GS #44, 439-40.

[58] MdHR 17,438, 1-23-3-38, Robert Smith, survey for Fox's Last Shift, Oct. 5, 1764, 72 acres. MSA BC & GS #27, 311.

[59] WCLR, Elias Butter to Philip Laypole, Aug. 23, 1824, for 142 perches of Fox's Last Shift. This deed indicates a number of lots were laid out on this tract of land, apparently for a town.

[60] MdHR 17,472, 1-23-4-28, John Mansberger, resurvey of Fox's Last Shift called Newcomer's Purchase, Jan. 5, 1786, 101 acres. MSA IC #1, 713.

[61] MdHR 17,473, 1-23-4-29, John Mansberger, resurvey of Newcomer's Purchase called Partnership, Aug. 20, 1794, 685 acres. MSA IC #K, 343-4.

[62] MdHR 17,430-1, 1-23-3-26, Jacob Hessing, survey for Racon, Apr. 10, 1762, 50 acres. MSA BC & GS #19, 310-1.

[63] MdHR 17,456, 1-23-4-10, John Summer, patent for Raccoon, Aug. 27, 1770, 253 acres. BC & GS #45, 10-1.

[64] MdHR 17,443, 1-23-3-43, John Summer, patent for Kizer's Lowden, May 26, 1763, 110 acres. MSA BC & GS #22, 89-90. Probably adjacent to Contentment and Resurvey on Jerrico Hills. See MdHR 17,441, 1-23-3-41, survey for Contentment, Aug. 20, 1764. MSA BC & GS, 259-61.

[65] Archives of Maryland, Article XCV, 58:543.

[66] B. Williams, *Old South Mountain Inn*, 70.

[67] Tracey Collection records in the Historical Society of Carroll County, Westminster, Maryland.

[68] MdHR 17,395-1, 1-23-2-28, Daniel Dulany Esqr., survey of Ram's Horn, April 14, 1744, 600 acres. MSA LG #E, 346-8. See Rice, *New Facts and Old Families*, 114-5, for the plotting of the Rams Horn tract, Interstate 70, U.S. 40, and the old Hagerstown Road.

[69] MdHR 17,395-2, 1-23-2-29, Daniel Dulany Esqr., survey of Hoggyard, Oct. 7, 1742, 100 acres. MSA LG #E, 397.

[70] Tracey Collection records.

[71] Frederick County, Maryland, Robert Evans Administration Account, B-2-169, July 6, 1771.

[72] MdHR 17,415, 1-23-3-9, Robert Evans, survey of Betty's Good Will, Oct. 20, 1727, 50 acres. MSA BC & GS 4, 195-6.

[73] MdHR 17, 412-2, 1-23-2-37, Robert Evans, survey of Cuckholds Horns, Oct. 14, 1747, 150 acres. MSA BY & GS #1, 611-2.

[74] Tracey and Dern, *Pioneers of Old Monocacy*, 245.

[75] Maryland Archives, *Acts of Assembly, 1737-1740*, 19:220, 307, and 308. "Saturday Morning May 12th 1739."

[76] FCLR, B-172, Thomas Whitaker to Nicholas Fink, Prevention, May 19, 1750, 50 acres.

[77] FCLR, O-540, Nicholas Fink to Thomas Welch, Goose Cap, recorded Sept. 2, 1771, 66 acres. See MdHR 17,456, 1-23-4-10, survey of Goose Cap, Oct. 10, 1770. MSA BC & GS #45.

[78] FCLR, JS-39-260, John Stemple et ux to George Baltzell, recorded July 5, 1832, 273 1/2 acres.

[79] MdHR 17,408, 1-23-3-1, Joseph Chapline, patent for the Resurvey on Watson's Welfare, July 28, 1752. MSA Y & S #7, 192.

[80] MdHR 17,443, 1-23-3-43, Philip Keywhaughvor, Resurvey on Whiskey Alley, May 12, 1762. MSA BC & GS #32, 480-3.

[81] See Tracey and Dern, *Pioneers of Old Monacacy*, 245. They mention Prevention, Forrest, and Wooden Platter. See MdHR 17, 412-2, 1-23-2-37, Resurvey on Wooden Platter, surveyed Sept. 1, 1748, MSA BY & GS #1, 604-5. Also, MdHR 17,412, 1-23-3-6, Resurvey on Prevention, surveyed May 10, 1752, MSA BC & GS #1, 155.

[82] FCLR, WR-4-179, Jacob Keefour to Members et al., Aug. 20, 1783.

[83] MdHR 17,394, 1-23-2-27, Ewen McDonald, patent for Watson's Welfare, August 27, 1744, 100 acres. MSA LG #C, 56-7.

[84] Millard M. Rice, *New Facts and Old Families*, 137-48. Also see, George C. Rhoderick Jr., *The Early History of Middletown, Maryland*, Middletown Valley Historical Society.

[85] Tracey Collection records.

[86] FCLR, N-560, Bartholomew Booker to Jacob Smith, recorded Jan. 23, 1772, 100 acres.

[87] FCLR, F-1077, Bartholomew Booker to Michel Shepfell, part of the Resurvey on Mend All, June 6, 1760, 100 Acres.

[88] The surveys for Kizer's Lowden, Jacob's Brune, and Marstone mention the location of Robert Turner's plantation.

[89] WCLR, B, 336-8, Robert Turner, patent for Nelson's Folly, recorded March 5, 1750, 500 acres. ". . . according to the certificate of survey thereof taken and returned into our land office bearing date the fourth day of June seventeen hundred and thirty four . . ."

[90] Land tract analysis by the author and material supplied by Doug Bast of the Boonsborough Museum of History.

[91] Tracey Collection records.

[92] MdHR 17,420, 1-23-3-14, Samuel Ogle, survey for Charlemount Pleasant, January 1, 1745, 100 acres.

[93] MSA B, pp. 336-8, Robert Turner, patent for Nelson's Folly, March 5, 1750. The certificate of survey date was June 4, 1734.

[94] MdHR 17,465, 1-23-4-19, Henry Poulis, survey of Jacob's Brune, March 27, 1772. MSA IC #B, 301.

[95] MdHR 17,456, 1-23-4-10, Peter Pecker, survey for Martsome, May 26, 1763. MSA BC & GS #45, 27.

[96] The reader may find the following article of interest. "The Old National Pike," *Harper's New Monthly Magazine*, Vol. LIX, 1879.

[97] *Laws, Documents and Judicial Decisions, Relating to The Baltimore and Fredericktown, York and Reisterstown, Cumberland and Boonsborough Turnpike Road Companies* (Baltimore: John D. Toy, 1841).

[98] *American State Papers: Miscellaneous* 1:901-7.

[99] *American State Papers: Miscellaneous* 1:909. "Answers to the queries respecting artifical roads, so far as relate to the Baltimore and Fredericktown Turnpike road, by Jona. Ellicott."

[100] *Maryland Herald and Hagerstown Weekly, 1805-1809,* MSA Special Collections, MSA M 8099.

[101] *Maryland Herald and Hagerstown Weekly, 1805-1809,* MSA Special Collections, MSA M 8099.

[102] MdHR 19,999-059-006 1/8/5/48, 59/3, 4, and 6. MSA S 1005-7887.

[103] WCLR, 74-264, George F. Smith to Madeleine Dahlgren, Apr. 19, 1876, 60 acres. Part of Addition to Friendship, part of Partnership, part of Swearingen's Disappointment, and part of Flonham.

[104] FCLR, WBT-10-143, Susan Miller et al. to Daniel Beagley, Apr. 21, 1849, 14 acres. Part of Addition to Friendship.

[105] FCLR, JS-39-264-8, George Baltzell to Henry Miller, Apr. 1, 1833, 189 1/2 acres. Part of Addition to Friendship.

[106] MdHR 17,487-1, 1-23-4-44, Jacob Fulwiler, survey for Apple Brandy, Oct. 31, 1791, 14 acres. MSA IC F, 307. Patented to John R. Magruder, May 8, 1815.

[107] MdHR 17,476, 1-23-4-32, Henry Beagley, Resurvey on The Gap, July 16, 1798, 219 1/2 acres. MSA IC #N, 467-8.

[108] FCLR, JS-25-372, Philip Sheffer to Henry Miller, July 6, 1826, 5+ acres. Part of Flonham.

[109] WCLR, 74-264, George F. Smith to Madeleine Dahlgren, Apr. 19, 1876, 60 acres. Part of Addition to Friendship, part of Partnership, part of Swearingen's Disappointment, and part of Flonham.

[110] FCLR, JS-39-264-8, George Baltzell to Henry Miller, July 5, 1832, 189 1/2 acres. Part of Addition to Friendship.

[111] WCLR, 172-524, "St. Mary's Academy" of Notre Dame to Otho Hewitt, Charles M. Hewitt, and Robert W. Hewitt, recorded Sept. 11, 1925.

[112] FCLR, WBT-10-143, Susan Miller et al. to Daniel Beagley, May 7, 1844, 14+ acres. Part of Addition to Friendship.

[113] FCLR, BFG-5-516, John W. Derr et al. to Adam Koogle, Mar. 16, 1854, 25 1/10 acres. Part of Addition to Friendship.

[114] FCLR, JS-38-194, Jacob Routzah to Henry Miller, recorded Feb. 18, 1832, 67 acres. Part of Addition to Friendship and part of Fredericksburg. Also see FCLR, JS-30-58-61, Jacob Routzong to George Routzong, recorded Aug. 8, 1828.

[115] FCLR, JS-39-264-8, George Baltzell Atty. to Henry Miller, May 31, 1832, 189 1/2 acres. Part of Addition to Friendship. Baltzell was attorney for the heirs of Joseph Swearingen.

[116] FCLR, WR-32-26-8, Frederick Fox to Joseph Swearingen, Sept. 21, 1807, 202 acres of Addition to Friendship and 30 acres of Fredericksburg.

[117] MdHR 17,478, 1-23-4-34, Frederick Fox, patent of Addition to Friendship, May, 9, 1797, 202 acres. MSA IC #P 672-3.

[118] *American State Papers: Miscellaneous* 1:738; *Laws, Documents and Judicial Decisions, relating to the Baltimore and Fredericktown, York and Reisterstown, Cumberland and Boonsborough Turnpike Road Companies.* (Baltimore: John D. Toy, 1841).

[119] FCLR, JS-25-372, Philip Sheffer to Henry Miller, July 6, 1826, 5+ acres. Part of Flonham.

[120] MdHR 17,458, 1-23-4-12, Philip Jacob Shafer, survey for Flonham, Aug. 27, 1770, 36 acres. MSA BC & BS #47, 496-7.

[121] J. G. de Roulhac Hamilton, ed., *The Papers of Randolph Abbot Shotwell* (Raleigh: N. C. Historical Commission, 1929), 1:305-71.

[122] MdHR 17,405-1, 1-23-2-42, William Steuart, patent for The Vineyard, Oct. 10, 1750, 154 acres; warrant of George Steuart, The Vineyard, April 7, 1739, 154 acres. MSA BC & GS #4, 181-3; See HS, *Correspondence*, 6:16. Perhaps Dr. George Stewart and his brother, William, who are mentioned in a letter from Lord Glencairn to HS, Dec. 24, 1753.

[123] See Otto B. Smith to Daniel R. Berry, transferred between 1867 and 1869, on the west side of the Antietam Creek and the south side of the stone bridge on the road from Keedsyville to Bakersville, next to Jacob Hammond's, Jos. Hoffman's, Daniel Miller's, and Dr. Kennedy's.

[124] MdHR 17,412, 1-23-3-6, William Stewart's assignment and Benjamin Tasker Sr.'s patent for the Resurvey of The Vineyard, Sept. 10, 1752, 506 acres. MSA BC & GS #1, 164.

[125] MdHR 17,456, 1-23-4-10, Joseph Chapline, Resurvey on Hills and Dales and The Vineyard, Nov. 9, 1771, 2256 acres. MSA BC & GS #45, 22-5.

[126] Tracey and Dern, *Pioneers of Old Monocacy*, 54-5.

[127] Tracey and Dern, *Pioneers of Old Monocacy*, 98.

[128] Rice, *This Was The Life*, 258.

[129] Williams and McKinsey, *Frederick County*, 1:60. "Orderly Book of General Braddock," orders of Apr. 28, 1755.

[130] MSA BC & GS 1-355, Edward Dorsey, Dorsey's Resque, Dec. 14, 1754, 158 acres.

[131] Little Meadow, Thomas Walker, Sept. 26, 1756, 200 acres.

[132] *Western Maryland Genealogy*, January, vol. 3, #1, (Middletown, Md.: Catoctin Press, 1987).

[133] Maryland Historical Magazine, 1914, 9:356.

[134] Robert Dinwiddie to Charles Dick, Jan. 25, 1755, Virginia Historical Society, *The Official Records of Robert Dinwiddie*, 2 vols. (Richmond: The Society, 1883-4), 2:479.

[135] Williams and McKinsey, *Frederick County*, 1:59-60. Orders, Apr. 27 and 28, 1755.

[136] Charles Hamilton, *Braddock's Defeat* (Norman: University of Oklahoma Press, 1959), xi.

[137] C. Hamilton, *Braddock's Defeat*, xi.

[138] C. Hamilton, *Braddock's Defeat*, 12.

[139] William J. Hinke, transl., "Report of the Journey of Francis Louis Michel, October 2, 1701, to December 1, 1702" *Virginia Magazine of History and Biography*, 24:1-43, 113-141, 275-303.

[140] Williams and McKinsey, *Frederick County*, 1:57. Orders, April 7th at Alexandria.

[141] HS to Robert Dinwiddie, Dec. 10, 1754, *Correspondence*, 6:140.

[142] Rice, *This Was the Life*, 186.

Afterword

Pages 177 through 182.

[1] Howard K. Beale, ed., *Diary of Gideon Welles*, 3 vols. (New York: Norton, 1960), 1:143.

[2] Roy P. Basler, ed. *The Collected Works of Abraham Lincoln*, 9 vols. (New Brunswick, N. J.: Rutgers Unviersity Press, 1953-55), 4:419. Remarks by the president, reported at a meeting at Bryan Hall in Chicago on September 20, 1862.

[3] Jacob D. Cox, *Military Reminiscences of the Civil War*, 2 vols. (New York: Charles Scribner's Sons, 1900), 1:278.

[4] Daniel Harvey Hill, Jr., *Bethel to Sharpsburg*, 2 vols. (Raleigh: Edwards & Broughton Co., 1926), 1:365. Hill Jr., 1:364, footnote 1 cites *Battles and Leaders*, 2:564. The four corps within Hill's view were the 1st and 9th under Reno and the 2nd and 12th under Sumner. The 6th under Franklin was at Crampton's Gap. Fitz John Porter's Corps was en route from Washington. Daniel Harvey Hill Jr. was the son of Major General Daniel Harvey Hill.

[5] Hill Jr., *Bethel to Sharpsburg*, 1:365.

[6] Cox, *Military Reminiscences*, 1:281.

[7] Cox, *Military Reminiscences*, 1:281-2.

[8] *The Middletown Valley Register*, September 19, 1862.

[9] Morgan, H. Wayne, *William McKinley and his America* (Syracuse, N.Y.: Syracuse University Press, 1963), 24.

[10] Charles Richard Williams, *Diary and Letters of Rutherford Birchard Hayes* (Columbus: The Ohio State Archaeological and Historical Society, 1926), 2:355-7.

[11] United States War Department, *The War of the Rebellion: A Compilation of the Official Records of the Union and Confederate Armies including Atlas*, 70 vols. (Washington, D.C.: U. S. Government, 1880-1891), Series 1, Vol. 19, Part I. See the *Atlas to Accompany the Official Records*, map of the Battlefield of South Mountain.

[12] Middletown newspaper, issue of Sept. 19, 1862. These reports also are in the *Official Records*.

[13] This passage was taken from a speech by Orlando Wilcox at the dedication of the Reno Monument.

[14] Jerome M. Loving, ed., *Civil War Letters of George Washington Whitman* (Durham, N. C.: Duke University Press, 1975), 67.

[15] Cox, *Military Reminiscences*, 1:297-8.

[16] Beale, *Diary of Gideon Welles*, 1:143.

[17] Basler, *Collected Works of Abraham Lincoln*, 4:424.

[18] Also see Salmon P. Chase, *Inside Lincoln's Cabinet: The Civil War Diaries of Salmon P. Chase*, ed. David Donald (New York: Longmans, Green, 1954), 133-58.

[19] Basler, *Collected Works of Abraham Lincoln*, 438.

[20] George B. McClellan, *McClellan's Own Story* (New York: Charles L. Webster & Co., 1887), 27.

Appendix A - Maps

Pages 183 through 186.

[1] Edward Bennett Mathews, *The Maps and Map-Makers of Maryland* (Baltimore: The Johns Hopkins University Press, October, 1898), 388-90.
[2] Mathews, *Maps and Map-Makers of Maryland*, 391.
[3] Mathews, *Maps and Map-Makers of Maryland*, 398.

Appendix C - Land Tract Analysis

Pages 189 through 199.

[1] Addition to Friendship was a resurvey obtained by Frederick Fox out of the western shore land office by a special warrant of proclamation to resurvey and affect the vacancy included in a *resurvey* made for him on the eighth day of June seventeen hundred and ninety five by the name of Friendship, the caution money for which had not been paid within the time limited by law. In pursuance whereof a resurvey was made and a certificate thereof returned containing two hundred and two acres and called Addition to Friendship.
[2] Peter Ludy acquired 58 acres from Joseph Swearingen at the time he acquired 10 acres from William Bottenberg. See WR-34-315-317.
[3] This transfer was an apparent attempt by Jacob Routzong to avoid confiscation of the property by the County Court. The sheriff confiscated the property under court order in 1832 and auctioned it to the highest bidder. The 1832 deed from Sheriff Brengle to Henry Miller indicates the court awarded a judgement on the first Monday of August 1827 against Jacob Routzong in favor of Peter Sower and Philip Hunsslmen. The April 5, 1889, deed from James W. Coffman et ux to Jonas Gross, however, refers to the Jacob Routzong and George Routzong deed.
[4] The court apparently voided the deed from Jacob Routzong to George Routzong and transferred the land to Henry Miller.
[5] No record of a will of Henry Miller was found. He probably died intestate.
[6] The heirs at law of Henry Miller were: Susan Miller, widow of Henry Miller; John W. Derr and Elizabeth Derr, his wife; John Miller and Susan Miller, his wife; Adam Koogle and Catharine Koogle, his wife; Phineas Williams and Ann Maria Williams, his wife; Joseph Nyman and Jane Rebecca Nyman, his wife; and Henrietta Miller.
[7] Jonas Gross recorded three deeds at 9:00 AM on April 5, 1889. WIP-9-148 from James W. Coffman et ux to Jonas Gross, 6 and 1/2 acres; WIP-9-148 from George H. Kefauver et ux to Jonas Gross, 5 and 1/2 acres; WIP-9-149 from John W. Wise et ux to Jonas Gross, 4 and 3/4 acres. The deeds to Jonas Gross from James W. and Mary Coffman and from George H. and Mary R. Kefauver both state they are part of a tract called "Fredericksburg." The tracts probably became confused when Peter Ludy

obtained 10 acres from William Bottenberg and 58 acres from Joseph Swearingen. These two tracts became part of one tract of 68 acres, containing portions of both Fredericksburg and Addition to Friendship. The deed to the United States government states, "said land (i. e. the 40 foot by 40 foot tract of the Reno Monument) being a part of the same land that was conveyed to said Jonas Gross by John W. Wise and wife by a deed dated the 9th day of June A. D. 1879, and recorded in Liber W I P No. 9, folio 149."

[8] MdHR 17,438, 1-23-3-38, Daniel Dulany Esqr., survey for The Exchange, Oct. 5, 1742, 100 acres. MSA BC & GS #27, 578.

[9] This tract was originally for 100 acres, but actually contained only 75 acres. Also see MSA BY & GS #2, 239.

[10] See FCLR, G-17. Casper Shaff, a merchant, acquired Boble (Bubble), for 50 acres, from Michael Jesserong, an innholder, on June 4, 1761.

[11] FCLR, E-1026, sale to Conrad Young, March 18, 1756, 125 acres.

[12] Fidler also obtained Boble (Bubble) for 50 acres with this deed.

[13] George Fidler probably inherited the property on the death of Valentine Fidler.

[14] "Fidler's Purchase being part of two tracts of land the one called the Resurvey on Exchange and a tract call'd Buble."

[15] "part of two tracts of land the one called The Resurvey on Exchange and the other called Bubble."

[16] "part of two tracts of land the one called the Resurvey on Exchange and the other called Bubble Beginning at the original Beginning tree of Exchange and running thence . . . Also one other piece or parcel of land being part of a tract called Mount Pleasant." The Mt. Pleasant tract contained 18 acres.

[17] "Fidler's Purchase, being part of two tracts of land, the one called the Resurvey on Exchange and the other called Bubble."

[18] The deed is from Sidney Ringer, widow of John Ringer. The property was left to Sidney Ringer as a life estate. Daniel Ringer, son of John and Sidney, improperly transfered the property to Jacob Everhart Jr. and his wife Eliza. The deed mentions Jacob Everhart Sr. and Eliza his wife, Jacob Everhart Jr. and Eliza L. Everhart, and the land tracts named Fidler's Purchase, the Resurvey on Exchange, and Bubble.

[19] "part of a tract of land called Fidler's Purchase, part of a tract called The Resurvey on Exchange, part of a tract called Bubble and a tract called Deefer Snay." Vincent Sanner acquired Deefer Snay from George Routzahn.

[20] This tract is substantially the same as the tract sold by Vincent Sanner to Samuel Ausherman in 1868. Lines 4, 5, 6, 7, and 15 are along the old Sharpsburg Road. The Fox Inn stands at approximately 35 perches directly west of the end of the third line of this tract at the intersection of Marker road (to Burkittsville) and the old Sharpsburg Road.

[21] There is no course number 39 indicated on this map. The author believes this missing line in the written description of the road should be South, about 81 Degrees East, about 40 to 45 perches.

[22] MdHR 17,458, 1-23-4-12, Philip Jacob Shafer, survey for Flonham, Aug. 27, 1770, 36 acres. MSA BC & BS #47, 496-7. MdHR 17,455, 1-23-4-

9, Philip Jacob Shafer, patent for Flonham, April 20, 1774, 36 acres. MSA BC & GS #44, 439-40.

[23] This transfer was from the heirs of Henry Miller. This deed conveyed two parcels: the "Homestead" of 40 acres and Lot No. 5 consisting of 18 1/8 acres.

[24] This transfer was from Edward L. and Prudence C. Boteler. This deed mentions the tracts of Addition to Friendship, Partnership, Swearingen's Disappointment, Flonham, and Knave's Good Will. It mentions "the Boonsboro and Middletown turnpike," "north side of the public road leading from said turnpike to Daniel Rent's farm," and "a stone wall." The deed indicates George Baltzell was an agent for Henry Miller. This deed indicates portions of the 60 acre tract lie on both sides of the turnpike road.

[25] This transfer was from George F. Smith. "Being part of a tract of land called Addition to Friendship, part of Partnership, part of Swearingen's Disappointment, and part of a tract called Flonham." It identifies "Madelein V. Dahlgren of Washington City in the District of Columbia," "the Boonsboro and Middletown turnpike," "north side of the public road leading from said turnpike to Daniel Rent's farm," and "a stone wall." This tract contained "60 acres of land more or less it being the same land that Edward L. Boteler and wife conveyed to the said George F. Smith by deed bearing date March 27th 1867 and recorded in L B N No. 2, folio 133, one of the land records of Washington county."

[26] Will of Madeleine Sarah Vinton Dahlgren, recorded in Frederick County and also recorded in Washington County, Liber I, folio 357.

[27] Saint Mary's Academy of Notre Dame, St. Joseph's County, Indiana.

[28] ". . . SECOND. Deed from GEORGE F. SMITH TO MADELEINE V. DAHLGREN dated April 19th 1876 and recorded in Liber T. G. No. 5 Folio 708, one of the land records for Frederick County it being also recorded in Liber No. 74 Folio 264 one of the land records for Washington County and containing 60 acres of land, more or less." Later, "ALSO EXCEPTING, 10 acres of land, upon which is located the Chapel, said 10 acres being part of the 60 acres more or less conveyed to MADELEINE VINTON DAHLGREN BY GEORGE F. SMITH by deed dated April 19th 1876 and recorded in Liber T. G. No 5, folio 708 one of the land records for Frederick County, it being the second of the above thirteen deeds."

[29] This deed created a 3.7 acre tract. The tract was "situate along the South side of U. S. Route No. 40A at the summit of Dahlgren Mountain, in District No. 6, Washington County, Maryland."

[30] "Situate along the South side of U. S. Route No. 40A at the summit of Dahlgren Mountain, in District No. 6, Washington County, Maryland."

[31] "being situate along the South side of U. S. Route 40A at the summit of Dahlgren Mountain, in Election District No. 6, Washington County, Maryland."

[32] This deed mentions the following tracts: David's Will, a resurvey called Security, Flonham, Knave's Good Will, Turkey Ramble, and Bowser's Addition.

[33] This deed transfered all 202 acres of the original tract called Addition to Friendship as well as 30 acres of a tract named Fredericksburg.

[34] The heirs of Joseph Swearingen were Joseph Van Swearingen, Eleanor (and John) Stemble, Elizabeth Swearingen, Marcia Swearingen, Margaret W. Swearingen, and Ruth D. Swearingen. Joseph Van Swearingen, son of Joseph Swearingen, appointed George Baltzell his attorney at law.

[35] Eleanor and her husband, John Stemble, sold the one sixth interest of Eleanor to attorney George Baltzell.

[36] This transfer consisted of two parts: Part One, "the first part of the whole tract aforesaid wherein before mentioned and lying south of the said turnpike road," consisted of 75 1/2 acres. Part Two, "the second tract of the aforesaid land called 'Addition to Friendship' lying north of the turnpike road," consisted of 114 acres. Henry Miller acquired a portion of Fox's Last Shift from Michael Easterday in 1824-1827. He acquired five acres of Flonham from Philip Shafer in 1824, deed WC JS-25-372. He acquired a portion of Swearingen's Dissapointment from John Shafer in 1824-1827.

[37] Henry Miller probably died intestate. There is no will of Henry Miller on record at either the Washington or Frederick County Courthouses.

[38] This transfer was from Edward L. and Prudence C. Boteler. The deed mentions the tracts of Addition to Friendship, Partnership, Swearingen's Disappointment, Flonham, and Knave's Good Will. It mentions "the Boonsboro and Middletown turnpike," "north side of the public road leading from said turnpike to Daniel Rent's farm" and "a stone wall." The deed indicates George Baltzell was an agent for Henry Miller. The deed indicates portions of the 60 acre tract lie on both sides of the turnpike road.

Appendix D - The Fox Inn

Pages 200 through 205.

[1] Daniel Gebhart Fox, *The Fox Genealogy including the Metherd, Benner, and Leiter Descendants* (n.p., 1914).

[2] Byron L. Williams, *The Old South Mountain Inn* (Shippensburg, Pa.: Beidel Printing House, Inc., 1990).

[3] *Ohio D.A.R. Soldiers Rosters*, 2 vols., 1:146.

[4] Fox, *Fox Genealogy*, 13. MdHR 17,430-1, 1-23-3-26, Frederick Fox, patent for Turkey Foot, March 13, 1794, 6 acres. MSA IC #G, 361.

[5] MdHR 17,471, 1-23-4-27, Frederick Fox, patent for Mt. Pleasant, May 27, 1793, 23 acres. MSA IC #H, 298.

[6] See FCLR, WR 32-30, George Fox to John Ringer, recorded Oct. 7, 1807, 100 acres for £1800. Also see FCLR, WR-32-28, Frederick Fox to John Ringer, recorded Oct. 7, 1807, 50 acres for £300; and, FCLR, WR-31-319, George Fox to Frederick Fox, Aug. 1, 1807, Mt. Pleasant.

[7] MdHR 17,412-2, 1-23-2-37, Daniel Dulany of the city of Annapolis Esqr., survey for The Exchange, Sept. 9, 1742, 100 acres. MSA BY & GS #1, 177.

[8] FCLR, WR-13-49, Jacob Smith Sr. to Jacob Smith Jr., Exchange, Feb. 10, 1795, 30 1/2 acres.

[9] FCLR, E-339, Joseph Chapline Sr. to Casper Shaff, Exchange, recorded Dec. 11, 1753, 75 acres.

[10] See Tracey and Dern, *Pioneers of Old Monocacy*, 244-5. They identify the Exchange tract as being along a route "To Opequon."

[11] MdHR 17,438, 1-23-3-38, Daniel and Walter Dulaney, The Exchange, patented Sept. 29, 1765, 100 acres. MSA BC & GS #27, 578.

[12] MdHR 17,402-3, 1-23-2-37, Robert Evans, The Exchange, surveyed April 22, 1747, 50 acres. MSA BY & GS #1, 610.

[13] FCLR, WR-23-286, Joseph Chapline [Jr.] to Frederick Fox, recorded Aug. 9, 1802, 25 acres.

[14] Maryland Archives, Chancery Records, B 49 - 243, Frederick Fox. Joseph Chapline [Jr.] vs. William W. Chapline and Jacob Smith. The court case runs from pages 241 to 259 and mentions Frederick Fox.

Appendix F - Biographical Listing

Pages 207 through 222.

[1] Daniel Gebhart Fox, *The Fox Genealogy including the Metherd, Benner and Leiter Descendants* (n.p., 1914), 13.

[2] FCLR, WR 9-607, Agreement regarding Resurvey on Wooden Platter, Deposition of Bartholomew Booker.

[3] Ralph Beaver Strassburger, *Pennsylvania German Pioneers*, ed. by William John Hinke (Baltimore: Genealogical Publishing Co., 1966), 269. Lists 71 - 73 B. Loyal Judith, Sept. 3, 1739, Capt. Paynter, "Peter Bucher, Bardoll Bucher".

[4] Frederick County, Maryland, Register of Wills Records, GM-3-126, will of Margaret Book (Booker). Witnesses to the will included Joseph Chapline [Jr.], Catharine Fox, and two names in German.

[5] Robert Dinwiddie to Charles Dick, Jan. 25, 1755, *The Official Records of Robert Dinwiddie* (New York: AMS Press, 1884), 1:53-4.

[6] Kenneth P. Bailey, *The Ohio Company of Virginia, a chapter in the History of the Colonial Frontier, 1748-1792* (Glendale, Calif.: The Arthur H. Clark Company, 1939), 51.

[7] Calvin E. Schildknecht, "Which Charles Carroll?" *The News* Frederick, Maryland, April 4, 1990. Also see Edward C. Papenfuse et al., *Biographical Dictionary of the Maryland Legislature, 1635 - 1789*, 2 vols. (Baltimore and London: The Johns Hopkins University Press, 1982), 1:193-9.

[8] Herbert L. Osgood, *The American Colonies in the eighteenth century*, 4 vols. (Gloucester, Mass.: P. Smith, 1958), 2:192, 201-2 and 3:6-8, 10, 25.

[9] Osgood, *American Colonies in the Eighteenth Century*, 3:6. Osgood cites Maryland Archives, 30:375.

[10] Papenfuse, *Biographical Dictionary*, 1:244-5.

[11] T. J. C. Williams and Folger McKinsey, *History of Frederick County*, 2 vols. (Baltimore: Regional Publishing Company, 1967), 1:31.

[12] John Bakeless, *Daniel Boone* (Harrisburg, Pennsylvania: Stackpole Company, 1939), 21.

[13] Stanley Pargellis, ed. *Military Affairs in North America 1748 - 1765* (New York: D. Appleton-Century Company, 1936), 109.

[14] Papenfuse, *Biographical Dictionary*, 1:284-6. Also see Aubrey C. Land, *The Dulanys of Maryland* (Baltimore: Maryland Historical Society, 1955).

[15] Papenfuse, *Biographical Dictionary*, 1:286-7. Also see Land, *Dulanys of Maryland*.

[16] Fox, *Fox Genealogy*, 12.

[17] FCLR, WR-19-206, mortgage from Christian Benner to Frederick Fox, recorded April 11, 1799, Shaff's Purchase and Mount Sinai. "Between Christian Benner Sen. of Frederick County farmer of the one part; and Frederick Fox of the same county farmer of the other part."

[18] Lemoine Cree, *A Brief History of the South Mountain House* (Boonsboro, Md.: Dodson, 1963); *Ohio D.A.R. Soldiers Rosters*, 2 vols., 1:146; also see Fox, *Fox Genealogy*, 13-4.

[19] Frederick S. Weiser, ed., Maryland German Church Records, Vol. 2, *Zion Lutheran Church 1781-1826* (Manchester, Md.: Noodle-Doosey Press, 1987), 77. The Death Register of Zion Lutheran Church indicates "Catarin, wife of Friedrich Fuchs, bur. 4 Nov. 1800. Heb. 4:9."

[20] Frederick County, Maryland, Register of Wills Records, GM-2-431, will of Bartholomew Booker, Oct. 21, 1791.

[21] *Ohio D.A.R. Soldiers Rosters*, 2 vols., 1:146.

[22] Will of Frederick Fox, Will Book C, case #1444, Montgomery County, Ohio. Dec. 10, 1833. Mary and Elizabeth, daughters of Frederick Fox, are mentioned in the will of Margaret Booker.

[23] S. Eugene Clements and F. Edward Wright, *The Maryland Militia in the Revolutionary War* (Silver Spring, Md.: Family Line Publications, 1987), 241. Maryland Historical Society Records for Washington County. Militia Lists of Daus. of Founders and Patriots.

[24] Washington County, Maryland, Patriot's Oath, March Court, 1778. Sharpsburg Hundred, March 2, 1778, Christopher Cruss's Returns.

[25] National Archives, card numbers 37404176, 4837, 37188278, and 39144421; National Society of the Daughters of the American Revolution, 17th Report, *Pierce's Register*, #67913. Also see Pennsylvania Archives, Series 5, 3:487, 529, 533, and 572.

[26] The author is a member of The Society of the Descendants of Washington's Army at Valley Forge.

[27] Weiser, *Zion Lutheran Chruch 1781-1826*, Maryland German Church Records, 2:4.

[28] Fox, *Fox Genealogy*, 15.

[29] Fox, *Fox Genealogy*, 18.

[30] *Ohio D.A.R. Soldiers Rosters*, 1:146.

[31] I. Daniel Rupp, *Thirty-Thousand Names of Immigrants* (Baltimore: Genealogical Publishing Co., 1971), 280-1.

[32] R. B. Strassburger and W. J. Hinke, *Pennsylvania German Pioneers, Lists of Arrivals* (Norristown, Pa.: Pennsylvania German Society, 1934), 488-9.

[33] Clements and Wright, *Maryland Militia in the Revolutionary War*, 241. Michael Fox also was a member of Joseph Chapline's Company.

[34] Will of John Fox, Book A Liber 102, Washington County, Maryland. Jan. 17, 1784.

[35] Fox, *Fox Genealogy*, 12.

[36] Frederick County, Maryland, The Account of Joseph and Jennett Chapline Executors of Moses Chapline late of Frederick County Deceased.

[37] See WCLR, K-703, K-1231, J-1400, K-1278, and K-1279 in the years 1766 to 1769.

[38] Letter from Jacob Reel to Michael and Frederick Fox, dated at Sharpsburg, Aug. 9, 1812, from a copy obtained from Robert H. Fox of Cinicinnati, Ohio. "The following letter received and forwarded from Lebanon, Warren County, Ohio, Sept. 8, 1812, addressed to Msrs. Fredric(k) & Michael Fox, Franklin Township, Warren Co. Ohio"

[39] Dinwiddie, *Records*, 1:7-8.

[40] Bakeless, *Daniel Boone*, 21.

[41] Julia Angeline Drake and James Ridgely Orndorff, *From Mill Wheel to Plowshare, The Story of the Contribution of the Christian Orndorff Family to the Social and Industrial History of the United States* (Cedar Rapids, Iowa: Reprinted by the Maryland Historical Society, 1971), 294.

[42] Winthrop Sargent, ed., *The History of An Expedition against Fort Duquesne, in 1755* (Philadelphia: J. B. Lippincott & Co., 1856), 136-7.

[43] George Athan Billias, ed., *George Washington's Generals* (New York: Morrow, 1964), 25.

[44] North Callahan, *Daniel Morgan, Ranger of the Revolution* (New York: Holt, Rinehart and Winston, 1961).

[45] Sargent, *History of an Expedition*, 240.

[46] Papenfuse, *Biographical Dictionary*, 2:618-9.

[47] Sir Henry Asgill Ogle, *Ogle and Bothal* (Newcastle-upon-Tyne, England, 1902). DAB.

[48] Papenfuse, *Biographical Dictionary*, 2:726-8.

[49] Lady [Matilda Ridout] Edgar, *A Colonial Governor in Maryland: Horatio Sharpe and his Times, 1753-1773* (New York: Longmans, Green, and Co., 1912).

[50] Sargent, *History of An Expedition*, 285.

[51] Pargellis, *Military Affairs*, 58.

[52] Maryland Historical Society marker at Rumsey Bridge.

[53] Berkeley County Historical Society, *The Berkeley Journal*, Issue Thirteen, 1989, 9-21.

[54] Papenfuse, *Biographical Dictionary*, 2:799-801.

[55] Bakeless, *Daniel Boone*, 21.

[56] Grace L. Tracey and John P. Dern, *Pioneers of Old Monocacy* (Baltimore: Genealogical Publishing Company, 1987), 44. Prince George's County Wills, 1:520, probated August 20, 1760.

Bibliography

Contemporary Sources

Andersen, Patricia Abelard. "Jacob Fluck of Middletown, Frederick County, Maryland, and his Flook and Fluke Descendants." *National Genealogical Society Quarterly*, September 1984, Volume 72, Number 3, 163.

American State Papers: 1, *Miscellaneous.*

Balch, Thomas. *Letters and Papers relating chiefly to the Provincial History of Pennsylvania with some Notices of the Writers.* Philadelphia: Privately Printed, 1855.

Basler, Roy P., ed. *The Collected Works of Abraham Lincoln.* 9 vols. New Brunswick, N. J.: Rutgers Unviersity Press, 1953-55.

Beale, Howard K. ed., *Diary of Gideon Welles.* 3 vols. New York: Norton, 1960.

Browne, William H. et al., eds. *Archives of Maryland.* Baltimore: Maryland Historical Society, 1888.

Browne, William Hand, ed. *Letters to Governor Horatio Sharpe.* Archives of Maryland. Vol. 30. Baltimore: Maryland Historical Society, 1911.

Browne, William Hand, ed. *Correspondence of Governor Horatio Sharpe, 1753-1771.* Archives of Maryland. Vols. 6, 9, 14, 31. Baltimore: Maryland Historical Society, 1888-1911.

Burke, Sir Bernard. *Burke's American Families with British Ancestry.* Baltimore: Genealogical Publishing Company, 1975.

Chase, Salmon P. *Inside Lincoln's Cabinet: The Civil War Diaries of Salmon P. Chase.* ed. David Donald. New York: Longmans, Green, 1954.

Clark, Walter, ed. *Histories of the Several Regiments and Battalions from North Carolina in the Great War 1861-1865.* 5 vols. Raleigh: State of North Carolina, 1901.

Clements, S. Eugene and Wright, F. Edward. *The Maryland Militia in the Revolutionary War*. Silver Spring, Md.: Family Line Publications, 1987.

Culbertson, Sidney Methiot. *The Hunter Family of Virginia and Connections*. Denver, Colorado: n.p., 1934.

Darlington, William M. ed. *Christopher Gist's Journals*. Pittsburgh: J.R. Weldin & Co., 1893.

Davis, George B., Perry, Leslie J., and Kirkley, Joseph W. *Atlas to Accompany the Official Records of the Union and Confederate Armies*. Washington: Government Printing Office, 1891-5.

Dulany Jr., Daniel. "Military and Political Affairs in The Middle Colonies in 1755," *Pennsylvania Magazine of History and Biography* (1879), 3:14.

Etting Collection. *Ohio Company Papers*. Philadelphia: Pennsylvania Historical Society.

Evans, Lewis. *Geographical, historical, political, philosophical and mechanical essays, the first containing an analysis of a general map of the middle British colonies in America, and of the country of the confederate Indians; a description of the face of the country; the boundaries of the confederates; and the maritime and inland navigations of the several rivers and lakes contained therein*. Philadelphia: Franklin and Hall, 1755.

Fitzpatrick, John C., ed. *The Writings of George Washington from the Original Manuscript Sources 1744-1789*. 39 vols. Washington, D.C.: U.S. Government Printing Office, 1933.

Fox, Daniel Gebhart. *The Fox Genealogy including the Metherd, Benner, and Leiter Descendants*. N.p., 1924.

Fry, Joshua. *The Fry and Jefferson map of Virginia and Maryland; facsimiles of the 1754 and 1794 printings with an index*. 2nd ed. Charlottesville: University Press of Virginia, 1966.

Green, Karen Mauer. *The Maryland Gazette 1727-1761 Genealogical and Historical Abstracts*. Galveston: The Frontier Press, 1989.

Hamilton, Charles. *Braddock's Defeat*. Norman: Univ. of Oklahoma Press, 1959.

Harrison, Fairfax, ed. "With Braddock's Army: Mrs. Browne's
        diary in Virginia and Maryland." *Virginia Magazine of
        History and Biography*. October, 1924, 32:305-20.
Hazard, Samuel, et al., ed. *Pennsylvania Archives*. 138 vols. to
        date. Philadelphia and Harrisburg: The State, 1644-.
Hening, William Waller, ed. *Hening's Statutes at Large of
        Virginia*. 13 vol. Richmond: Samuel Pleasants, 1809-23.
Hibbard, Francis Hamilton. Assisted by Stephen Parks. *The
        English origin of John Ogle, first of the name in
        Delaware*. Pittsburgh: n.p., 1967.
Hinke, W. J. *Pennsylvania German Pioneers 1727-1808, Lists of
        Arrivals*. Norristown, Pa.: Pennsylvania German
        Society, 1934.
Hinke, William J., transl. "Report of the Journey of Francis Louis
        Michel October 2, 1701 to December 1, 1702." *Virginia
        Magazine of History and Biography*. 24:1-43, 113-141,
        275-303.
Hinke, William J. *Ministers of the German Reformed
        Congregations in Pennsylvania and Other Colonies in
        the Eighteenth Century*. Lancaster: Rudisill and Co.,
        Inc., 1951.
Hinke, William J. and Reinecke, E. W., translated by.
        *Evangelical Reformed Church of Frederick, Maryland,
        1746-1800*. Silver Spring, Md.: Family Line Publications,
        1986.
Iscrupe, William L. and Iscrupe, Shirley G. M. *Early History of
        Western Pennsylvania and the Western Campaigns
        1754-1833*. Laughlintown, Pa.: Southwest Pennsylvania
        Genealogical Services, 1989.
Jackson, Donald, ed. *The Diaries of George Washington*. 6 vols.
        Charlottesville: University of Virginia Press, 1976.
Labaree, Leonard W. et al., eds. *The Autobiography of Benjamin
        Franklin*. New Haven, Conn.: Yale University Press,
        1964.
Lancaster, Pennsylvania. *A treaty, held at the town, by the
        honourable lieutenant-governor of the province, and the
        honourable commissioners for the provinces of Virginia
        and Maryland, with the Indians of the Six Nations, in
        June, 1744*. Philadelphia: n.p., 1744. (The Lancaster
        treaty served for the basis of both Virginia's and

Pennsylvania's claims to the Ohio region.)

Laws, Documents and Judicial Decisions, Relating to The Baltimore and Fredericktown, York and Reisterstown, Cumberland and Boonsborough Turnpike Road Companies. Baltimore: John D. Toy, 1841.

Lincoln, Charles Henry, ed. *William Shirley, Governor of Massachusetts and Military Commander in America, Correspondence, 1731-1760.* 2 vols. New York: n.p., 1912.

Link, Paxson. *The Link Family.* Paris, Illinois: n.p., 1951.

Loving, Jerome M., ed. *Civil War Letters of George Washington Whitman.* Durham, N. C.: Duke University Press, 1975.

MacDonald, William. *Select Charters and Other Documents Illustrative of American History, 1606 - 1775.* New York: The Macmillan Company, 1899.

Mason, Betty J. "Castle Bible Records." *Western Maryland Genealogy.* Middletown, Md., 1986.

Mathews, Edward Bennett. *The Maps and Map-Makers of Maryland.* Baltimore: The Johns Hopkins Press, October, 1898.

McClellan, George B. *McClellan's Own Story.* New York: Charles L. Webster & Co., 1887.

Morgan, H. Wayne. *William McKinley and his America.* Syracuse, N.Y.: Syracuse University Press, 1963.

Nichols, Franklin T. "*The Braddock Expedition.*" Ph.D. diss., Harvard University, 1947.

North Carolina. *The Colonial Records of North Carolina.* ed. William L. Saunders. 10 vols. Raleigh: The State, 1886-90.

O'Callaghan, E. B. and Fernow, B., eds. *Documents Relative to the Colonial History of New York.* 15 vols. Albany: n.p., 1853-87.

Ogle, Sir Henry Asgill. *Ogle and Bothal.* Newcastle-upon-Tyne: Andrew Reid & Company, 1902.

Older, Curtis L. *Documentation Related to Frederick Fox, including material on his descendants.* Unpublished.

Older, Curtis L. *The Land Tracts of Fox's Gap, including material on Crampton's, Orr's, and Turner's Gaps.* Unpublished.

Papenfuse, Edward C. and Coale III, Joseph M. *The Hammond-Harwood House Atlas of Historical Maps of Maryland, 1608-1908.* Baltimore & London: The Johns Hopkins

University Press, 1982.

Pargellis, Stanley, ed. *Military Affairs in North America 1748-1765*. New York: D. Appleton-Century Company, Inc., 1936.

Pennsylvania. *Minutes of the Provincial Council of Pennsylvania, from the organization to the termination of the proprietary government*. [March 10, 1683 - September 27, 1775] 10 vols. Philadelphia: The State, 1851-1852. (Commonly known as the *Pennsylvania Colonial Records*.)

Pennsylvania. *Votes and Procedings of the House of Representatives, 1754-1755*. Philadelphia: The State, 1755.

Pickering, Henry G. "An Unpublished Autograph Narrative by Washington." *Scribner's Magazine*. Vol. 13, 529-37.

Rice, Millard M. *New Facts and Old Families*. Redwood City, California: Monocacy Book Company, 1976.

Rice, Millard M. *This Was the Life excerpts from the judgment records of Frederick County, Md. 1748-1765*. Redwood City, California: Monocacy Book Company, 1979.

Rupp, I. Daniel. *Thirty-Thousand Names of Immigrants*. Baltimore: Genealogical Publishing Co., 1971.

Sargent, Winthrop, ed. *The History of an Expedition Against Fort Duquesne in 1755; under Major General Braddock*. Philadelphia: J. B. Lippincott & Co., 1855.

Strassburger, Ralph Beaver. *Pennsylvania German Pioneers*. ed. by William John Hinke. Baltimore: Genealogical Publishing Co., 1966.

United States War Department. *The War of the Rebellion: A Compilation of the Official Records of the Union and Confederate Armies*. 70 vols. Washington, D.C.: U. S. Government, 1880-1891.

Virginia Historical Society. *The Official Records of Robert Dinwiddie*. 2 vols. New York: AMS Press, 1884.

Weiser, Frederick S., ed. *Zion Lutheran Chruch 1781-1826*. Maryland German Church Records. Vol. 2. Manchester, Md.: Noodle-Doosey Press, 1987.

Willcox, William B., ed. *The Papers of Benjamin Franklin*. 30 vols. New Haven: Yale University Press, 1986.

Williams, Charles Richard. *Diary and Letters of Rutherford Birchard Hayes.* Columbus: The Ohio State. Archaeological and Historical Society, 1926.

Wright, F. Edward. *Western Maryland Newspaper Abstracts 1786-1798.* Silver Spring, Md.: Family Line Publications, 1985.

Secondary Sources

Bailey, Kenneth P. *The Ohio Company of Virginia, a chapter in the History of the Colonial Frontier, 1748-1792.* Glendale, Calif.: The Arthur H. Clark Company, 1939.

Bailey, Kenneth P. *Thomas Cresap, Maryland Frontiersman.* Boston: The Christopher Publishing House, 1944.

Bakeless, John. *Daniel Boone.* Harrisburg, Pennsylvania: Stackpole Company, 1939.

Barron, Lee and Barbara. *The History of Sharpsburg, Maryland.* Sharpsburgh, Md.: Barrons, 1972.

Bast, Doug. "William, George Boone Lay Out Boone's Berry." *Maryland Cracker Barrel, Inc.* Volume 20, No. 6. Boonsboro, Maryland.

Bowie, Lucy L. *The Ancient Barracks at Fredericktown.* Frederick, Md.: Maryland State School for the Deaf, 1939.

Callahan, North. *Daniel Morgan, Ranger of the Revolution.* New York: Holt, Rinehart and Winston, 1961.

Cox, Jacob D. *Military Reminiscences of the Civil War.* 2 vols. New York: Charles Scribner's Sons, 1900.

Craig, Neville B. *Washington's first campaign, death of Jumonville, and the taking of Fort Necessity; also Braddock's defeat; also the march of the unfortunate General explained by a distinguished historian, traced on the ground by a civil engineer, and exhibited on a neat and accurate map, prepared under his direction.* Pittsburgh: n.p., 1848.

Craig, Nevill B., ed. *The Olden Time.* Pittsburgh: n.p., 1846-8.

Cree, Lemoine. *A Brief History of South Mountain House.* Boonsboro, Md.: Dodson, 1963.

Cunz, Dieter. *The Maryland Germans, a History.* Princeton: Princeton University Press, 1948.

Dandridge, Mrs. Danske. *Historic Shepherdstown.*
Charlottesville: Michie, c1910.
Dare, Maria J. Liggett. *Chaplines from Maryland and Virginia.*
Washington, D.C.: The Franklin Print, 1902.
Drake, Julia A. and Orndorff, James R. *From Mill Wheel to
Plowshare.* Cedar Rapids, Iowa: The Torch Press, 1938.
Reprinted by the Maryland Historical Society, 1971.
Edgar, Lady [Matilda Ridout]. *A Colonial Governor in
Maryland: Horatio Sharpe and His Times, 1753-1773.*
New York: Longmans, Green, and Co., 1912.
Fiske, John. *Old Virginia and Her Neighbors.* Boston: Houghton
Mifflin Co., 1900.
Fox, Robert H. *Middletown Valley Register,* Aug. 19, 1932.
Frassanito, William A. *Antietam: The Photographic Legacy of
America's Bloodiest Day.* New York: Scribner's, 1978.
Gibson, John, ed. *History of York Co., Pennsylvania.* Baltimore:
Genealogical Publishing Company, 1975.
Hadden, James. *Washington's Expedition (1753-1754) and
Braddock's Expedition (1755), with history of Tom
Fausett the slayer of General Edward Braddock.*
Uniontown, Pa.: n.p., 1910.
Hamilton, J. G. de Roulhac, ed. *The Papers of Randolph Abbot
Shotwell.* Raleigh: N. C. Historical Commission, 1929.
Hays, Helen Ashe. *The Antietam and Its Bridges.* New York:
The Knickerbocker Press, 1910.
Heusser, Albert H. *In the Footsteps of Washington (Pope's Creek
to Princeton).* Paterson, N. J.: Privately Published, 1921.
Hill, Jr., Daniel Harvey. *Bethel to Sharpsburg.* 2 vols. Raleigh:
Edwards & Broughton Co., 1926.
Hough, Walter S. *Braddock's Road Through the Virginia
Colony.* Winchester, Virginia: Winchester - Frederick
County Historical Society, 1970.
Hotchkiss, Jedediah. *Make Me a Map of the Valley, The Civil
War Journal of Stonewall Jackson's Topographer.*
Archie P. McDonald, ed. Dallas: Southern Methodist
Press, 1973.
Hulbert, Arthur Butler. *Historic Highways of America.* vol. 4.
Braddock's Road. Cleveland: Arthur H. Clark Co., 1903.
Jennings, Francis. *Empire of Fortune. Crowns, Colonies & Tribes in
the Seven Years War in America.* New York: W. W.

   Norton & Company, 1988.
Johnson, Allen and Malone, Dumas. *Dictionary of American*
      Biography. New York: Charles Scribner's Sons, 1927.
Johnson, Bradley T. *General Washington*. New York:
      D. Appleton & Co., 1898.
Johnson, Robert Underwood and Buel, Clarence Clough. *Battles*
      and Leaders of the Civil War. Grant - Lee Edition.
      New York: The Century Co., 1887.
Koontz, Louis K. *The Virginia Frontier, 1754-1763*. Baltimore:
      Johns Hopkins Press, 1925.
Lacock, John Kennedy. *Braddock Road*. N.p., self-published,
      1912.
Land, Aubrey C. Land. *The Dulanys of Maryland*. Baltimore:
      Maryland Historical Society, 1955.
Livingston, William. *A review of the military operations in*
      North America. Dublin: n.p., 1757.
Lowdermilk, William Harrison. *History of Cumberland,*
      (Maryland) from the time of the Indian town
      Caiuctucuc, in 1728, up to the present day embracing an
      account of Washington's first campaign, and battle of
      Fort Necessity, together with a history of Braddock's
      Expedition. Baltimore: Regional Publishing Co., 1976.
Maryland Geological Survey. *Report on the Highways of*
      Maryland. Baltimore: The Johns Hopkins Press, 1899.
McCardell, Lee. *Ill-Starred General*. Pittsburgh: University of
      Pittsburgh Press, 1958.
McSherry, James. *History of Maryland*. Baltimore: Baltimore
      Book Co., 1904.
Mish, Mary V. *Jonathan Hager, Founder*. Hagerstown, Md.:
      Hagerstown Bookbinding & Printing Co., 1937.
Nead, Daniel Wunderlich. *The Pennsylvania-German in the*
      Settlement of Maryland. Lancaster, Pa.: The
      Pennsylvania-German Society, 1914.
Nixon, Lily Lee. *James Burd, Frontier Defender, 1726-1793*.
      Philadelphia: n.p., 1941.
"The Old National Pike," *Harper's New Monthly Magazine*.
      Vol. LIX, 1879.
Osgood, Herbert L. *The American Colonies in the eighteenth*
      century. 4 vols. Gloucester, Mass.: P. Smith, 1958.

Papenfuse, Edward C. et al. *Biographical Dictionary of the Maryland Legislature, 1635 - 1789.* 2 vols. Baltimore: The Johns Hopkins University Press, 1982.

Pargellis, Stanley M. "Braddock's Defeat," in *American Historical Review,* Vol. 41, No. 2.

Parkman, Francis. *Braddock's Defeat, 1755. The French and English in America.* New York: Harper, 1890.

Pennsylvania-German Society. *"The Braddock Expedition."* Proceedings at Lancaster, Vol. XXV, Nov. 13, 1914. Historical Society of Pennsylvania. *Pennsylvania Magazine of History & Biography.*

Rhoderick Jr., George C. *The Early History of Middletown, Maryland.* Middletown Valley Historical Society.

Rouse Jr., Parke. *The Great Wagon Road.* New York: McGraw-Hill Company, 1973.

Scharf, J. Thomas. *History of Western Maryland.* 2 vols. Baltimore: Regional Publishing Co., 1968.

Schildknecht, Calvin E. "Which Charles Carroll?" *The News.* Frederick, Maryland, April 4, 1990.

Schildt, John W. *Drums Along the Antietam.* Parson, W.Va.: McClain, 1972.

State Roads Commission of Maryland. *A History of Road Building in Maryland.* 1958.

Stevens, Henry M. *Lewis Evans, His Map of the British Middle Colonies in America, A Comparative Account of 18 Different Editions Published between 1755 and 1814.* London: n.p., 1920.

Tracey, Grace L. and Dern, John P. *Pioneers of Old Monocacy.* Baltimore: Genealogical Publishing Company, 1987.

Wakelyn, Jon L. *Biographical Dictionary of the Confederacy.* Westport, Conn.: Greenwood Press, 1977.

Walker, Lewis B. *The Settlement of the Waggoners' Accounts Relating to General Braddock's Expedition.* N.p., 1899.

Wayland, John Walter. *The German Element of the Shenandoah Valley of Virginia.* Bridgewater, Va.: C. J. Carrier Company, 1964.

Williams, Byron L. *The Old South Mountain Inn, An Informal History.* Shippensburg, Pa.: Beidel Printing House, 1990.

Williams, T. J. C. and McKinsey, Folger. *History of Frederick County.* 2 vols. Baltimore: Regional Publishing Company, 1967.

Williams, T. J. C. and McKinsey, Folger. *History of Washington County, Maryland.* Baltimore: Regional Publishing Company, 1967.

Wroth, Lawrence C. *The Story of Thomas Cresap.* Columbus, Ohio: The Cresap Society, 1928.

Wyand, Jeffrey A. *Maryland Historical Magazine.* Vol. 67, No. 3, Fall, 1972, 303-4.

Index

Potomac Ferry 153
Potomac River 14, 70
Prevention 154
Prince George's County Court 167
Raccoon 152
Racon 152
Ram's Horn 153
Raystown-Ft. Cumberland road 63
Reno Monument 99, 103
Reno Monument Road 98, 111
Reserve Artillery 106
Resurvey of Security 87
Resurvey on Exchange 96
Resurvey on Hills and Dales and the Vineyard 167
Resurvey on Learning 96
Resurvey on Mend All 96, 155
Resurvey on Mount Pleasant 76, 86
Resurvey on Oxford 99
Resurvey on The Gap 151, 161
Resurvey on Tom's Gift 94
Resurvey on Watson's Welfare 94
Resurvey on Whiskey Alley 94, 155
Revolutionary War 106
Rice, Millard M. 140
Ringer, John 99, 135, 136
Ringer, Sidney 99
Ripley's Brigade 109
Ripley, Roswell S. 107
road between Winchester and Ft. Cumberland 5
road by Robert Evans 153
road commonly called the wagon road 86
road from Bartholomew Booker to Peter Beaver 156
road from Conestoga to Opequon 15, 37
road from Cumberland to Ohio 160
road from Hagerstown to Newcomber's Mill and Frederick County Line 135, 141
road from Frederick and York to Lancaster 37
road from Frederick Town to Fort Frederick 151
road from Frederick Town to Hagerstown 154
road from Frederick Town to Sharpsburg 87, 99
road from Frederick Town to Stull's Mill 140, 153
road from Frederick Town to Swearingen's Ferry 76, 77, 79, 80, 85, 109
road from Frederick Town to Williamsport and Hagerstown 145
road from Ft. Frederick to Ft. Cumberland 152
road from Middletown to Sharpsburg 96
road from Monocacy to Conococheague 167
road from Shippensburg 38
road from Stulls Mill to Monocacy 140, 155
road from Swearingen's Ferry to Fox's Gap 111, 136
road from Volgamots to Stull's 141

About the Author

Curtis L. Older was born in Danville, Illinois in 1947. His educational background includes Bachelor and Master of Science degrees in Accounting. He served as a Spanish interpreter in the United States Navy and has worked in public accounting and teaching. Presently, he works as a computer programmer. A descendant of Frederick Fox, he has been interested in the history of Fox's Gap, Maryland, for a number of years.

3850946

Made in the USA